LIVING RAMAYANAS

Azeez Tharuvana was born in 1974 at Tharuvana in the Wayanad district of Kerala. He earned his postgraduate and doctoral degrees in Malayalam from the University of Calicut. He has served as Editor, Kerala State Institute of Languages (2008–2011) and Assistant Director, Institute of Tribal Studies and Research (2011–2012). He is currently an assistant professor and the head of the Department of Malayalam at Farook College, Calicut, Kerala. He is also a research guide for Malayalam Studies at the University of Calicut, Kerala.

He has several books in Malayalam to his credit. They include the *Wayanadan Ramayanam,* about the different versions of the Ramayana in Wayanad; *Etrayetra Ramayanangal,* on the plurality of the Ramayana; *Osho Darshanikathayude Girisringam,* a study on Osho; *Basheer Phalithangal* and *Basheer Sambhashanangal,* about the Malayalam writer Vaikom Muhammad Basheer; *60 Gibran Kathakal,* a collection of short stories by Kahlil Gibran translated into Malayalam; *Wayanattile Adivasikal: Charitravum Varthamanavum* and *Adivasi Padangal,* studies on the Adivasis; *PK Kalan: Adivasi Jeevithathinte Samaramugham* (editor), a collection of essays on the Adivasi activist P.K. Kalan; and *Vidyabhyasa Chinthakal* (editor), an anthology of essays by famous thinkers on education and pedagogy. He was awarded the Ambedkar National Excellency Award in 2014 for his work *Wayanadan Ramayanam.*

Obed Ebenezer S. is pursuing his doctoral degree in English at the University of Calicut, Kerala. He holds an MPhil in English (University of Calicut), and master's degrees in English (University of Calicut), linguistics (Annamalai University) and journalism and mass communication (Bharathiar University). His poem *Long Walk to Nowhere* received an honourable mention in the 2021 Stephen A. DiBiase Poetry Prize. He is also interested in the translation of poetry, and has translated the works of the Malayalam poets Veerankutty, Kalpetta Narayanan, Sunil Jose, and Nanditha K.S. into English.

LIVING RAMAYANAS

EXPLORING THE PLURALITY
OF THE EPIC IN
WAYANAD AND THE WORLD

AZEEZ THARUVANA

TRANSLATED FROM THE MALAYALAM BY
OBED EBENEZER S.

eka

eka

First published in Malayalam as *Wayanadan Ramayanan* in 2014 by Mathrubhumi Books

First published in English as *Living Ramayanas* in 2021 by Eka, an imprint of Westland Publications Private Limited

Published in English as *Living Ramayanas* in 2022 by Eka, an imprint of Westland Books, a division of Nasadiya Technologies Private Limited

No. 269/2B, First Floor, 'Irai Arul', Vimalraj Street, Nethaji Nagar, Allappakkam Main Road, Maduravoyal, Chennai 600095

Westland and the Westland logo are the trademarks of Nasadiya Technologies Private Limited, or its affiliates.

Copyright © Azeez Tharuvana, 2021, 2022

ISBN: 9789395073462

10 9 8 7 6 5 4 3 2 1

The views and opinions expressed in this work are the author's own and the facts are as reported by him, and the publisher is in no way liable for the same.

All rights reserved

Typeset in Minion Pro by SŪRYA, New Delhi
Printed at

No part of this book may be reproduced, or stored in a retrieval system, or transmitted in any form or by any means, electronic, mechanical, photocopying, recording, or otherwise, without express written permission of the publisher.

*Rama is born in countless ways,
and there are tens of millions of Ramayanas.*

–Tulsidas
[*Ramacharithamanas* 1; 33; 6]

CONTENTS

FOREWORD	ix
ONE TEXT, MULTIPLE ORAL NARRATIVES	xiii
PREFACE: WHY MULTIPLE RAMAYANAS?	xvii

PART ONE: WAYANAD AND THE RAMAYANA

THE ADIYA RAMAYANA	3
THE WAYANAD CHETTI RAMAYANA	15
THE WAYANAD SITAYANAM	23
THE AREAPALLY CHETTIS AND THE MARRIAGE OF LAVA AND KUSA	30
RAMAYANA CHARACTERS AND NATURAL PHENOMENA IN WAYANAD	33
THE RAMAYANA AND TOPONYMIC TALES OF WAYANAD	38
RAMAYANA TALES AND THE HILLS OF WAYANAD	48
RAMAYANA INFLUENCES ON THE WAYANAD COSMOGONIC TALES	55
RAMAYANA CHARACTERS AND THIRUNELLY	73
RAMAYANA TALES IN THE FOLK SONGS OF WAYANAD	77
WHY WAYANAD RAMAYANAS?	89

PART TWO: THE POLYPHONY OF THE RAMAYANA

FOREIGN RAMAYANAS	121
BUDDHIST AND JAIN RAMAYANAS	138
MUSLIMS AND THE RAMAYANA	149
THE ADIVASIS OF INDIA AND THE RAMAYANA STORY	174
THE MANY VERSIONS AND VARIATIONS OF THE RAMAYANA	191
CONCLUSION	217
NOTES	219
GLOSSARY	231
SELECTED BIBLIOGRAPHY	249

FOREWORD

Dr K.N. Panikkar

Different 'tellings' of the Ramayana story exist in various parts of India as well as in foreign countries. However, most of the studies are based on the works of Valmiki, Tulsidas, Thunchath Ezhuthachan, or other texts which have gained literary recognition. Many regard the Ramayanas in regional languages as variant texts of the *Valmiki Ramayana*.

Variant texts of the Ramayana are found not just in the tens and hundreds, but in the thousands. A.K. Ramanujan, the renowned scholar, is of the view that these are not variant texts of the *Valmiki Ramayana*, but largely independent 'tellings'. A limited cross-section of this view can be found in his essay 'Three Hundred Ramayanas: Five Examples and Three Thoughts on Translations' published in the book *Many Ramayanas* edited by Paula Richman. The other essays in that book are responses to this view. Richman's book deals with the Ramayana story according to the Buddhist tradition, the *Ramakiya* of Thailand, the *Streemaymozhi* in Telugu and the *Pavakoothu* of Kerala. The articles in it not only draw our attention to the plurality of the Rama story, but also point out the need as well as scope for further research in this field. For this to become a reality, the first step is to reclaim the tellings prevalent among different communities.

Even in our age, when printing has become widespread, Rama's story lives on in the minds of the people through its oral or visual performative narration and singing. The Ramleela of north India and the numerous folk dance forms popular in almost every part of the country are good examples of this. These have been formed as a result of the confluence of the life experiences of the local communities. The study by Anuradha Kapur on the Ramleela of Benares throws light on the local nature of the celebrations of the Rama story. H.D. Sankaliya, the renowned archaeologist, says that the events described in the Ramayana might have happened among two tribes of Madhya Pradesh. Numerous variations of the Ramayana exist in tribal regions. In Kerala itself, there are several unwritten Ramayanas. These range from the *Adiya Ramayana* of Wayanad to the *Mappila Ramayana* popularised through singing by D.H. Kunjiraman Nambiar. Collecting these texts and doing research on them will greatly contribute to a deeper understanding of the pluralistic nature of our culture.

It is in this context that the book written by Dr Azeez Tharuvana on the Wayanad Ramayanas assumes importance. This work is the result of painstaking and prolonged research. The Ramayana stories that have been collected and edited as part of this effort provide insights into the cultural consciousness and ideological world of the many communities in Wayanad. The general understanding is that the Ramayana story happened in Wayanad. The names of places and community consciousness corroborate this belief. It is believed that the ashram at Ashramkolly near Pulpally is Valmiki's ashram. Jadayattakavu is the place where Sita went down into the earth. People recognise the scar left by the tail of Hanuman, which he used to encircle the hill. These are only samples of the numerous beliefs prevailing in Wayanad that lend credence to the assumption that Wayanad is the field of action of the Ramayana. But there are several Ramayanas in Wayanad, not just one. Among them there are differences in the matter of details and the style of narration. The source of these differences is the life experiences of each place. In them are reflected the social relations of each community. The *Adiya Ramayana*, *Chetti Ramayana* and *Sitayana*, collected and edited by Azeez, are, as Ramanujan has put it, innovative tellings. These are the local variations of the *Valmiki Ramayana* and the *Adhyatma Ramayana* of Ezhuthachan. It is difficult to pinpoint when and how these started to be narrated. But one thing is certain, they originated in the soil of Wayanad. Azeez clearly points out this local nature of the Ramayana. To quote the author, 'Almost all the Ramayana stories of Wayanad are inextricably interwoven with the cultural, social, local and environmental peculiarities of Wayanad.'

The *Adiya Ramayana*, with all its variations, is different from the other Ramayana stories. It is tightly linked to the cultural and social conditions of Wayanad. Rama sees Sita, tripping over hills and dales, carrying all her belongings with her in the bamboo basket, and falls in love with her. But Sita falls in love with Ravana whom she meets on the way. Ravana, through a ruse, wins Sita's heart and takes her to Lanka in a bullock cart. Sita lives in Lanka on the condition that Ravana will not touch her or even her dress for twelve years. While staying in Lanka, Sita is not Rama's wife. She does not even know the reason for the burning down of Lanka by Hanuman. Thus, the Rama story is narrated differently here. We may say that this difference is a feature of all the tribal Ramayanas.

The Wayanad Ramayanas are only a section of the diverse narratives found among different communities across our country. They are an indication of the cultural plurality of India. In this sense, the Ramayana is not a religious text. It is a social text, a text that reflects the life of the communities in which these tellings are born.

This study on the Wayanad Ramayanas has been undertaken against the backdrop of the Ramayanas that exist in other parts of the world. In the first part of this book, Azeez Tharuvana analyses the Ramayanas of Wayanad, and in the second part, he shines a light on the narratives popular in the rest of India and abroad, beginning with the *Valmiki Ramayana*, thus paving the way for a comparative study of the plurality of the epic.

Undoubtedly, this is a profoundly meaningful contribution to the study of the Ramayana. I am delighted at having been given the opportunity to introduce this work, which will be interesting not only to scholars but to the general reader as well.

ONE TEXT, MULTIPLE ORAL NARRATIVES

Dr A. Nujum

It is through chance encounters with other races, that the past memories of a particular race are spread. It is part of history's dynamics that the development of livelihoods (agriculture, craft, tending of cattle and so on) of some ancient civilisations exert influence and exercise domination over other 'lesser' and 'inferior' civilisations. Their ethnic legends gain the upper hand and eclipse the genesis as well as survival stories of the subjugated races. Interactions between ethnic and 'caste' civilisations can happen in the context of domination, subjugation or cordiality.

The vitality and creativity of the Indian epics lies in their folk nature. Only communities which have not completely lost their identity can lay claim to this dynamism. This is conveyed well by the epic texts found in the oral traditions of Wayanad. In the reciprocity between civilisation and culture, we see that while civilisation depends on written texts, culture spreads through oral traditions. The written texts of the epics are the ideological products of civilisations, constructed by individuals with extraordinarily gifted minds. However, in oral traditions, the authorship rests with community spirit and tradition. Since the stories are not written down and are retained in memory alone, they are constantly reconstructed and revived. They are built and re-built based on the exigencies of time and space, as well as race and individuals. As opposed to the monologicity of a written text, they are polyphonic, with constantly changing polarities. The staticity of the written epic is continually demolished by oral traditions.

The authenticity of an epic lies in its continuity. When the interests of a civilisation confine it to a single text, the epic becomes a mere literary creation. 'Formal literature' is the concept and product of civilisation. It is in the nature of folklore to reconstruct history on the basis of the experiences and the worldview of the current times. They exist not as formal literature, but in the form of ritualistic arts and practices as well as narrations of the rural folk. As a civilisation advances and becomes dominant, it gains the tendency to swallow up other smaller civilisations and subcultures. So, almost as if in a spontaneous revolt against dominant civilisations, folk traditions, by their very nature, produce a thousand oral narrations.

In rural and tribal cultures the world over, epics are created by the local communities. The Kalevala in Finland is a good example of this. In the case of all the local written texts (varamozhi) of Kerala, the origin of the epics can be traced to the oral narrative (vaamozhi). It's the same in Wayanad, which, too, is an inexhaustible mine of folk epics. Azeez Tharuvana has conducted his study by closely interacting with the tribal-Dalit-religious communities. His work has resulted in an enquiry into the history, geography and cultural heritage of Wayanad. This study is guided by the political and ideological stance of reconstructing the cultural history of marginalised communities.

No doubt, this work has the capacity to intervene in the contemporary discourse on cultural history. One of its main aims has been to present findings in a simple, direct and transparent idiom, without falling into the trap of verbosity, use of dead words, as well as mystification, which are the creations of post-modernism, itself the result of imperialistic civilisation.

We hope that this work will be a model for a constructive and dialogical, alternative reading of culture and for a reconstruction of the text by the marginalised. I would like to believe that the researcher in Azeez Tharuvana has only initiated the process, and that many such studies will follow.

PREFACE

WHY MULTIPLE RAMAYANAS?

Azeez Tharuvana

> It spreads, ceaselessly various,
> one and many at once
>
> –Kampan

A.K. Ramanujan, in his essay 'Three Hundred Ramayanas: Five Examples and Three Thoughts on Translations', cites a folk story:

> One day when Rama was sitting on the throne, his ring fell off. When it touched the earth, it made a hole in the ground and disappeared into it. It was gone. His trusty henchman, Hanuman, was at his feet. Rama said to Hanuman, 'Look, my ring is lost. Find it for me.'
>
> Now Hanuman can enter any hole, no matter how tiny. He had the power to become the smallest of the small and larger than the largest thing. So he took on a tiny form and went down the hole.
>
> He went and went and went and suddenly fell into the netherworld. There were women down there. 'Look, a tiny monkey! It's fallen from above.' Then they caught him and placed him on a platter (*thali*). The King of Spirits (*bhut*), who lives in the netherworld, likes to eat animals. So

Hanuman was sent to him as part of his dinner, along with his vegetables. Hanuman sat on the platter, wondering what to do.

While this was going on in the netherworld, Rama sat on his throne on the earth above. The sage Vasistha and the god Brahma came to see him. They said to Rama, 'We want to talk privately with you. We don't want anyone to hear what we say or interrupt it. Do we agree?'

'All right,' said Rama, 'we'll talk.'

Then they said, 'Lay down a rule. If anyone comes in as we are talking, his head should be cut off.'

'It will be done,' said Rama.

Who would be the most trustworthy person to guard the door? Hanuman had gone down to fetch the ring. Rama trusted no one more than Laksmana, so he asked Laksmana to stand by the door. 'Don't allow anyone to enter,' he ordered.

Laksmana was standing at the door when the sage Visvamitra appeared and said, 'I need to see Rama at once. It's urgent. Tell me, where is Rama?'

Laksmana said, 'Don't go in now. He is talking to some people. It's important.'

'What is there that Rama would hide from me?' said Visvamitra. 'I must go in, right now.'

Laksmana said, 'I'll have to ask his permission before I can let you in.'

'Go in and ask then.'

'I can't go in till Rama comes out. You'll have to wait.'

'If you don't go in and announce my presence, I'll burn the entire kingdom of Ayodhya with a curse,' said Visvamitra.

Laksmana thought, 'If I go in now, I'll die. But if I don't go, this hotheaded man will burn down the kingdom. All the subjects, all things living in it, will die. It's better that I alone should die.'

So he went right in.

Rama asked him, 'What's the matter?'

'Visvamitra is here.'

'Send him in.'

So Visvamitra went in. The private talk had already come to an end. Brahma and Vasistha had come to see Rama and say to him, 'Your work in the world of human beings is over. Your incarnation as Rama must now he given up. Leave this body, come up, and rejoin the gods.' That's all they wanted to say.

Laksmana said to Rama, 'Brother, you should cut off my head.'

Rama said, 'Why? We had nothing more to say. Nothing was left. So why should I cut off your head?'

Laksmana said, 'You can't do that. You can't let me off because I'm your brother. There'll be a blot on Rama's name. You didn't spare your wife. You sent her to the jungle. I must be punished. I will leave.'

Laksmana was an avatar of Sesa, the serpent on whom Visnu sleeps. His time was up too. He went directly to the river Sarayu and disappeared in the flowing waters.

When Laksmana relinquished his body, Rama summoned all his followers, Vibhisana, Sugriva, and others, and arranged for the coronation of his twin sons, Lava and Kusa. Then Rama too entered the river Sarayu.

All this while, Hanuman was in the netherworld. When he was finally taken to the King of Spirits, he kept repeating the name of Rama. 'Rama Rama Rama …'

Then the King of Spirits asked, 'Who are you?'

'Hanuman.'

'Hanuman? Why have you come here?'

'Rama's ring fell into a hole. I've come to fetch it.'

The king looked around and showed him a platter. On it were thousands of rings. They were all Rama's rings. The king brought the platter to Hanuman, set it down, and said, 'Pick out your Rama's ring and take it.'

They were all exactly the same. 'I don't know which one it is,' said Hanuman, shaking his head.

The King of Spirits said, 'There have been as many Ramas as there are rings on this platter. When you return to earth, you will not find Rama. This incarnation of Rama is now over. Whenever an incarnation of Rama is about to be over, his ring falls down. I collect them and keep them. Now you can go.'

So Hanuman left.

Just like the rings of Rama, there are innumerable Ramas. Multiple texts of the Ramayana exist in written form as well as in oral traditions. All these texts, both written and oral, are tributaries entering the great river of the Ramayana. Modern Ramayana scholars reject as absurd the contention that among these multiform Ramayana traditions, some are more exalted than others. They consider the multiform nature of the Ramayana not a limitation, but as offering immense scope.

In her foreword to *Questioning Ramayanas: A South Asian Tradition*, edited by Paula Richman, Romila Thapar reminisces about the famous Pakistani writer Intizar Hussain, who, at a gathering of writers at Kathmandu, notably stated that he had never known that Ayodhya actually existed on a map. For him, 'it had always been a fabulous kingdom, a sound, a resonance. After the demolition of the Babri Masjid, he was compelled to remap his geography as a writer'. Hussain's perception of the Ramayana and his concept of Ayodhya are just one among the numerous ideas and varied interpretations. Thapar's words are a criticism and an admonition against the tendencies to reject or ignore the textual possibilities of a polyphonic Ramayana; they point to the fact that there can be numerous versions and different interpretations of the Ramayana.

The Ramayana literature is a great banyan tree that is constantly growing. It has deep roots and many branches.

Though its roots are Indian in origin, its branches have grown beyond India's borders and spread throughout the Asian nations, and have played decisive roles in the formation of the cultures in those regions. It can be said without doubt that there is no other story that has so influenced the oral and written literatures in India and its surrounding territories.

Mythologies are immortal texts that lend themselves to new meanings and interpretations as they are read across ages. They are handed down over generations, exerting influence on the reader or listener, leaving lasting imprints on their mind. They continue to exist in the abstract, impacting the subconscious of the individual and society. The Ramayana and the Mahabharatha are illustrations of this.

It is not possible to state the exact time period when the Ramayana story came into existence. However, there is no doubt that Valmiki's Ramayana was not the first version of the Rama story. Many oral narrations were in circulation even before Valmiki's time, as is evident in the Drona Parva and Shanti Parva of the Mahabaratha, which are condensed versions of the Rama tale. Camille Bulcke, who has the distinction of being known as India's most renowned Christian Hindi scholar, and was conferred the Padma Bhushan in 1974, has studied the origin and development of the Rama tale in his work *Ramkatha: Utpatti Aur Vikas*. He opines in his book that since the many oral narrations of the Ramayana were not available in textual form, Valmiki's version obtained the status of being the original, 'ancient' text of the Ramayana.

The archaeologist H.D. Sankalia, who has conducted an extensive study of the geographical sites mentioned in Valmiki's Ramayana, opines that an incident that occurred between two tribes in what is now Madhya Pradesh could be the source for the basis of the Ramayana.

The Ramayana, as we know it today, is a story of

considerable length. It was probably a short tale originally, which was expanded on by oral storytellers and wandering folk singers and minstrels. It was common for these singers to embellish the parts they liked. Indications that these bands of travelling singers used to sing these tales are evident in the *Valmiki Ramayana*. Such groups that eke out their living by singing and reciting folktales have always been present in India.

The disciples of Valmiki learnt the Ramayana by heart. Kusa and Lava might have captured the imagination of their listeners by reciting the Ramayana. The singers who were skilled in the craft of poetry would introduce refrains or enhance the lyrical and dramatic beauty of portions that had popular appeal, incorporating their own embellishments and interpretations in an attempt to make the tale more impressive. The more fantastic parts would grab the attention of listeners and viewers, instantly investing the tale told with a fresh lease of life.

The influence of the Ramayana is prevalent in varying degrees among the Hindu, Buddhist, Jain, Muslim and tribal communities. Each community has reconstructed the Rama story and made it their own. The Ramayana has spawned numerous texts and even more unofficial textual variations with diverse points of view. There exist caste-based, Dalit, tribal and feminist interpretations.

Several insertions have been added to the text of the *Valmiki Ramayana* to buttress and reinforce the concept of caste or Brahmin supremacy. The Vedas, Itihasas and the Puranas were thought to be the exclusive heritage of the upper castes, and were denied to the Dalits, including the Shudras. The Dalits were not permitted to read them or even to listen to them. Those who disobeyed this injunction were severely punished. Nevertheless, surmounting the obstacles created by these restrictions, various texts emerged among the Dalits. These were not copies of the texts of the upper caste or their mutilated imitations. Rather, they were authentic texts born of the Dalit communities themselves. Later, they evolved into survival strategies for overcoming their existential and identity crises. Dalit communities reimagined the personality of Rama that had been created by the upper castes, by setting him as a deity on par with their own deities, and sometimes below them too. They subjected him to trial and absorbed him within the boundaries of the tribal universe and within their concept of social justice. The ending of the *Adiya Ramayana*, where Rama is tried before the elders of the community for his failure to take care of Sita, is a glowing example of this. It is remarkable that in the first part of this folk or oral form of the Ramayana, Rama is a character who is accessible to the community of storytellers in the theatre of Wayanad.

The folk narrations of the Rama story develop in detail what was left out by written texts such as the *Valmiki Ramayana*, and throw to the winds all logic and objectivity. They demystify the supernatural and other-worldly elements introduced and established by the written texts and present gods and goddesses as ordinary human beings.

Like the Dalit Ramayanas, there have also been Ramayanas centred on women in India. Why is it that these have never been the subject of studies? There have been interpretations focused on Sita, just like the presentations or stories about Rama. The reading of Ramayana is not merely of Rama, it includes Sita as well. Such approaches have been attempted in recent times.

The *Chandrabathi Ramayana*, composed by Chandrabathi, who lived in the Maimensing region of East Bengal in the sixteenth century, is a remarkable woman-centric Ramayana. There's no mention of this work even in Camille Bulcke's

Ramkatha: Utpatti Aur Vikas, which is unanimously accepted as the encyclopaedia on Ramayana. Ignored by scholars in Bengal, the *Chandrabathi Ramayana* has survived across four centuries through the oral tradition. This work, which attempts to reconstruct the Ramayana from a woman-centric point of view, has several special features. Sita symbolises the despised, humiliated and downtrodden woman. In one instance she says, 'I have heard the cries of millions of women, the plaintive cries of millions of women who have lost their husbands and children.'

Chandrabathi traces Sita's journey, right from her birth through all the stages of her life, in a way very different from the one adopted by Valmiki. This is how she narrates the birth of Sita: Ravana had preserved the blood of the holy sages in a box, intending to use it as a poison to neutralise the immortality of the gods and thus reign as the unchallenged king of the three worlds. Ravana spent all his time with the women he stole from the land of the gods. His wife Mandodari, who was fed up of seeing and hearing about his debauchery, decided one day to die by consuming poison. But instead of poison, she drank the blood of the sages that Ravana had saved in the box. As a result, she did not die. Instead, she conceived. After a few months, she delivered an egg. The soothsayers of Lanka predicted that the egg contained the ruin of the rakshasa race. Hearing this, Ravana wanted to destroy the egg, but Mandodari would not allow it. She put the egg in a box made of gold and threw it into the sea. The box drifted up the Bay of Bengal, and was discovered by a poor, honest fisherman named Madhabjaliya, whose wife was called Sata. They worshipped the egg with great devotion. Lakshmi, the Goddess of wealth, who was hidden in the egg, blessed Sata, and the couple became rich. One night, Sata had a dream in which she was told to present the egg to King Janaka. Sata went to the king's palace and presented the egg. She prayed that the child born out of the egg be given the name of Sita, resembling her own name. So Sita was brought up by King Janaka. The *Chandrabathi Ramayana* makes it clear that though Sita was the daughter of Mandodari, Ravana was not her father.

The Adivasi deities, such as Valliyoorkavu Bhagavathy, Pulpally Bhagavathy, Pakkatheyyam, Thirunelly Perumal, Sidhappa, Nenchappa and Mathappadaivam, make an appearance in the *Adiya Ramayana*. Forest fairies, such as Athirukalan, Arupuli, Kandanpuli, Bammadan, Kaikolan and Tampiratti, are also important characters in the *Wayanad Chetti Ramayana*. In the same way, the local deities of Bengal, such as Mangalpandi, Manasa, Banadurga, Sulapani, Shithala and Shashthi, are introduced as characters in the *Chandramathi Ramayana*.

Such local interpretations have been attempted not only in India but also in all the Asian countries. The Wayanad Ramayanas are dominated by Sita and Lava and Kusa, who grow up without the protection of their father. A notable feature of all these stories is their pro-woman stance. These stories focus on the life of Sita and Lava and Kusa during the time of their abandonment.

The local oral and written texts in India and Asia, including the Wayanad Ramayanas, question and dismantle the argument about a single Ramayana. In fact, Sita must have been the first person to realise the plurality of the Ramayana. There is a scene in the Ayodhya Kanda of the *Adhyatma Ramayana* of Ezhuthachan in which Sita insists on going with Rama into the forest. She is not deterred by the possibility of the hardships she might face during the long exile. Finally she says:

Ramayanangal palavum kavivara-
ramodamodu paranju kelpundu njan

> *Janakiyodu kudathe Raghuvaran*
> *Kananavasathinennu poittullu?*
>
> I have heard the Ramayanas
> composed by several poets.
> Has the great Rama ever gone
> to the forest without Sita?

Sita is giving Rama a cue to ensure that the story is proceeding along the proper lines. The existential distinction between the story and the storyteller is being done away with here.

Kumaravyasa, the Kannada poet who lived in the fourteenth century, decided to compose a new Mahabharatha. His reasoning was that innumerable Ramayanas have already been composed, and that Adishesha, the king of serpents, is being smothered by the weight of the countless Ramayanas.

A large number of communities have been enriched by these creative interpretations. The process is an ongoing one; new Ramayanas come into existence all the time, whether in the oral or written form. India is not the only country where this happens—this is the case all over the Asian continent. These diverse texts are rich with the elements of human experience, social verities and the lives and cultures of the people among whom they are born. These Ramayanas are capable of conversing with each individual and the world around them. They encompass multiple voices from diverse contexts. They can reveal many truths. In brief, through the constantly evolving, vibrant Rama stories, a new space is created for understanding the cultural pluralities of India.

By analysing the folklore of the Ramayana in Wayanad, we do not intend to reconstruct history. Instead, we are aiming at the identification of the 'self' among the carriers of folk stories and their rich experiences. Ramayana is not a historical text; it is a myth. Myth and history are two separate things. 'Myths are sources of history; at the same time they are not history. By turning myth into history, the historian is bidding goodbye to history,' says Dr K.N. Panikkar.

In the present context of invading global cultures swallowing up small cultures, communities and their subcultures, understanding and protecting the history of local communities is of great importance. It is necessary to understand the role played and contributions made by the Puranas and Itihasas in the lives of such communities. It is my hope that this study will trigger reflections on how to ensure the survival of local and indigenous communities, including tribal societies, at a time when small cultures are being swallowed up on a global scale.

It can be said that it was during the capitalist phase of writing and printing, and the sovereignty of global media, that the canonisation of the Ramayana took place. The advent of printing served to establish a particular textual version of the Ramayana as the canon, thereby invalidating the other versions which existed in oral form. This canonisation was a kind of a colonisation of the simple and humble traditions of the Ramayana. An easy way to marginalise and make invisible whole communities is to block out their narratives. This is how Pulpally and Areapally were shoved aside, and Ayodhya firmly established its presence as the land of Rama. Dr K.M. Anil, who reviewed this manuscript, observed that the goal of this book is to weaken the structure of this canonisation from within.

A reflection on how marginalised communities, including the Adivasis, approach the Ramayana is essential for us to identify folk literatures and the beliefs and ritual systems of the tribal communities, which are on the path to extinction.

This work is a partial record of the research conducted under the guidance of Dr A. Nujum. The topic of the study was 'Ithihasa Kathakalude Nadodi Roopangal Wayanadu Jillayil' (Folk Forms of Mythical Stories in the Wayanad District). The oral forms of the Mahabaratha have not been included in this work. Therefore, Living Ramayanas is only a segment of my research thesis.

I received help from many people in preparing this work. I would like to express my heartfelt thanks to all those who have guided or assisted me in one way or another: the narrators who provided the data; the renowned historian Dr K. N. Panikkar, who wrote the foreword; Dr A. Nujum, who provided valuable guidance during every phase of the study; and all my other friends, who have been pillars of support in many different ways.

PART ONE

WAYANAD AND THE RAMAYANA

Among the tribal communities in Wayanad, there exist unique beliefs relating to the Ramayana story. What is more remarkable is that even within one tribe, there are many different versions of the same story. The tribal people of Wayanad use these versions of the Ramayana to justify their ritual beliefs, to trace their ancestry and to glorify their lineage.

Toponymical stories, belief systems, oral narratives, genesis accounts, art forms, temple-centric concepts, legends related to particular hills and many other such segments linked to Indian mythology exist in Wayanad. The first part of this book deals with an analysis of these.

THE ADIYA RAMAYANA

Kali Mathei is an elder and traditional healer of the Adiya tribal community of Thrissilery in the northern part of Wayanad district. He narrates the Ramayana story, which he inherited from his father, in the following manner:

> We believe our Pakkatheyyam (Lord of Pakkam) resides in the Pulpally region. One day, Pakkatheyyam confronted Sita, who was staying in Pulpally. 'Look, Sita, don't stay here. This area belongs to me. You can choose any place outside my area and build your hut there.' Pakkatheyyam then planted a boundary stone and measured out his land. (It was customary for the devas [deities] in ancient days to establish their control over lands. The jurisdictional limits of each God were clearly demarcated, and they also had their own temples. They set up dominions in places such as the Kottiyoor temple, the Thirunelly temple and the Valliyoorkavu temple, and settled there.)
>
> So, Sita left Pulpally and walked through the forest, crossing hills and dales, carrying all her belongings in a bamboo basket. Rama and Lakshmana were returning the same way, after a battle. Sita stepped aside for them. Rama's eyes fell on Sita. A flame leapt up in his heart. He said to Lakshmana, 'Lakshmana, what a stunning beauty she is! I would like to marry her.' By this time, Sita had disappeared among the trees.
>
> Rama had already lost his heart to her. She had to be won over at all costs. But how would he tell her what was

in his heart? Who else could speak to her? And what if she rejected him? Rama shared these thoughts with Lakshmana. Lakshmana replied, 'Brother, you are an archer without parallel. You are the king designate. Why feel diffident? We will meet Sita and tell her our wish. If she does not agree, we will use force and subdue her.'

Meanwhile, Sita had reached another hill, where Rama and Lakshmana could not see her. Ravana was travelling along the same path. Gently persuading her to pause en route, Ravana befriended Sita. Eventually, Ravana won Sita's heart over and took her to the city of Lanka in a bullock cart.

Lanka lay beyond a river, and to cross over, a bridge was needed. Hanuman and his friend the Bear built one. They encountered a problem while constructing it: Hanuman brought huge blocks of stone using both his mighty hands, but with much difficulty; Bear, on the other hand, took the stones in one hand with great ease and built the bridge. Hanuman was enraged by this. 'You are a woman, I am a man. How dare you carry with one hand the stones I bring with both?' In a fit of rage, he encircled the hill with his long tail and shouted, 'I will pull down this hill.'

Sita was at this time planting millet in the valley below. Hearing Hanuman's threat, she implored, 'O revered Hanuman, please do not pull the hill down now. We will be buried under the earth.' Hanuman yielded to her request and desisted. In return, Sita blessed Hanuman. 'O revered Hanuman, hereafter, you will not need to eat food from the ground. I have prepared food for you on the trees. You can eat that. Don't drink warm water, drink only fresh water. That is better for you and your progeny.' Accordingly, the monkeys, even to this day, live by eating fruits from the trees and drinking clear water from the streams.

Crossing the bridge, Ravana and Sita entered the city of Lanka. Ravana put Sita up in the topmost room of a twelve-storeyed tower. Sita said, 'Until twelve years have passed, you should not touch my body, not even my clothes. I shall become your wife only after that. Till that time, I will sit here and meditate.' Ravana agreed.

Meanwhile, Rama and Lakshmana were wandering around on the hill slopes and riverbanks. Rama's desire to marry Sita was growing stronger by the day. He told Lakshmana that he could not imagine a life without her. They combed Pulpally and Thirunelly, asking everyone they met if they had seen her. Finally, they landed at Pakshipathalam, where they saw Hanuman and his companions resting. Rama asked them if they had seen Sita.

Some of the monkeys reported having seen Sita and Ravana cross the bridge. Rama was not familiar with Lanka, the city across the bridge. He had never been there. But he knew that Ravana was the ruler of Lanka and that he was a bad character. So Hanuman spoke up: 'Wasn't it Sita who blessed me? I will go over there and bring her.'

Rama replied, 'You are a monkey. Won't that scoundrel arrest you and put you in chains?'

Hanuman said, 'Don't insult us by calling us monkeys. We will show you how strong and clever we are.' So saying, Hanuman leapt onto the adjacent tree, and then, to the next one. Leaping from tree to tree in this manner, he reached the top of a palm tree near the bridge. From there, the city of Lanka could be clearly seen. Hanuman did not land on the ground, nor did he cross the bridge. Instead, he leapt from the palm tree onto an areca nut tree on the other side of the bridge.

Rama was not sure where Hanuman had gone and whether he would find Sita. Rama and Lakshmana thought that he had left in protest against their speaking ill of the monkeys. So the brothers continued their search.

After a long search, Hanuman discovered that Sita was in a room at the top of Ravana's palace. But how would he reach her? Looking around the palace precincts, he saw a small pond. He devised a clever plan.

An Adiya woman (a member of the Adiya community) was washing Sita's clothes at the pond. Hanuman stopped nearby, pretending that a thorn had pierced his foot. 'Hey monkey, what are you doing here?' asked the Adiya woman.

'A thorn has pierced my foot. I am trying to pull it out,' replied Hanuman, leaping onto the coffee tree nearby. He observed the woman, who was humming while washing the clothes. After a while, when the cleaned clothes had dried, she put them in a basket. When the attention of the woman was elsewhere, Hanuman quickly entered the basket unseen, and hid under the pile of clothes. Unaware of this, the woman hoisted the basket onto her head and walked away. On reaching the room where Sita was staying, she put the basket down and left. Hanuman leapt out of the basket. Sita, who was lost in reverie, was startled at his appearance. Recognising him, she said, 'You are the fellow who wanted to pull the hill down on us. You better go away. If people see you here, they will kill you. If Ravana comes to know you are here, he will throw you into a cage.'

Hanuman climbed out through the window and sat on top of a coconut tree. Looking around, he saw children playing marbles in the courtyard and people walking through the by-lanes. To attract their attention, he played a trick. He plucked some coconuts and started hurling them down. The people walking on the streets saw this. Those in the palace heard the sound. They came out to see what the commotion was about. 'Who is this madcap, plucking the ripe and unripe coconuts? Catch that rascal and kill him.' Hanuman paid them no attention; he continued throwing the coconuts down. Soon, the trees started to look bare, and the city was in chaos. Bows and arrows in hand, people started surrounding the tree on which Hanuman was perched. Hanuman shouted, 'If you want to catch me, you will first have to cut down all the trees, coconut, areca, banana, coffee, everything. I will come down only when all the trees have been cut.'

The people conferred among themselves for a while, and decided to cut down the trees. They came armed with axes, scythes, knives, whatever they could get hold of, and cut down all the trees in sight. Their first target was the tree on which Hanuman sat. When that tree was about to fall, he leapt to the next. When that too was felled, he jumped onto another. In the end, there was only one coconut tree left. Perched on that, Hanuman surveyed the graveyard of fallen trees and the agitated group of people with their sticks and knives. He shouted, 'I will come down. But no one should touch me or abuse me. I will tell you how you can kill me.'

'Interesting fellow,' the crowd muttered, curious and angry at the same time. 'Tell us, you bloody monkey! How should we kill you?'

Hanuman did not appreciate being cursed. 'Don't you dare insult me. There may be many of you and I am alone, but you won't be able to even touch me. I will show you who I am.' The crowd fell silent. He continued, 'I will tell you how you can kill me. Bring the clothes of all the people in this town and two cans of kerosene. Wrap the clothes around my tail, then pour kerosene and set fire to it. You are not to beat, kick or stab me. I will die only by fire.'

The people were overjoyed hearing this. They clapped their hands and laughed and shouted. Hanuman spoke again, in a derisive tone this time. 'When I am dead, you can collect my ashes and smear them on your foreheads. It will bring you God's blessings.' In a frenzy, the townspeople ran to their homes and the textile shops on the streets. They returned with all the clothes they could lay their hands on. Those who were rich exhibited their wealth by bringing exquisite clothes in bullock and buffalo carts. The poor, who had no clothes except the ones on their bodies, stood at a distance, watching all the drama. They hadn't lost any trees because they were landless.

Hanuman descended to the ground and showed his

tail. People stood in a queue to drape it with clothes. The first man who wrapped the clothes he had brought around Hanuman's tail was an important personality in the town. He had brought a cartload of clothes, seeing which the others thought that would be more than enough to cover the monkey's entire tail. But as he kept winding the clothes around the tail, Hanuman kept lengthening it. It got longer and longer, and the clothes brought by the rich man proved insufficient to cover even a small patch of Hanuman's long tail. He felt embarrassed and stepped back.

The second man, also rich and important, had brought in a full cartload as well. But he too had to withdraw, humiliated, as his offerings could only cover a fraction of the tail. A third man followed and a fourth. But the situation remained the same. The more they tried to cover it, the more the tail kept getting longer and only the end remained covered. All those present hung their heads in shame at being outwitted by a monkey. Those who had brought no clothes save the ones they were wearing, burst into laughter looking at their predicament. Hanuman looked at them and said, 'If you have used up all the clothes you have brought, pour kerosene and set fire to my tail. In just a few minutes, I will be reduced to ashes. Then you can collect my ashes and smear them on your forehead. You will receive God's blessings.'

The sarcasm in his words was not lost on the people, but they still followed his directive. The flames leapt up. The townspeople told themselves that they would be rid of Hanuman now. When the flames grew as tall as a hill, they moved away to avoid being scorched by the heat, while Hanuman leapt onto the roof of a house thatched with dry grass. When the house started to burn, Hanuman jumped onto the roof of the next house. He then jumped from one rooftop to the next, and in no time, all the houses in the town were reduced to ashes. Meanwhile, the people forgot they were supposed to catch Hanuman and kill him. They started to run helter-skelter, crying aloud, 'Our homes have been burnt down, our wives and children are dead.' A heat wave engulfed the town. When all the houses were gutted, Hanuman jumped into the pond near the palace where Sita was staying and put out the fire on his tail. Then he ran into the room Sita was resting in, oblivious to the mayhem outside. She was feeling nervous. Like the town of Lanka, her mind too was on fire. Ravana was out of town on some important business. On seeing Hanuman, Sita became enraged and started hurling abuses at him. He chose not to reply, and sat down in a corner of the room, feigning ignorance of the incident outside. Finally, Sita asked him, 'Why did you come to Lanka? What do you want? Who sent you over here?'

Unperturbed, Hanuman replied, 'I came to take Sitadevi with me. Rama sent me. I see that you have fallen into a trap.'

'Why has Rama sent you? What has Rama to do with me?'

To this Hanuman replied, 'Rama is in love with you. He wants to marry you. He is a king-designate.' He then waxed on about Rama's qualities and exploits.

Sita was a little mollified listening to Hanuman. 'What will I say to Ravana? He will be come looking for me.'

'Ravana is a wicked fellow,' said Hanuman. 'He has a wife and yet he philanders.'

Sita did not try to contradict Hanuman. She had heard some of the stories circulating about Ravana, and they flashed through her mind now.

That same night, she left with Hanuman for Iruppu (in Kudagu district in Karnataka, adjacent to Wayanad), where Rama was living at the time.

On meeting Rama, Hanuman said, 'I would like to make a request. Hereafter, please do not call me and my kith and kin monkeys. Now you know there are strong people among us.'

Rama said to Hanuman, 'Then I shall take all the strong monkeys into my army, and I will make you the leader of the Monkey Brigade.'

On hearing this, Hanuman was delighted. He agreed to join Rama's army.

All this while, the shy Sita sat, eyes averted, not knowing what to say or do. Then Rama approached her and declared his love. He also narrated the details, to her amazement, of all his wanderings in search of her. Sita silently accepted Rama's proposal. They started their life together as man and wife. Lakshmana accepted Sita as the wife of his elder brother.

As the days passed, some disagreements cropped up between Rama and Sita. While in Lanka, Sita had become used to the luxuries in Ravana's palace, where every conceivable comfort had been made available to her. While at Iruppu, they had to live in a hut. She had no companions, no maids-in-waiting, no servants. She was also very lonely, as there were no other houses near their hut. All this started affecting her behaviour.

Rama and Lakshmana went hunting with their bows and arrows daily, returning with the deer and wild boar they killed in the forest. As soon as they returned, Sita would serve them hot coffee. Quite often, Rama did not like the coffee. He would find a hair or something similar in the coffee she made or the sweets she prepared. 'O Sita, what is happening? Do you not love me?' he would ask. Sita would silently retreat into a corner.

Days and months went by in this fashion. Meanwhile, Sita became pregnant. Though on the surface they seemed happy, Rama began to be plagued by nagging doubts. Some people had seen Sita going to Lanka with Ravana. For a while now, there had been murmurs at the bathing ghats and near the drinking water wells where people gathered and talked.

No one was aware of Ravana's assurance that he would

not touch Sita's body, or even her clothes, for twelve years. The scandalous tattle had reached Rama, but he did not pay heed. But, as the news of Sita's pregnancy travelled far and wide, so did the gossip. Soon the rumours made it unbearable for Rama to even step out to the bazaar. But he did not mention them to Sita.

One day, after Rama returned ravenous from hunting, Sita served him rice and curry. There were stones and sand in the rice. Rama lost his temper and hurled abuses at her. Unable to bear her grief, Sita retaliated. Leaving the meal unfinished, Rama walked out. This quarrel was overheard by some gossip-mongers passing that way, and the pair became the talk of the town. Rumours spread thick and fast that Rama and Sita had fallen out over the issue of Sita's pregnancy. As the days went by, the rumour gathered strength, spreading like wildfire. Women who came to visit Sita whispered their suspicions to each other. All this took a toll on Rama's mind. One day, he told his brother, 'Lakshmana, Sita is a fallen woman. I am fed up with her. Take her to the hill and slay her.'

Lakshmana was as devoted to Sita as he was to his elder brother. He was in a fix. How could he disobey his older brother's command? How could he kill his brother's wife? That too a pregnant woman? Lakshmana was plunged into unbearable grief. Going against Rama's wishes, given the state he was in, could lead to grievous consequences. Rama handed Lakshmana a gleaming new sword, and commanded, 'Kill her today itself!' Having uttered these terrible words, Rama went into his room, bolted the door and lay down.

Lakshmana and Sita travelled through the forest by horse cart, then bullock cart, then on foot, and reached the foot of Garshimala. On approaching the hill, Lakshmana unsheathed his sword and looked at its shining blade. Suddenly, the image of the twins in Sita's womb flashed in the gleaming blade of the sword as if in a mirror. What a terrible sin he was about to commit. He let out a piteous cry. On seeing him cry, Sita asked, 'Lakshmana, why are you crying?'

With a loud cry of anguish, he replied, 'Rama has asked me to kill you. I cannot do it. I will not obey my brother's orders. I see two children playing on the blade of this sword. No, I cannot kill you. I will kill myself instead.'

Wiping Lakshmana's tears with the end of her sari, Sita said, 'You need not kill me, nor do you need to kill yourself. We both can live. There is a way out of this quandary. I will show you.' Pointing to a tree she said, 'Make a cut on that tree with your sword.'

Lakshmana hacked at the tree with all his might.

Sita asked, 'What do you see flowing from the tree trunk?'

'Milk,' he replied.

'That is nourishment for the babies in my womb,' said Sita. 'Trees such as jackfruit, fig and koli have milk.' Pointing to another tree, she said, 'Make a cut on that tree.' It was a Malabar kino tree.

Lakshmana made a cut on the trunk of the tree.

'What is coming out?' she asked.

'Blood,' replied Lakshmana.

'Take that blood, smear it on your sword and clothes, and go back to Rama.'

Lakshmana followed Sita's instructions and returned.

Sita gave birth to twins in Valmiki's ashram at Ashramkolly near Pulpally. As the children grew up, they learnt to read and write and acquired general knowledge. They also started farming near the ashram. They grew rice, elephant yam and taro, and planted coffee and pepper trees. They also grew bitter gourd and beans on their farm. The crops flourished. The plants flowered and bore fruits.

One day, a huge horse that belonged to Rama came and destroyed their crops. No one dared complain or question when this horse entered farmlands and ruined the standing crops. No one ever stopped it or drove it away, as they all feared the wrath of Rama, the most skilled archer in the world.

But the twins could not bear the sight of their crops being destroyed. They caught hold of the horse and tied it to a tree. When the horse did not return to the fold by evening, Rama, Lakshmana and Hanuman set out in search of it. They went in different directions. Hanuman heard the distressed neighing of the horse from afar. He was surprised to see the horse tied up to a tree and made to free it. But the children chased Hanuman away. When Hanuman reported this to Rama and Lakshmana, they were furious and rushed to the spot. 'Who has trapped this horse?' they shouted.

Unperturbed, the children came forward and replied, 'We caught it.' There followed a verbal duel. Rama did not realise that he was arguing with his own children. The angry exchange of words developed into a fight. The children defeated Rama, Lakshmana and Hanuman and tied them to trees. Sita watched all this from the window and wondered how a compromise could be reached.

She sent letters to Valliyoorkavu Bhagavathy, Pulpally Bhagavathy, Pakkam Theyyam, Kottiyoor Perumal, Sidhappa, Nanchappa and Mathappa Daivam. As soon as they received the letter, they rushed to the spot. They discussed the various aspects of the matter. Then they cross-examined Rama and Lakshmana, making them aware of who the children really were. The elders said, 'These are your own children. You did not even recognise that.' Others said, 'Children growing up away from their father will usually behave worse than this.' Rama and Lakshmana were willing to come to a compromise, so the elders untied them from the trees and released them. Despite the defeat and humiliation, Rama and Lakshmana were happy that they had found the children.

These were the terms of the agreement—'Do not fight, do not encroach, accept Sita and the children.' The elders also decided on authorities for each of the territories and localities. 'No one should violate these norms'. The rulers and deities were decided in the following fashion—Pakkatheyyam for Thirunelly and Cheruvali regions; Pookkarimage Theyyam for Vadaku Manram region; Karichathan for Evila regions, Jogiyachan for Kuppathodu regions, Ulankattu for Ulankattu Muthukattu regions, Malakkan for Katchalevelappa regions, Pookkarimage Theyyam for Puthurila regions, Kallarache Theyyam for Kallilamarigod region, Kandappeeli for Madasserimala region, Kalappan for Kalamkottu Muthiramattila region, Thirumuna Theyyam for Seythe Thirumunda regions, Pandinadu Thamprakkanmar for Pandinadu region. The deities then said, 'They should not encroach on our territory. If they do, all will resist them united.' Rama and Lakshmana were informed about this.

This arrangement is maintained even today. After examining all the aspects of the case, Sita was summoned. She and Rama came face to face. Rama admitted that he had made a mistake. Sita narrated to the twins the story of their birth and the sequence of events that had transpired before that. They were delighted that their father and mother were re-united. Finally, Sita agreed to go to Iruppu[1] along with Rama. All the elders along with Hanuman accompanied them to Iruppu. Sita lives in Iruppu even today, where there is a temple in her name.

The above story, told by Kali Mathei, has several versions within the Adiya community itself.

THE WAYANAD CHETTI RAMAYANA

Kalankandy Ravunnichetti, a member of the Chetti community of Muthanga near Sulthan Bathery in Wayanad district, is an elder of the community and a farmer. He narrates their Ramayana story:

It was Thretha Yuga. Rama, after his forest exile and the execution of Ravana, reached the city of Ayodhya accompanied by Sita and Lakshmana. The coronation ceremony was conducted shortly and Rama took over the reins of the country. The people of Ayodhya were happy with Rama's rule. However, they remained suspicious of Sita's faithfulness. In a sense, they were justified, as the image of Sita in their mind was associated with her abduction by Ravana, the wicked and womanising king of the rakshasas. It would be unreasonable to expect the common folk to believe that Sita, the epitome of feminine beauty, the object of every man's desire, could retain her chastity in Ravana's palace.

The conjectures and gossip spread throughout the country and reached Rama's ears too. Rama, who loved his wife dearly, was deeply distressed. He decided that the best way to distance himself from the scandal and protect his reputation was to abandon Sita. But the decision virtually paralysed him, causing much grief and giving him many a sleepless night. Finally, he sent for Lakshmana and informed him of his decision to send Sita away.

With a heavy heart, Lakshmana got ready to carry out

his elder brother's wishes. He told Sita that he would take her to visit the hermits in the forest to seek their blessings. The unsuspecting Sita was excited at the prospect of enjoying the pure air and sylvan beauty of the ashram precincts. Sumantra, Rama's able minister, drove the chariot in the direction of the forest. Sita couldn't help but notice that Lakshmana and Sumantra did not share her enthusiasm and joy for being in the midst of nature. On the way, she saw several bad omens and unknown fears gripped her. 'O Prince Lakshmana! Why are you both silent? I see bad omens everywhere. What is the matter? Tell me.'

Containing the sea of sorrow within, Lakshmana said, 'Dear sister, don't be frightened. Everything will be fine.' Lakshmana's words could not comfort Sita. The journey forward was like a funeral procession. Lakshmana's anguish at having to follow Rama's orders to abandon Sita in the forest knew no bounds. To avoid having to speak to her, Lakshmana sat with his face turned away. They reached the banks of the Ganga at sunset and halted there for the night. Early next morning, they crossed the river and continued their journey. As they neared their destination, Lakshmana was unable to hold back his tears any more and cried aloud. Sita asked, 'Why do you cry, young prince? What is the matter? Is it because you are separated from your elder brother for a night? Look at me. I was separated from my husband for a year, when I was abducted. Don't grieve this way, Lakshmana. Be at peace!' Sita's consolation only doubled Lakshmana's grief. Gripped by suspicion, she demanded the truth. Lakshmana could no longer hide it and told her everything. Sita, who was deeply devoted to her husband, fainted from the shock of hearing what he had planned. When she recovered consciousness, she wept bitterly. 'O my Lord, why did you abandon me? How will I bear this? Oh God, what am I hearing? Is this true? I would rather die than face this. If I choose to jump into a fire, it would not help me. It will refuse to burn me. How am I to embrace death? Lakshmana, please go back to your brother. Give him my good wishes. Tell him I want him to rule the country well.' She fainted again and fell to the ground. Lakshmana, who had got her permission to return to Ayodhya, walked around her thrice, then, whimpering, he turned and slowly walked away. Sita, the abandoned daughter of Mother Earth, lay on the ground and sobbed like a child on the lap of its mother. Her cries could be heard even at Valmiki's ashram, some distance away. The young hermits came to the spot to see what had happened. They found Sita and informed Sage Valmiki about the incident.

Touched by Sita's suffering, the forest fairies gathered around her. They were at a loss as to how to console her. An oppressive silence enveloped the forest.

Sage Valmiki, accompanied by the hermits, arrived at the place where Sita was lying. 'Take it as part of fate and be at peace. Come with us to the ashram. We will take care of you.' The great sage's comforting words gave Sita some solace. She slowly walked to the ashram with them. But even though she was safe there, her grief knew no bounds. Her hot tears scalded Mother Earth's bosom, and pooled together in a spot without being absorbed into the ground. In the course of time, this pool of tears turned into a lake. Even today, devotees believe that the lake known as Sitakulam at Ponkuzhy on the Wayanad border was born of Sita's tears.

The young hermits and forest fairies watched over Sita at Valmiki's ashram, but nothing could assuage her grief. Days passed this way, and when it was time, Sita gave birth to a baby boy. The little one brought her some happiness. Soon the toddler started taking his first steps.

One day, Sita went out to fetch water from the stream, taking along the baby with her. The little one was playing and dancing. Suddenly she saw that a leech had attached itself to the baby's foot. A pang went through Sita's heart.

Pain turned to rage and made her utter a curse. 'May all the leeches in this place be damned,' she said. Ever since, that particular area in Pulpally has been free of leeches.

On another day, when Sita went to the stream to get water, she left the little one behind in the ashram, requesting Sage Valmiki to keep an eye on the baby. When she reached the banks of the stream, Sita saw a touching sight. A monkey was holding its baby to its breast. Overcome by maternal love, she returned to the ashram, took her baby, and went back to the stream. Valmiki was immersed in his daily activities and did not notice that Sita had taken the child with her. After a while, he looked for the baby and found, to his horror, that he was missing. The sage was in a fix. Sita would soon return. How would he face her if her precious child, her only comfort through those dark and difficult days, was missing? There was no time to lose. He plucked a blade of kusa (halfa) grass and, using his spiritual powers, created a baby that looked exactly like Sita's son. Valmiki seated the baby he had created in his lap and waited for Sita to return. When she did, he was astonished to see that the boy was with her, holding on to the hem of her sari. Sita was equally bewildered to see a baby that looked exactly like her own with Valmiki. Realising the slip, the sage narrated what had happened. Sita embraced the baby created by Valmiki. When the time to name the babies came, Valmiki named Sita's natural-born Lava and the boy he had created from the strand of kusa grass 'Kusa'.

One day, Sita and the young boys, accompanied by Valmiki and the forest deities, reached Ashramkolly near Pulpally to meet the sages in those areas. During their stay there, Valmiki took Lava and Kusa to the high mountains of Sisumala, now known as Sasimala, and trained them in the martial arts. The boys became experts in the martial arts, including the *divya-astras* (supernatural weapons).

In those days, the Vanavedans (forest hunters) used to

live in large numbers in Pulpally and the surrounding areas. The Vedans, who took to hunting and gathering of forest-produce as a means of livelihood, were devoted to their king and to God. One day, the Vedan king, along with his retinue, went on a hunting expedition. As the hunt progressed, the reverberating sound of bows and arrows could be heard from a distance. The Vedans traced the source of the sound and reached Sisumala, where they saw Valmiki training the boys in martial arts. The Vedans bowed and prostrated themselves before the trio. Then they descended the mountain to meet Sitadevi. They touched her feet and attained liberation. The Vedan king who ruled the forests gifted suitable plots of land to Sita, Lava and Kusa. In that place today stands the Sitadevi temple of Pulpally.

During this period, Sri Rama was ruling Ayodhyapuri, and the people there were prosperous and happy. Rumours about Sita had been forgotten by now. Besides, in Rama's mind, she still reigned as his dutiful wife and royal queen. It was at this time that he decided to conduct the Aswamedha yajna. Among the invitees to the yajna were sages and the great monkeys Sugriva and Hanuman. Following the prescription of the royal preceptor Vasishta Maharishi, a golden statue of Sita was installed in the yajna hall. Gifts were given to the sages and the Brahmins in attendance. Lakshmana reached the venue with the yajna horse. People had gathered there in the thousands, and they chanted Rama's name. The yajna horse started its triumphal march to conquer the lands in all the eight directions.

The rule of the yajna was that if anyone stopped the horse on its way, a battle would ensue. If the horse was allowed to pass through any territory unhindered, it would amount to the other king recognising the sovereignty of Ayodhya, and be taken as a sign of his readiness to pay tribute to the king, Rama. A proclamation to this effect was hung round the neck of the horse. As it went along the prescribed route, no one stopped it. Finally, it entered the forest on the western side of Valmiki's ashram, near Ponkuzhy on the Wayanad border. Lava and Kusa stopped the horse there and tied it to a banyan tree. Then they went and informed their guru, Valmiki. When days had passed with no news of the horse reaching Rama, he sent Lakshmana and Hanuman in search of it. They searched for the horse in several countries and were told that it had indeed passed through those territories. Finally, following its hoofmarks, Lakshmana and Hanuman reached Ponkuzhy and consulted the Vanadevathas (forest deities)—Athirukalan, Arupuli, Kandanpuli, Dammadan, Kaikkolan and Thampuratti. They were told that Lava and Kusa had accosted the horse, so Lakshmana and Hanuman proceeded to meet the boys. They reached and asked them to release the horse. But Lava and Kusa said, 'We haven't tied the horse to release it. The plaque that hangs round its neck reads, "Pay tribute, else fight". We are prepared to fight.'

Both the camps remained resolute, and so they fought a battle. The boys won. Hanuman was caught, chained and imprisoned. Lakshmana sent word to Rama, informing him of the unhappy developments. Rama was furious. 'Who are those boys? Are they the Rudra of Kailasa, or Devendra or the Divine Guards of the eight directions? Or are they incarnations of Ravana, whom I killed with my arrows?' Rama's imagination went wild. He took up his bow and arrows and, accompanied by his chosen soldiers, started walking through the forests. As they crossed Ponkuzhy on the Kerala border, they heard the plaintive neighing of the yajna horse and the shouts of Hanuman. Rama flared up, and when he reached Rampalli in Wayanad, he took his bow and pulled the string. The sound of the taut bow reverberated through the forest and reached the ends of the earth, frightening all living beings. All nature was plunged into silence and gloom. Lava and Kusa heard the reverberations and prepared for battle. Striding into the battleground, Rama ordered them to release Lakshmana, Hanuman and the yajna horse. Lava and Kusa showed no signs of fear, nor did they cow down. Handing over to Rama the proclamation hung round the horse's neck, they said, 'Who has written this? You should know there are others more skilled than you in archery. Get ready for battle. Else be prepared to pay us tribute, instead.'

Rama went to war with Lava and Kusa. His arrows were burnt down in the fire of Sita's faith, and Lava and Kusa defeated him. The boys took the captured Hanuman to their mother. Sita was pained to see her husband, Lakshmana and Hanuman crushed by the defeat, and asked Lava and Kusa to stop fighting. But they said they could not stop without the consent of their guru. The two informed Valmiki about the battle, who then asked them to release Hanuman and the horse. He went over to the battleground, greeted Rama and Lakshmana and took them to his ashram. Valmiki then revealed to Lava and Kusa that Sri Rama was their father.

Lava and Kusa were amazed to hear this, and excited. The place where Valmiki seated Rama and Lakshmana near the ashram is where the Ponkuzhy temple stands today. He seated Lava and Kusa on the battleground and Sita under a banyan tree. Sitadevi offered holy, life-giving water to devotees and all living things in the forest from the Sitakulam pond. Earlier, she had collected water from the stream nearby, Valmiki had bathed in it and Rama and Lakshmana had also washed themselves in it. Sita declared that all those who visited her, Rama, Lakshmana, Lava and Kusa would obtain moksha (liberation) if, after a dip in the holy waters, they circumambulated around Rama and Sita and had a holy bath in the Sitakulam. Rama gave moksha to the Vanadevathas and made them subsidiary gods. He blessed them and said that whenever other devotees offered oblations to him and the Sitadevi, they too would get a share of the benefits of the pooja.

After this, Rama and Lakshmana made arrangements

to return to Ayodhya. They invited Sita to the palace, but she wasn't prepared to go to Ayodhya, the place that had humiliated her and turned her away. Instead, she prayed to Mother Earth to receive her back. The earth split open, and Sita disappeared into it. As she was disappearing into the gorge that had opened up in the earth, Rama caught hold of her hair. A tuft of it came off in his hand. The spot where Sita disappeared came to be known as Jadayattakavu, near Pulpally in Wayanad.

THE WAYANAD SITAYANAM

Balan Puzhamudi is an upper-caste Hindu from Puzhamudi near Kalpetta in the central region of Wayanad, and an expert craftsman who works with coconut shells. He is an ardent devotee of Hanuman, and many people in Wayanad believe his version of the Ramayana story, which is known as the Sitayanam. The stories he tells are connected to historical sites like temples and mountains, which are to this day associated with Rama. These tales are summarised below:

> During Sita's sojourn in the forest with Rama and Lakshmana, Ravana abducted and took her to Lanka. Rama sent his monkey contingent in all directions in search of Sita. The search party that went southwards under Hanuman's command had to cross dense forests. They deliberately chose this path so that food would be readily available, abundant in the form of fruits and tubers (the Sita-phalam and Rama-phalam, the Sita fruit and Rama fruit, of the forests of Wayanad are famous). When they reached Brahmagiri through Coorg, Hanuman and his followers saw cranes, water dripping from their feathers. This was a sign that there was water nearby. So the monkeys followed the birds and reached the famous Pakshipathalam. Pakshipathalam, meaning birds' valley, is located eight kilometres from Thirunelly.
>
> In those days, the vulture Sampathi, Jatayu's brother, was doing tapas (penance) at Pakshipathalam (the people

of Coorg refer to Pakshipathalam as Muniyara; 'muni' meaning sage). Sampathi narrated several incidents relating to the abduction of Sita to the search party under Hanuman. Hearing what Sampathi had to say, the group was convinced that Ravana had abducted Sita and that she had been taken to Lanka. Sampathi also gave them clear directions to reach Lanka. They passed this information on to the other search parties. After all of them reached Pakshipathalam, they rested there for some time, before proceeding along the route indicated by Sampathi, which went from Pakshipathalam to Thirunelly, then on to Mananthavady, Pongini, Muttil, Puthoorvayal, Meppadi, Meenmutti, Anappuzha, Nilambur, Mannarkkad, Palakkad, Pollachi, Palani, Madurai, Rameswaram and, finally, Sri Lanka.

After offering prayers to Vishnu at the Thirunelly temple, the search party reached Mananthavady, where a Vishnu temple is also believed to have existed. Next, they stopped at the Pongini temple of Bhadrakali near Panamaram. After worshipping there, they proceeded to the Vishnu temple at Muttil, and worshipped the deity there. Then they started for the Umamaheswari temple of Shiva and Parvathy at Puthoorvayal. From there, the search party travelled through the hills and reached Mannarkkad via the Nilambur forests without descending from the hills (the path to Nilambur through the mountains is a very old one. Once upon a time, it was the royal path, according to Balan Puzhamudi). Proceeding from there, the party reached Palakkad, and after travelling though Palani and Madurai, they reached Rameswaram. They stopped and prayed at all the sacred shrines that fell en route. From Rameswaram, Hanuman and the party left for Lanka.

Sita's Sojourn in the Forest

People started to spread scandalous rumours about Sita because she had lived in Ravana's palace in Lanka. The tales were started by a rajaka, a washerman who was the reincarnation of a parrot Sita had once caged. Hearing the rumours, Rama abandoned Sita. Lakshmana was deputed to take Sita into the forests beyond the jurisdiction of Rama and his vassals. Wayanad in those days was ruled by the asura kings. Today's Gundlupet in Karnataka was at that time known as Kondalpuram and fell within the kingdom of Rama and his vassals. Therefore, Lakshmana abandoned Sita at Ponkuzhy, which was a dense forest outside the jurisdictional territory of Kondalpuram palace.

The Kanneerthadakom (pool of tears) was formed by Sita's tears, during her stay at Ponkuzhy. The hermits who saw Sita living alone in Ponkuzhy took her to Valmiki's ashram in Ashramkolly near Pulpally. There, she gave birth to Lava and Kusa. Sita and her sons lived in hermitages on eight hills near Pulpally. These hills are known today as Sasimala. Sita is known to have lived in Pulpally for sixteen and a half years. Lava and Kusa grew up in Pulpally and the surrounding areas. The Adivasis in those areas provided Sita with food items, such as thena, finger millets and little millets, during her stay there.[2]

Sita's Disappearance at Pulpally

Sri Rama conducted the Aswamedha yajna when he was sixty years old. Hanuman followed the horse to ensure its safety. As soon as the horse entered the Wayanad region, beyond the jurisdictional area of Kondalpuram palace, near Ponkuzhy, Lava and Kusa chained the horse. (There is a Lava and Kusa temple near Ponkuzhy, where the incident is supposed to have taken place. An annual festival is held here). They took Hanuman hostage and brought him to Sita. 'Mother, look, we caught this old monkey.' Sita, who regarded Hanuman as her first son, was seeing him after sixteen long years. They recognised each other. Though Sita asked Lava and Kusa to release him, Hanuman did not agree to it. Instead, he sent a message to Rama, saying that the monkeys who followed him had chained him, and urged him to reach Pulpally at the earliest.

On arriving, Sri Rama recognised Sita and his children at once. He expressed his intention to take Lava and Kusa to Ayodhya. Sita wasn't prepared to go to Ayodhya with Ram. Instead, she ardently prayed to Mother Earth to receive her. Accordingly, the earth split open and Sita, along with the Saptha Mathas, the seven divine mothers, went down into the bowels of the earth. As Sita plunged down into the earth, Sri Rama caught her by her hair, which came off in his hand. The place in Pulpally where this happened is named Jadayattakavu after the incident. Following Sita's disappearance, Sri Rama was plunged into deep grief. Finally, along with Lava and Kusa, he returned to Ayodhya. There, they lived together for about ten years.

Sita's Stay and Disappearance at Pulpally

Prabhakaran is the caretaker of the Valmiki ashram at Ashramkolly, and a member of the Ezhava community. He narrates a belief regarding Sita's stay at the Valmiki ashram after being abandoned by Rama on suspicions of her purity:

Sita in the Valmiki Ashram at Pulpally

After the burning down of Lanka, Sita returned to Ayodhya with Rama and Lakshmana. One day, an inquisitive woman requested Sita to share her experience in Lanka. Among other things, Sita mentioned that Ravana had ten heads. The woman then asked Sita if she could make a sketch of Ravana for her. Sita drew the figure of Ravana on a stool that was nearby to illustrate his ten heads. When Rama came that way, the gossipmonger told him that Sita had drawn the sketch of Ravana, which showed she was still thinking of him. She went out and set off a rumour mill.

After this, one day, while cursing his wife and referring to her waywardness, a washerman in Ayodhya said, 'Don't behave like Sita in Lanka.' This remark somehow reached Rama's ears. The rumour that Sita had been unfaithful started spreading like wildfire wherever people assembled. This created difficulties for Rama, who ruled the state as per the wishes of his subjects. He started to reflect. How could he overcome this scandal? Finally, he arrived at a solution: put Sita to death. Lakshmana was entrusted with the task. At first, Lakshmana was reluctant. But Rama's distress got the better of him and at last, much against his own will, he obliged.

The following day, Lakshmana set out with Sita to carry out Rama's wish. Sita was pregnant at the time and soon tired of walking. She said, 'Lakshmana, you are killing me by making me walk.' Those words proved to be prophetic.

Lakshmana tactfully made Sita sit down. Smearing his sword with the blood of a lizard, he left Sita behind and returned to Ayodhya. The experts at the palace examined the blood on the sword. Their verdict was that it was not human blood. Rama was furious. He commanded Lakshmana to go and carry out his orders. This time Lakshmana had no option. Sita said, 'Lakshmana, come on, do your duty!' Lakshmana refused. He asked for a drop of blood from her thumb and smeared that on the sword. After he returned to Ayodhya, Sita was alone in the forest. Overcome by grief and exhaustion, she sat under a tree. The forest was dense, and wild animals could pounce on her at any time. She was gripped by great fear. Her mental agony was compounded by birth pangs.

At this time, Sage Valmiki had been searching for a suitable location for his ashram in south India. After visiting several places in Wayanad, he had started living in a small ashram at Ashramkolly near Pulpally. From his ashram, Valmiki heard Sita's cries. He asked his disciples to find out who it was. The disciples found Sita writhing in pain. They informed Valmiki about the matter and Sita was brought to the ashram at once. There were no medical facilities there, but by this time, word had spread among the local people, including the tribals, and they came rushing to the ashram. A woman among them, belonging to the Uralikuruma sect, said to Valmiki, 'There are only men in the ashram. We will take Sita with us to our hut. That will be the best way of ensuring post-delivery care.' Valmiki did not object. The Uralikuruma women took Sita to their hut. Before long, she gave birth to a son. Maharishi Valmiki assigned the gods Nagarajan and Kuruma to protect Sita.

Even today, we can see the spot in Ashramkolly where, the local Hindus believe, Sita gave birth to Lava. There were two hibiscus plants in front of the hut where Sita is said to have given birth to Lava. It is believed that two flowers are found in full bloom on this plant throughout the year. Some believe that these flowers are for Sita to adorn her hair. The Munikallu (sage's rock), believed to be the spot where Valmiki performed tapas, is on the banks of a rice field near the hut, and is considered to be the place where Lava was born. Legend has it that under the Munikallu, there was a cave, which was later blocked by a landslide. It is said that if you pressed your ear on the Munikallu in olden days, you could hear the chanting of Ramanama (Rama's name). It was also believed that if you poured water collected in a taro leaf over the sage's rock and rubbed it, you would get sandalwood paste. This does not happen now. A tiny stream flows near the rock. The sandalwood paste thus obtained would be visible only till the stream was being crossed; once the stream was crossed, the paste would disappear. Many people here believe that Sita makes an annual visit to this site.

Sita's Disappearance at Pulpally and the Aswamedha Yajna

After the burning of Lanka, Rama returned to Ayodhya and decided to conduct the Aswamedha yajna. Respecting the sentiments of his subjects, Rama had already abandoned Sita. As a prelude to the yajna, he sent out a horse to travel through the country. No king dared stop the horse. But Lava and Kusa stopped the horse near Ponkuzhy and chained it. Rama reached the place of the incident, and came face to face with Sita. He invited Sita to Ayodhya, but Sita declined. 'What guarantee is there that you won't abandon me once again to please the public?' Rama tried to persuade her several times, but Sita stood her ground.

The shashtra prescribed that during the Aswamedha yajna, the royal queen should be seated near the king. Many racked their brains as to how this could be made possible. Many advised Sita to return to Ayodhya. But she remained firm in her decision. Finally, they decided to use force and tried to drag her. Sita fervently prayed to Mother Earth to come to her rescue. The earth split open and Sita jumped into the crevice. Rama tried to keep her from falling by pulling her by the hair. A clump of hair came off in his hand when Sita fell into the earth. The chasm that appeared in the earth closed. A pall of gloom spread everywhere. Rama drowned in sorrow.

After Sita's disappearance, Rama returned to Ayodhya. The Aswamedha yajna demanded the presence of the royal consort beside the king. What was to be done now? Finally, some sages advised Rama to have an idol of Sita made. The yajna would be valid even with the symbolic presence of the royal consort. And so, an idol of Sita was made from wheat flour and placed beside Rama on the dais during the yajna.[3]

THE AREAPALLY CHETTIS AND THE MARRIAGE OF LAVA AND KUSA

Areapally lies between Sulthan Bathery and Pulpally in Wayanad. It is mostly inhabited by members of the Chetti community. There are a number of stories related to the Ramayana in this community, with the same story often having different versions. One of them, narrated by Raman Chetti, goes like this:

> Once upon a time, Areapally was a dense forest. In those days, a poor, childless old couple, belonging to the Chetti community, lived there. One day, two boys of heavenly radiance came to their hut. They said, 'We are feeling thirsty. Please give us something to drink.'
>
> There was nothing at all in the hut. The old couple told them, 'We have nothing to offer you—no buffaloes to give you buttermilk, no sugar to make tea.'
>
> 'Then give us plain water,' said the boys.
>
> 'We have no water, either.'
>
> 'Then give us a pitcher for fetching water.' The old couple did so, and the boys collected water from outside and drank it. On returning, they said, 'Please make a shed for buffaloes. When we come next, you must give us milk and buttermilk to drink.'
>
> The old couple replied, 'What is the use of making a shed when we have no buffaloes?'
>
> 'Don't worry about that. You just make a shed. Everything

will be fine,' replied the boys as they departed. The very same day, the old couple built a shed. The following morning, they saw two people sitting in front of it. When they came close, they saw the shed was full of buffaloes. They were spellbound at this miracle, and realised that the boys were not ordinary humans. The two people in front of the shed were a man and a woman belonging to the Paniya community. They had been given charge of looking after the buffaloes. The next day, the boys, along with their mother, came to the hut. The couple received them with folded hands and gave them milk and fruits. When the mother and children had left, the old couple built pedestals where they had sat.

Every year, on the tenth of the month of Makaram, a religious festival is held in which members of the Paniya community participate. Special rights are reserved for the Chetti tharavadu (ancestral family) in the festival at the Sitadevi temple at Pulpally, which has close connections to Lava and Kusa.

It is said that the Pulpally devaswom land is registered as a 'minor property',[4] due to its legendary connections to Lava and Kusa. It is believed that after the disappearance of Sita, the property came into the hands of the boys, who were minors, and that tradition continues to this day.[5]

Many maintain that in the olden days Wayanad was a thick forest and that the asuras used to roam around freely in it. In those days, women and children lived in fear of the asuras, who were believed to abduct and molest girls. Areapally was especially frequented by the asuras. Lava and Kusa are thought to have saved the locals several times from them. Joseph Munjad, in his article 'Wayanadan Chettimar', records the belief that, once, Kusa saved Chandikadevi, the daughter of Erumappally Chetti, from molestation at the hands of the asuras. Such acts often led to marriage, and thus, at Hanuman's request, Kusa married Chandikadevi, and Lava married Sunithadevi, the younger sister of Chandikadevi.[6]

Transformation of the Names of Lava and Kusa

In different regions of Wayanad, Lava and Kusa are called by different names. In oral narratives, they are variously referred to as Murikens, Lavakuchan, Atharalar and so on. While in Pulpally, Lava and Kusa were known by their own names; in Althara, they were called Mookkuvas. In Porakkady, they were known as Poomalas. In Chingeri, their names were transformed into Raram Kaliyachan. In Irulam, they became Ilavally. In Manikkavu (beyond Meenangadi), they became Kalinmel Tampran. When Lava and Kusa reached Thurimunda, they became Thalachil, and in Sulthan Bathery, their name changed to Melethalachil.[7]

RAMAYANA CHARACTERS AND NATURAL PHENOMENA IN WAYANAD

Among the different communities in Wayanad, there exist many legends that link natural phenomena such as streams, waterfalls, natural springs, rocks and other geographical features with the characters of the Ramayana, whether Sita, Lakshmana, Ravana or Rama. A brief description of these phenomena and the beliefs linked to them is given below.

Sita and Natural Phenomena

Kannarampuzha is a tributary of the river Kabani. The traditions among the Wayanad Chetti, Mandadan Chetti, and Edanadan Chettis connect this stream with the story of Sita's abandonment by Rama. The tributary is believed to be formed of the stream of tears that flowed from Sita's eyes as she sat alone in distress. It is also called Kannuneerpuzha, the stream of tears.[8] The water in the Kannarampuzha was once yellow in colour. Some devotees believe that was because Sita had bathed in this river with turmeric smeared all over her body.[9]

Fifteen kilometres away from Meppadi, near the town of Mundakai, is a place called Sitammakuzhy (Sita's valley). There is a beautiful waterfall and a pond here. Devotees connect Sitammakuzhy to Jadayattakavu.[10] It is believed that this is the spot where the earth split and Sita went down into it.

Kappikunnu is a village near Manikkavu, in central Wayanad. There is a perennial spring here. The locals believe that this is the flow of tears from Sita's eyes.[11]

Kandathuvayal is situated near Vellamunda, in the northern part of Wayanad district. The name is derived from the instance where Rama came across Sita in a rice field many years after he had abandoned her, on suspicions of her purity (kandathi means discovered, and vayal means paddy field). As soon as she saw Rama, the one who had deserted her, Sita fervently prayed to Mother Earth, 'Divine Mother, kindly take me back into your womb. Save me from those who insulted me.' At once, the earth split, and as Sita went down, Rama tried to grab and pull her back by the hair. A tuft of her hair came out and later on became the mani grass. People use this plant to make brooms.[12]

Lakshmana and Natural Phenomena

Lakshmana Thirtha is a river originating at Coorg (Kodagu) in Karnataka, on the border of Wayanad in Kerala. As it reaches the Brahmagiri mountain (it is believed that Brahma did tapas on this mountain, hence the name), it becomes the Irupu Falls. Narayanan, the pujari of the Irappa Rameswaram Shiva temple, narrates the story of the origin of the Lakshmana Thirtha river thus:

> When Lakshmana and Rama reached Brahmagiri after the burning of Lanka, it struck Lakshmana, 'I have been serving Rama and Sita for many years. Why shouldn't I also lead an independent life?'
>
> But after leaving Brahmagiri, Lakshmana felt guilty about having such an unholy thought, and decided to do penance. 'Why did I entertain such thoughts? Rama is my elder brother. Sita is the wife of my brother.' Without revealing

his thinking, Lakshmana asked Rama, 'Brother, if one has entertained evil thoughts, what penance should he do?'

Rama said, 'He should walk through fire and be purified.' As Lakshmana got ready to do this, Rama asked, 'What was your evil thought?' Lakshmana revealed it and Rama replied, 'You are not responsible for that thought. It was due to the influence of the place we were in. We were in Bhargava Kshetra (referring to Wayanad). Now we are in Brahma Kshetra (referring to Kodagu, Karnataka). The evil thought left you as soon as you entered Brahma Kshetra. So there is no need for purification by fire. You can be purified by bathing in two holy ponds.'

Hearing this, Lakshmana released the Varunastra, his divine arrow. Water started flowing from the two places touched by the arrow. One spring so created is the beautiful waterfall at Iruppu, near the Kerala border. This is known as Lakshmana Thirtha (Lakshmana's holy spring). The locals there say that this water has medicinal properties. The other spring is the Rama Thirtha, located near the Lakshmana Thirtha in Poojakkal on the Kerala border. After taking a dip in these streams, Lakshmana continued his journey with Rama and Sita.[13]

Rama and Natural Phenomena

There is a rock near Papanasini stream that has the impression of a foot on it. It is known as Rama Padham (Rama's footprint). The story regarding this rock is as follows:

> With the intention of informing Rama and Lakshmana of their father's death, Bharatha and his retinue came to Wayanad, which in those days was a dense forest. They combed the entire forest, crossing hills and dales in search of Rama and Lakshmana. At last, Bharatha met his brothers at Thirunelly. A small contingent of soldiers had accompanied Bharatha. On seeing the soldiers, Rama and Lakshmana

thought they had come to fight. When they readied their bows to shoot, Bharatha came forward and said, 'Rama, I have not come to fight. I have come to inform you of the demise of our father. You should come back and assume the role of king.' After a brief conversation, Rama, Lakshmana and Bharatha went to the Papanasini temple to offer prayers for the departed soul of their father. The footprint seen on the rock in a pond near Papanasini marks the spot where Rama stood.[14]

There is another belief regarding the Thirunelly temple. It is said that Rama visited the Vishnu temple in Thirunelly after the slaying of Ravana, on the instruction of the sages. It is also believed that on seeing Vishnu in full battle gear, Rama was ecstatic and he prostrated before the deity.[15]

Malakkari, the Avatar of Shiva, and Natural Phenomena

Ambukuthi and Ambukuthimala are two places in Wayanad that are believed to have been formed by Shiva. Here are some of the beliefs related to these places, and Malakkari, who is the avatar of Shiva.

Malakkari is the principal deity of the Kurichya tribe who are found all across Wayanad, and means 'one who resides in the hills'.[16] A number of beliefs and legends about him exist in the Kurichya community. One such legend says Malakkari was born of Shiva and Parvathy in the Wayanad forest and hence he was appointed by Shiva as the God of those living in the hills.[17]

Another belief regarding the origin of Malakkari is found in the *Kumbha* song sung by the Kurichyas of Wayanad. The song says Malakkari was born of the third eye of Paramashiva to save the people from the evil deeds of the rakshasa-demons. The Kurichyas believe that Malakkari, with his bow and arrows, neutralised all the wicked gods and evil creatures on earth and threw them into the sea. Seawater entering the land is seen as a sign that the wicked gods and evil creatures are trying to stage a comeback. But since Malakkari is present in the kavus (sacred groves) on land, the sea will never be able to swallow the land.[18]

Maramayappattu is a song describing the descent of the Malakkari deity. Mahabali, the benevolent and legendary king of Kerala, features in this song. The story, according to the song, goes that Malakkari came down to the earth and asked Mavothi for a gift of three steps of land. Mavothi agreed. After Malakkari measured out two steps, he placed the third foot on top of Mavothi's head, and pushed him down into the northern sea. The Kurichyas have no doubt that Mavothi and Mahabali are the same person.[19]

Malakkari dispenses blessings—those that liberate from the effects of black magic, release from possession by evil spirits, and enable better hunting. Some traditions connect Malakkari to the Banasura–Krishna war that is believed to have been waged on the Banasura hill in north-west Wayanad. During the battle, Shiva sent two arrows in tandem through the sky. At that time, two boys were playing marbles near the Peechankod temple of Malakkari, near Mananthavady in the northern part of Wayanad. They saw the two arrows moving together through the sky, and threw marbles at them. Both the arrows were hit and veered from their planned route. One fell at a place near Mananthavady, which is known as Ambukuthi (the place where the arrow fell). The other arrow fell on a hill near Ambalavayal near Sultan Bathery in south Wayanad, a place now known as Ambukuthimala (the hill where the arrow fell). Later, Shiva demarcated the area between these arrows as the area of Malakkari's jurisdiction.[20]

THE RAMAYANA AND TOPONYMIC TALES OF WAYANAD

The names of a large number of places in Wayanad are related to the Ramayana. The local communities have several beliefs that link their origins to this epic. Some such places and the tales about how these places came into existence, or the beliefs regarding how they got their names, are listed below.

Wayanad

Wayanad is not the name of a village or town; it is the name given to a larger area, a district. The present Wayanad district was formed in 1980. The name, however, existed prior to that. The Hindus of Wayanad believe that Wayanad was created by Mayan, the asura (demon) architect who worked for both the devas and asuras. Named after him, Wayanad was known as Mayakshetra, the temple of Mayan, in ancient times. [21] In his *Wayanad Rekhakal*, wherein the history of Wayanad is traced, O.K. Johnny, historian, journalist and documentary film-maker, opines that the Sanskrit word was later on changed to Mayanad, land of Mayan, by the Malayalam-speaking population, and in the course of time, its pronunciation became Wayanad.[22]

Ponkuzhy

The Noolpuzha panchayat in Kerala shares borders with Karnataka on the north-east side and Tamil Nadu on the south.

It has the distinction of being located at the junction of three states, Kerala, Tamil Nadu and Karnataka. Ponkuzhy, located on the Karnataka border near Muthanga on the Kozhikode–Mysore highway, falls in the Noolpuzha panchayat. The Wayanadan Chettis believe that a story related to Sage Valmiki is behind the name Ponkuzhy.

The origin of the name Ponkuzhy is traced back to the word 'penkili', meaning female bird.[23] It is believed that Valmiki, seeing a savage hunter shoot down one of a pair of krouncha (crane) birds, was anguished and uttered the words 'Manishada' (desist, o hunter!), which became the first sloka, or verse, of the *Valmiki Ramayana*. It is thought that the place where the incident happened was named Penkili after that, which later evolved into Ponkuzhy.

Althara

Althara is a village near Ponkuzhy on the Kerala–Karnataka border. The existing belief among the Wayanad Chettis is that this is the place where Sita, crushed by distress and loneliness on being abandoned by Rama, sat under a banyan tree. Althara means the area under a banyan (aal) tree.[24]

Alinkulam

Alinkulam is a place close to Althara. People living here believe that when Rama conducted the Aswamedha yajna after he defeated Ravana, the unleashed horse reached this place, where Sitadevi was living with Lava and Kusa. The boys chained the horse to a banyan tree. They defeated Lakshmana and Hanuman and the army that followed the horse and tied them too to trees. Sri Rama came looking for them and recognised Sita, Lava and Kusa. But Lava and Kusa, who did not recognise their father, got ready for battle. Sita intervened and stopped the battle between the boys and their father. The horse was released too. There was a pond near the banyan tree to which the horse had been tied. This is where the name Alinkulam originated—'aal' means banyan tree, 'kulam' means pond.[25] Valmiki is said to have walked through these areas with Lava and Kusa when they were children, reciting Rama stories.[26]

Rampalli

Upon learning that the yajna horse as well as Lakshmana and the army were chained at Alinkulam, Sri Rama rushed to the spot from Ayodhya. Rampalli, which is a small village near Sultan Bathery in the south-eastern part of Wayanad, is believed to be the place where he rested before reaching Alinkulam. Rampalli means 'where Rama slept'.[27]

Irulam

After being abandoned by Sri Rama due to his suspicions regarding her chastity, Sita was on her way to Valmiki's ashram. It became dark and she could not travel further. She spent the night sitting alone under a tree. The place where the tree stood is now known as Irulam—dark place.[28] Irulam is on the eastern side of Wayanad, near the Kerala–Karnataka border.

There are some variations to the story about the origin of the name of the place. One version, narrated by Prabhakaran, the caretaker of the Valmiki ashram at Ashramkolly, runs like this:

> One day, when Sitadevi was staying at the Valmiki ashram, she went to the place now known as Irulam to collect flowers—it was famous for the large variety of flowers growing there. Sita got absorbed in plucking flowers and lost track of time. It was dark before she knew it. In the pitch darkness, she could not find her way back to the ashram.

So she spent that night under a tree. That place came to be known as Irulam.[29]

Another version, narrated by Jayaraj of Pariyaram, goes thus:

> During her stay at Pulpally near Valmiki's ashram, after having been abandoned by Rama, Sitadevi was walking through the place now known as Irulam. It was very dark. When she found that the onward journey was not possible in the pitch dark, she stopped there along with her sons. Later on, the place came to be known as Irulam.[30]

Ashramkolly

Ashramkolly lies near Pulpally, on the eastern side of Wayanad, near the Kerala–Karnataka border. It is believed that Maharishi Valmiki's ashram was located here, and that is how the place came to be known as Ashramkolly. The area still has an ashram called Valmiki ashram with a hut with a thatched roof. The common belief among the community living in these parts is that Sita gave birth to Lava in this hut. A few feet down from the ashram, on the bank of a small stream, is a large rock. It is believed that Valmiki meditated under this rock and that the chanting of the name of Rama could be heard from within the rock until quite recently.[31]

Yogimoola

Yogimoola is situated near Ashramkolly. The word Yogimoola is derived from the idea that sages lived here—it translates to yogi's corner ('moola' means corner). But it is not clear who these sages were.[32]

Sasimala

Sasimala is believed to be the site where Lava and Kusa played during their childhood while they were staying at Valmiki ashram. Earlier, it was known as Sisumala. 'Sisu' means child, and 'mala' means hill. There is a temple dedicated to Lava and Kusa at Sasimala. The Wayanad Chettis believe it was here that Sage Valmiki trained Lava and Kusa in the art of archery.[33]

Varadur

In the *Valmiki Ramayana*, Ravana abducted Sita by setting a trap. Ravana did this when Rama and Lakshmana went away, leaving Sita alone. Before departing, Lakshmana drew a line and told Sita, 'Keep strangers outside this line.' Sita did not follow this instruction. That is why she fell into Ravana's trap. Varadur is the site where Lakshmana drew the line. The name Varadur originated from the words meaning 'beyond the line'—'vara' means line, 'dur' means far.[34] The place is located near Meenangadi, which is near Sultan Bathery on the southern part of Wayanad.

Chethalayam

Chethalayam is near Pulpally. It is believed that the original name of this place was Sitalayam, meaning the place where Sita lived.[35] Some others claim that its original name was Sitalamma. Over the course of time, the pronunciation of the word 'Sita' shifted to 'Chetha'.

Pulpally

Pulpally is a prominent agricultural centre in Wayanad. Pulpally is also home to the Wayanad Chetti community. It has a number of stories about Sri Rama. It is believed that Sri Rama lay down and rested on a bed of 'pul', or grass, here. The etymology of the name Pulpally comes from here—'lying down on a bed of grass'.[36]

There is also another myth regarding the origin of this place-name. It is believed that Lava and Kusa had their lessons inside a small hut made of grass. Thus, the place became known as Pulpally ('pul' is grass, and 'pally' means school).

Areapally

Areapally is near Pulpally. The tale related to the origin of Areapally has already been narrated in the chapter 'The Areapally Chettis and the Marriage of Lava and Kusa'. It is related to Sita, Lava and Kusa as well as the Chettis.

When Lava and Kusa got to know that the Chetti couple had no buffaloes or cows, they asked them to build a shed. After the shed was built, buffaloes and cows appeared inside it.

In remembrance of the visit of Sita, Lava and Kusa, people here even today observe a kolukodukkal (banquet). The miraculous appearance of cows and buffaloes in the shed built by the Chettis became big news and travelled far and wide. That is how this place came to be known as Erumappally (village of buffaloes). Over the course of time, Erumappally became Areapally.[37]

Seetha Mount

Located near Pulpally, prior to 1950, Seetha Mount was called Sitamadi. Sita, Lava and Kusa, during their stay in Pulpally, lived on a group of eight hillocks.[38] Sitamadi represents that phase in their lives. The word 'madi' means lap, and Sitamadi probably refers to the fact that the boys often sat in their mother's lap in this place. Sitamadi must have become Seetha Mount after the arrival of Christian settlers in Wayanad.

Ambukuthi

There is more than one Ambukuthi in Wayanad. After Sita was abducted by Ravana, Rama searched for her in various forests, including the Wayanad forests. The search party included the monkey brigade, and different contingents came at different times. Rama and his retinue led the way and the others followed. Rama planted arrows on hilltops to guide those who came after him. Those spots came to be known as Ambukuthi—a place where the ambu, arrow, was planted.[39] This is a story common to all the Ambukuthis.

At the same time, each Ambukuthi has its own story to tell. For instance, the story behind the Ambukuthi near Mananthavady in the northern part of Wayanad is related to the Banasura–Krishna war. This is believed to be the place where Krishna's arrow fell during the battle on the Banasura hill.[40]

The Ambukuthimala near Ambalavayal in the southern part of Wayanad, where the Edakkal cave is situated, also has its own stories related to the Indian epics. In the Edakkal cave, there is a large rock vertically split into two. This rock is believed to have been split by Rama's arrows, lending the hill the name Ambukuthimala.[41]

Kandathuvayal

Kandathuvayal is the name of a place near Vellamunda in north Wayanad, near the Banasura hill. The members of the Kurichya community here believe that this is the place where Sitadevi disappeared into the earth. They also believe that this is the place where, after a long separation, Rama met Sitadevi. It is believed that the name Kandathuvayal originates from this incident. Kandathuvayal is a corruption of 'kandethiya vayal', meaning the field where (Sita) was found.[42]

Jadayattakavu

Jadayattakavu near Pulpally is famous, as the Hindus and the Adivasis here both believe that this is the place where Sitadevi disappeared into the earth. The Wayanad Chettis even connect the origin of the name of their community to this place. It is believed that while Sitadevi was going down into the earth, Sri Rama grabbed her hair and a tuft (jada) came off. In the course of time, the word jada became corrupted as cheda. Sita is worshipped in this form as Chedathilamma. Chedathinkavu is the moola sthanam, the place of origin, of the Lava-Kusa temple at Pulpally.[43]

Thirunelly

There are a number of stories related to the origin of the name Thirunelly, considered the Kashi of the south. Here are a few of them.

> Once, when Lord Brahma came that way (to Thirunelly), he felt the presence of Mahavishnu in the nelli (gooseberry) tree among the bushes on the hillside and heard a heavenly voice saying that an idol of Mahavishnu should be consecrated there. Accordingly, Brahma consecrated an idol of Vishnu on that site. This is how the temple at Thirunelly came to be.[44]

Another story goes something like this:

> A long time ago, before this part of the forest in northern Wayanad came to be called Thirunelly, three Namboothiris (Malayali Brahmins) set out on a pilgrimage to worship at the temple of Vishnu. In those days, one had to traverse long tracts of dense forest, infested with man-eating wild animals. The only protection for the travellers was their faith in God. Thirunelly could be reached from Mananthavady via the Shiva temple at Trissileri in the northen part of Wayanad, by crossing the the Narinirangi hill that lay in between. The journey lasted several days and one had to face many obstacles en route. Trusting in the Lord Vishnu, the

trio continued their trek. Their food reserve was exhausted. Hungry and tired, they felt totally at a loss. They looked up at the trees for something to satisfy their hunger, and their eyes fell on a gooseberry tree on the side of the path they were walking on. From that tree, laden with fruits, symbolising the blessings of Mahavishnu, they collected plenty of berries. Thinking that it would be better to eat after cleansing their bodies, they took a dip in the nearby stream. After bathing, they ate one berry each. To their amazement, their hunger and thirst ceased at once, and they felt revived, and more energetic than they had ever been. They meditated on the presence of Mahavishnu whose bounty they had just experienced. Then they saw a wonderful sight on the banks of the stream. There stood Mahavishnu, the protector of all things, and the crescent moon-adorned Paramashiva. They realised that what they had eaten was no ordinary gooseberry but the gift of the divine beings, Shiva and Vishnu. This prompted them to name this place Thirunelly, meaning the divine (thiru) gooseberry tree (nelli).[45]

Yet another story goes like this:

Once, a devotee felt very hungry and tired on his journey to Thirunelly. He got three berries from the gooseberry tree he saw on the way. Leaving the berries on the bank of a stream nearby, he went into the water for a bath. As soon as he entered the holy water, his hunger vanished and he felt fully refreshed. The berries he had left on the bank of the stream turned to stone. That is how the place came to be known as Thirunelly. The spot where the gooseberries turned to stone is known as Gundika.[46]

In Sanskrit, Thirunelly is also known as 'Amalagrama'. Amala is another name for gooseberry or nellika. Therefore, the Thirunelly temple is also referred to as Amalakshetram.[47]

Mananthavady

Mananthavady is a prominent town in the northern part of Wayanad. Some ascribe the etymology of Mananthavady to Varadur, which means beyond the line ('vara' means line, 'dur' means far). When Sitadevi crossed the line drawn by Lakshmana, it led to her abduction. What motivated Sita to do so was the sight of a deer. Sita ran after the deer till she reached the place now known as Mananthavady. The name is derived from 'maan' + 'antha' + 'vadi', meaning the place where Sita's running after the deer ended (maan means deer, antha means end, vadi means the spot).[48] According to some traditions, Mananthavady is derived from 'maha ananda vadi', meaning the garden of great bliss (maha means great, ananda means bliss, vadi means garden).

RAMAYANA TALES AND THE HILLS OF WAYANAD

The folk interpretations of mythological tales in Wayanad are inseparably linked with its landscape—the mountains and forests of the mythologies have been transplanted into the backdrop of Wayanad. This is similar to the relationship the Indian epics have with Mount Kailash and the Himalayas, and with the forest and forest dwellers.

Banasura Mala

The Banasura hill, in the western region of Wayanad, is one of the highest hills in the Western Ghats. The hill is named after Banasura, a legendary king with thousand arms, and the son of the great asura king Mahabali. There are several tales related to Banasura and the hill. One of them, as recorded by K. Panur, an eminent writer and activist in Kerala, in his book *Keralathile Africa*, is as follows:

> Banasura, mentioned in the epics, is believed to be the king of the aboriginal communities who ruled Wayanad in ancient times. The son of Mahabali, Banasura was, like all other asuras, a ferocious person. He ruled from the fort on Banasura hill. It is said that owing to the extraordinary powers granted to him for his penances, Banasura got Shiva to guard his fortress. One day, Anirudha, the grandson of Krishna, chanced to pass that way and saw the beautiful

daughter of Banasura. They fell in love. On getting to know of this, Banasura ordered Anirudha to be caught and thrown into prison. When Sri Krishna heard this, he reached the place along with his forces, resolving to defeat Banasura in battle. But, based on the agreement between Banasura and Shiva, the latter could not refuse to wage war against Sri Krishna. And so began a battle between two parties of equal strength. None winning, none losing, it continued for days. Finally, Shiva used his weapon known as the Ushnajwaram (hot fever). To stop Shiva's weapon in its tracks and wipe out Banasura's army, Krishna used his weapon known as the Sheethajwaram (cold fever). Banasura had to either surrender to Krishna or be prepared to perish. Banasura agreed to release Anirudha and give him his daughter. The battle ended. As a result of the use of the cold-fever arrow by Sri Krishna, Wayanad was caught in the grip of malaria for centuries.[49]

There is more than one version of this story related to the Banasura hill. Another story goes like this:

A fortress stood on the peak of the Banasura hill at 6,762 ft. Bana was a prominent and powerful asura emperor. Shiva was a guard at his fortress. Banasura had a very beautiful daughter named Usha. Once, she dreamt of Anirudha and woke up agitated in the middle of the night. Seeing her condition, Chandralekha, her maid-in-waiting and daughter of Banasura's minister, asked her the reason for her waking up so anxious. Usha said, 'I saw a very handsome man in my dream. I don't know who he is, but I won't be able to live without him now.' Chandralekha was a good painter, and she was adept in magical practices. She drew sketches of several kings. When Usha saw the sketch of Anirudha, she fell into a swoon. Using her magical powers, Chandralekha then had Anirudha (who was sleeping in his palace) brought to Banasura's palace without anyone's knowledge, and placed him near Usha.

On learning that his grandson had been imprisoned in Bana's palace, an enraged Sri Krishna came with Balabhadra to wage a war. A very fierce battle took place. Despite Lord Shiva's help, Banasura was defeated. Sri Krishna cut off Banasura's arms but desisted from killing him on the grounds that Banasura was born in the same clan as Prahlada. Bana gave his daughter in marriage to Anirudha.[50]

A second version of this tale says that the severed arms of Banasura fell from a cliff into the valley, and a temple was constructed where the arms fell; this temple is now called the Karabanasseri temple ('karabana' means the arms of Bana). Since that time, an annual festival has been celebrated here, when, it is said, one of the deities appears in the guise of Shiva. Twelve kilometres away from the Banasura hill, near Tharuvana, is a place called Mazhuvannoor (Mazhuvannoor means the place of the axe). It is believed that this is the place where Shiva's axe fell during the war with Krishna. There is a Shiva temple here.[51]

According to another version, the Ambukuthi near Mananthavady is the place where the arrow of Krishna fell during the battle with Banasura.[52]

A number of such stories relating to the Banasura hill are in circulation. Evidence of these are found in the folk songs belonging to the Kurichya and Adiya communities. K.K. Annan (a Kurichya leader and former MLA) and P.K. Kalan (an Adiya leader and Gaddika artist) have recorded that they have seen the ruins of Bana's fortress on the top of the hill. There is a belief among the Adivasis that a special type of hornet will attack anyone climbing up the mountain. These are believed to represent the guards of Bana.[53]

Muneeswara Mala/ Muneeswara Kovil

Muneeswara Mala (also called Muneeswara Kovil) is a hill that is situated within the Makkimala village, near Mananthavady in the northern part of Wayanad. It is said that this hill is located midway between the Thirunelly temple on the north-eastern border of Wayanad and the Kottiyoor temple in Kannur. On the slope of this hill is a cave where Sage Vasishta is thought to have done tapas. According to local belief, Sri Rama and Sita came here to visit Vasishta Maharshi. It is said that a footprint belonging to Rama has been discovered in the forest near Muneeswara Mala.

The hilltop has a temple without a roof that is in the possession of the Kurichya community. The principal deity here is Malakkari. The upper castes at some point began to believe that Malakkari is an incarnation of Shiva. This temple has since been frequented by the upper castes too. Pooja is offered only once a month. A festival is conducted on the fourth of Meenam (the Malayalam month corresponding to March-April).[54]

Brahmagiri

Brahmagiri is believed to be the place where Brahma conducted a yajna. The story, as recorded by O.K. Johnny in *Wayanad Rekhakal*, goes like this:

> One day, Brahma started touring the world, seated on his vehicle, the swan. When he reached the Western Ghats, he was struck by the beauty of the mountains. There were dense evergreen forests extending across several miles. The valleys were full of flowering trees and shrubs. Lofty peaks merged with the azure skies. Silvery mountain streams meandered around the hills. Captivated by the forests, Brahma descended on the hills now known as Brahmagiri mountains. For a moment, he thought that he was in Vishnuloka, the heavenly abode of Vishnu. A palpable sweetness pervaded the air. Brahma surmised that he was standing in a place filled with the heavenly presence of Vishnu. All of a sudden,

> Brahma's eyes fell on a finely adorned idol of Vishnu kept on a gooseberry tree. But before he could get a full view of it, the idol vanished. Brahma heard a voice then. 'O Brahma, the idol you saw is of Vishnu. You must install it in a suitable place.' Accordingly, Brahma installed the idol of Vishnu, the Lord of the Universe. The holy sages such as Thara anointed the idol with a thousand pots of holy water. The devas (gods) chanted the Lord's divine name. When Brahma paid his obeisance, Mahavishnu, the Lord of Lakshmi, made his appearance. Adorned with his divine conch, wheel, lotus and club, Mahavishnu stood before him and said, 'My home hereafter will be in this place on the Western Ghats. O Brahma, I will never leave this place that you have consecrated.'[55]

Hindus believe that the temple at Thirunelly stands on the very same spot where Brahma consecrated the Vishnu idol.[56] One can see, even today, the spot near the temple at Thirunelly, where Brahma performed his oblations. That area has been fenced off.

Bhoothathankunnu is located near the Brahmagiri hills. Bhoothathankunnu means hill of the ghost ('bhootham' means ghost, and 'kunnu' means hill). This hill is situated between the temples of Kottiyoor and Thirunelly. The story of Bhoothathankunnu is as follows:

> In the olden days, the rice needed for the festival at Kottiyoor was brought from Thirunelly. It is said that Lord Shiva's ghost army brought the stock of rice. One day, one of the ghosts who had been deputed to bring rice, fatigued by the rigorous work, happened to spill some of it on the way. For this unpardonable fault, the Perumal of Thirunelly cursed the ghost, turning him into a stone. That spot is called Bhoothathankunnu. In place of the ghost who had been transformed into a stone, another ghost was sent to Kottiyoor. Whatever may be the explanation, even today,

on the Visakha day of the month of Edavam (May–June), just before the festival at Kottiyoor, the ritual of sending a ghost to Kottiyoor is observed at Thirunelly. So is the ritual of returning the ghost back to Thirunelly after the festival.[57]

Another tale entrenched in the Brahmagiri hills is about Sage Agasthya. Responding to his prayers, and with the blessings of the Trimurti (Brahma, Vishnu and Shiva), the divine Ganga river flowed to Brahmagiri. It reappeared as Kaveri at Thalakkaveri in Coorg, Karnataka. The Papanasini (literally, the destroyer of sins) stream originating in the Brahmagiri hills is considered holy due to the belief that Ganga flows through Brahmagiri, unseen. Hindus believe that a dip in Papanasini leads to moksha (liberation), just as the case is with the river Ganga.[58]

Manikunnu Mala

Thrikkaipatta is a village near Kalpetta, the headquarters of Wayanad district, located in its central part. Manikunnu is a famous hill near Thrikkaipatta. It is believed that the sage Manu did penance on this hill, giving it its name. Over time, Manukunnu became Manikunnu. On the hill is a large, round rock, which is known as Kavanappara. 'Kavana' means sling and 'para' means rock. The locals believe that this is an enlarged form of the slingstone used by Lakshmana during his and Rama's stay in Wayanad. Once a year, a pooja is performed on the top of this hill. Devotees walk around this rock. It is believed that one attains moksha if they circumambulate this rock.

A story related to Manikkunnu Mala is as follows:

> Vishnu is said to reside on top of the Manikunnu Mala. But there is no temple here, only an idol of Vishu. It is believed that in the olden days, the priest would climb up the hill and

perform pooja. Since climbing the hill was an arduous task (it is situated at a height of 1,384 metres), one day, the priest stayed back after the evening pooja, with the intention of climbing down the hill after performing the morning pooja the following day. At midnight, he saw devas (gods) coming to perform pooja there. Then Mahavishnu appeared and told the priest that henceforth it was not necessary to climb the hill every day. Extending his hand, Mahavishnu said, 'It is sufficient to perform the pooja in the valley below.' That is how the Thrikkaipatta temple, which is considered a branch of the main spot of worship on the top of Manikunnu Mala, was built. The name Thrikkaipatta is derived from the legend that Vishnu gave his hand to the priest—'Thrikkai' means the hand of the Lord.[59]

RAMAYANA INFLUENCES ON THE WAYANAD COSMOGONIC TALES

Higher myths refer to mythological beliefs that exist across organised religions, and assume global significance, such as the concept of Heaven and Hell. On the other hand, lower myths are those beliefs that exist among smaller, tribal communities, and are local in significance. Genesis stories are found both in the higher myth and the lower myth traditions. There are scholars who believe that many myths are creation or cosmogonic myths. That is why the eminent folklorist Sir James Frazer has held that myths are stories that explain the origin of the world and the existence of nature.[60]

A number of stories relating to the origin of the world, the origin of mankind, as well as the origin of natural phenomena and objects, circulate among the different communities, such as the Mullukurumas, Adiyas, Kurichyas, Kusavas, Vedans, and Kurumas, in Wayanad. Of them, those related to the creation myths are narrated next.

The Origin of the Universe and the Trimurtis: The Mullukuruma Belief

The Mullukuruma tribe explains the origin of the gods and the mysteries of the universe through an oral story about a family:

> In the beginning, everything was a void. In the void, a mysterious object appeared in the shape of an egg. It split

into two. From the middle came forth Vellakaliyappan (Adimukhan, God) and his vehicle, the owl. The northern portion was transformed into the sky and the southern portion into the earth. The middle was filled with air. In the sky, millions and trillions of stars, the sun and the moon were formed. The earth was filled with water. Vellakaliyappan witnessed everything. The tired owl said, 'O Lord, I feel exhausted. I need some place to rest.' Suddenly, land emerged from the water. Vellakaliyappan created different types of trees, shrubs, fruits, birds and animals. The owl was pleased.

Vellakaliyappan, however, felt that his creation was somehow incomplete; it lacked something. Dejected, he began to perspire. God's wish was realised in his left armpit and Tworuvattamma was born from his sweat. The beautiful Tworuvattamma bowed before the Lord. Before long, Vellakaliyappan received Tworuvattamma as his consort. All the things on the face of the earth witnessed that blessed moment. They sang the praises of the Lord of the Universe. The sun went down. The stars shone in the dark. The moon shed its cool rays on the earth. It was the first night Vellakaliyappan and Tworuvattamma were to spend together.

Not knowing the mysterious ways of God's will, Tworuvattamma spoke sweet endearments to her husband, and then fell asleep. Vellakkaliyappan left his bride behind and went towards the east with his owl.

When morning came, Tworuvattamma could not find Vellakaliyappan anywhere. On enquiring, she came to know the truth about his disappearance. He was far far away, doing penance to sacrifice himself. The feminine spirit of the divine consort took form and travelled to Vellakaliyappan. Even though he was deep in meditation, the awareness of Tworuvattamma's spirit rekindled a desire in Vellakaliyappan that he could not contain. He ejaculated, and at once collected the semen in a peraka (guava) leaf and, through the owl, sent it to his consort. He instructed the owl to tell her it was poison and should not be consumed. The owl delivered the semen to the abandoned Goddess Tworuvattamma and conveyed the Lord's warning. The Goddess, unable to bear the painful separation from her husband, had resolved to end her life, and at once consumed the semen. She wasn't aware of the will of the Lord of the Universe. She conceived as soon as she drank the semen, and gave birth to three sons, one after the other, within a few hours. Brahma the creator, came through her mouth, Vishnu the protector, came forth from her navel, and Shiva the destroyer, was born from her vagina. The Goddess delivered her sons without anyone's assistance. She laid them on a peraka leaf. This was the origin of the spiritual embodiments of Vellakaliyappan. The sons grew up and, in the course of time, began to ask about their father. The Goddess told them the truth. They immediately started on a journey to the east in search of their father.

Vellakaliyappan sat deep in meditation. He could see his sons searching for him through his third eye. Before they could reach him, he separated his soul from his body and disappeared into water. With the help of the owl, the sons identified the corpse. To bury the dead body of their father, the boys started digging the earth.

To their utter surprise, they heard a voice speaking, 'My dear sons, my body should not be buried here. This land has been set aside for Panchanans, your descendants; it must be given to them. You should cremate me.' Since the cremation could not be performed by Brahma the creator or by Vishnu the preserver, the task was assigned to Shiva. Shiva made a pyre in his lap and burnt the body of his father. The leftover bones he wore around his neck. After cremating the body, the sons started searching for the soul of their father. They found his soul in the waters of a spring nearby. Brahma, Vishnu and Shiva fashioned a fishing basket (creel) and fished out the soul of their father, and with it they went back to their mother, Goddess Tworuvattamma.[61]

The Mullukurumas recognise and worship Vellakaliyappan as their father. They worship Brahma as the deity Munikalan Kalyar, Shiva as Vainnattan Kalyar and Goddess Tworuvattamma as Kathirngadevi.

The Origin of Mankind: The Adiya Belief

The Adiya tribe has many stories about how mankind came into existence. Some of them are narrated below. The first story is like this:

> Vishnu and Shiva jointly created the sun, the moon and the earth. Later, they made human beings with the soil on earth and infused life into them. However, despite having a tongue, these humans made by Vishnu and Shiva did not speak; despite having ears, they did not hear. What was to be done? The gods tried all kinds of tricks. None of the humans stood up and venerated them. Finally, the gods arrived at a strategy: they created Mali, a fierce God with blood dripping from his tongue. The humans were terrified and sprang up when they saw Mali charging towards them, screaming.
>
> Some of them asked Mali, '*Aareda*?' (Who are you?) Those who asked this question became the Thampurans (rulers). Those who shivered with fright and screamed '*eammi*' became the Paniya tribe. Those who exclaimed '*athava*' became the Adiya tribe. Those who uttered '*uyyi*' became the Thiyya caste and those who cried '*alloo*' became the Muslims. In this way, the human beings created by Shiva and Vishnu, who responded differently to the fierce Mali, formed the different castes, religions and tribes.[62]
>
> (*Eammi, athava, uyyi* and *alloo* are common expressions of astonishment, fear and surprise used by different tribes.)

The genesis story narrated above has several variations. One version goes like this:

Once, the gods stole the divine soil of the deity Maveli Manva (Mahabali). Maveli looked for it everywhere, but in vain. Finally, he and the gods decided to conduct an experiment to find the culprits. The material used in the experiment was the muddy water flowing in the river. It was decided that the culprits would be identified based on the direction in which the water flowed. If the water flowed upwards, the gods would be the guilty ones; if it flowed downwards, Maveli himself would be held responsible. The gods bathed upstream and Maveli downstream. Naturally, the muddy water flowed downwards. The gods declared that Maveli was the culprit. They beat him with a lime-pot. When Maveli fell, unconscious, the gods took out the soil they had hidden and fashioned human beings out of it. But the humans they made did not stand up. At once, the gods summoned Mali. Names were given to men based on their responses to Mali. Those who said '*athava*' came to be known as the Ravular tribe (another name for Adiyas). The others formed other communities and religious sects based on the nature of their reactions to Mali.[63]

Some versions link genesis with Maveli's tale. One of them goes like this:

There were two childless queens in the mel-lokam, the upper-world. To ensure that there would be someone to carry on their legacy, they brought two boys from Aryanad and Vaniyanad, raised them and crowned them kings. The boys went round to see their kingdom, and were well-received by their subjects. After the banquet, they lay down to rest on a cot made of gold. Suddenly termites appeared from nowhere and came crowding on the legs of the cot. The boys were amazed and asked what this meant. They were told, 'We are termites. We are going down to the keezh-lokam, the netherworld.' The young kings said they wanted to accompany them there. The termites told the kings that they could not go with them to the netherworld because of their large bodies. In reply, the kings said they could reduce the size of their bodies and become small like the termites. They did so and, passing through tiny holes, reached the land of King Maveli (Mahabali) in the netherworld. When Maveli was away, they stole his divine soil and hid it under their nails. On returning, Maveli found his soil missing and asked them about it. Playing a trick, the kings scampered away with the stolen soil. They put the soil they had brought in a coconut shell. The coconut shell was filled to the brim with the soil. From the coconut shell, they transferred the soil into a bamboo pipe. That too became choked with the soil. From there, they transferred it to a basket. The basket too was completely filled. Then they put it into a granary. The granary filled up as well. Earth was formed in this fashion by the multiplication of the stolen soil. When the earth's formation was complete, a bird was sent out to inspect if any pits or joints could be seen on its surface. The bird went round and round, trying to shake the earth and suss out fault lines. As a result of the shaking of the earth by this bird, the body of that bird (Oorakuluki bird) is shaking even now. The seeds of the stones, trees and living things brought from the netherworld were sowed on the earth in order to make it firm.[64]

Another variation to this story goes like this:

> Shiva and Parvathy fashioned human beings out of clay on the premises of the temple at Kuthirakottu, near Thirunelly. After making the human figures, Shiva and Parvathy fell asleep. As soon as they slept off, the Goddess Bhadrakali came and smashed with her foot the forms they had made. This happened several times. At last, Shiva and Parvathy found a solution to this. They fashioned a dog out of clay. The dog was put in charge of guarding the forms of men. Bhadrakali would come as soon as Shiva and Parvathy fell

asleep. Then the dog would bark, alerting Shiva and Parvathy, and Bhadrakali would have to go back. Thus, it was with the help of a dog that the creation of man took place. And it's quite true—dogs guard men to this day.

The description of Mali's arrival and the division of humans into different tribes, communities and religions based on their response on seeing Mali, is similar in all versions of the story of creation among the Adiyas.

The Origin of the Kurichyas

A variety of genesis myths pertaining to how they were formed exist in the culture of the Kurichyas, a prominent tribal sect of Wayanad. A few of them are recorded next:

> The Brahmins and the Kurichyas are the noblest of Brahma's creations. They are the only two 'pure' castes on earth.
>
> Brahma got ready for the act of creation by taking some earth and mixing it with water to make clay. He began to perspire from the effort, and wiped away his sweat with a flick of his hand. From the drops of sweat that fell to the ground, emerged a sect of humanoid beings. Brahma christened them the Adiyas. From the soil that remained after making man, he made the Paniyas. These became the Adiya and the Paniya tribes.
>
> The men created by Brahma with his hands were divided into two groups, and they were sent out to hunt in the forest. They were given a note with instructions to reassemble at a particular spot. The parties went into the interior of the forest to hunt. Brahma did not send them empty-handed. He gave them bows and arrows and trained them in archery. One of the two groups lost its way and did not reach the fixed spot, but wandered in the jungle. This upset Brahma who, in a fit of rage, named them Kadars (jungle dwellers). The Kurichyas believe that this was the origin of the forest-

dwelling populations in Wayanad. The second group reached the appointed spot on time. Brahma gave them the name Kurichyar (Kurichyar means those who followed the note; 'kuri' is note). Brahma selected the temple priests from among the Kurichyas.[65]

Since the Brahmins and the Kurichyas are the castes of temple priests, they believe that they are the only two 'pure' castes. Till recently, the Kurichyas followed the practice of 'untouchability' with all castes except the Brahmins.

Yet another version of the genesis story among the Kurichyas describes them as Sri Rama's soldiers. The story is as follows:

> When Sri Rama, accompanied by Sita, went to the forest for his self-imposed, fourteen-year exile, his brother Bharatha marked out a hilly area for the Kurichyas, who felt orphaned in the absence of Sri Rama and wished to be near him. Those who were given the place marked by Bharatha were called Kurichyas ('kuricha' also means the mark).[66]

There are also numerous tales and beliefs among the Kurichyas in which Sri Rama and Sita figure as characters. The bow and arrow is an integral part of their social and cultural life, remaining with the Kurichyas from the cradle to the grave. Not only while hunting, the bow and arrow also has a special place in the marriage hall. The Kurichyas justify the practice of carrying the bow and arrow to the marriage function by saying: '*Thairamassami chanakeene/Kootan poyath anganeya*' (Thus did Lord Sri Rama/ Go to wed Sitadevi).[67]

The Origin of the Vedars and the Kuruma Dynasties

The story regarding the origin of the Vedar and Kuruma communities, who were the rulers of Wayanad, is as follows:

With the intention of obtaining the all-powerful weapon Pasupathaastra, possessed by Paramashiva, Arjuna, the middle born of the Pandava brothers, did tapas at Poothadi in Wayanad. To test Arjuna, Paramashiva came down disguised as a vedan (hunter). A wild boar came between Paramashiva and Arjuna. Both of them shot at the animal. The boar fell down dead. They quarrelled over the carcass. Words led to blows. Arjuna, fearing defeat, struck Shiva's head with his bow and drops of blood began to ooze down from the wound. Two ghosts emerged from those drops of blood. Pleased with Arjuna's valour and devotion, Lord Shiva bestowed on him the Pasupathaastra and returned to Kailasa. The Lord, for unknown reasons, did not take the ghosts with him, but left them behind. The two ghosts born out of the two drops of Lord Shiva's blood became the originator of two communities: the Vedas and the Kurumas. These were the two dynasties who ruled Wayanad from the Veliyambam Kotta (fort).[68]

The Origin of the Kusavas

The Kusavas (potters) live in places such as Chulliyode, Kuppadi, Muthanga, Kaithakkal and Koyileri in the southeastern region of Wayanad. These people migrated to Wayanad in the twentieth century. A story circulating among the Kusavas related to their origin is as follows:

> Brahma, the God of creation, was in need of a pitcher. None of his creatures were capable of making one. So, Brahma approached Shiva with his wish. Shiva could not find a way, but Parvathy came to his rescue. She suggested that a being be created from his ear wax. Thus Kusava was born. Following Shiva's instructions, Kusava made a pitcher. Shiva blessed Kusava, 'May you be able to turn any form you visualise while turning the wheel into an object from the soils.' Since Kusava was alone, Parvathy arranged a partner

for him. But Kusava didn't speak to her, nor did he sleep with her. To change his mind, Sri Krishna appeared while Kusava would be at the potter's wheel, and danced to the rhythm of the wheel. One day, when there was a shortage of water, Kusava spat into the pot and continued his work. Krishna was disgusted and left in a huff. But before leaving, he reminded Kusava that he had given a plate to his wife, which was to be returned to him the next day. When, on the following day Krishna asked for the plate, Kusava searched for it everywhere but could not find it. In the end, he was left with no choice but to ask his wife about it. Thus Krishna brought the Kusava couple together with just a simple trick.[69]

The intent of this story may have been to demonstrate that the profession of potters is noble and divinely ordained.

The Origin of Flora in Wayanad: The Adiya Belief

The Adiya tribe hold that this is how different trees and crops came into existence:

At the beginning of time, the first father and mother of the Adiyas enquired this of all the gods:

Yeyamme, kalatheina
Chandrapagava, shuryapagava
Kamadeva, vellideva,
Noottavar pandavar
Ningalariveeli poomivaluthuva
Yengadakailariyappokamuriyathira
pinnangaruva poomi valuthava

Oh! Mother of the world,
Oh! divine Moon, divine Sun,
Oh god of Love, Oh god of Silver
Do you at least know
the art of harvesting gold from the earth?

> Do you perchance know
> how to till the earth and produce crops?

> The gods answered that they did not possess the knowledge of producing crops from soil. At last, the forefathers of the Adiyas, using their bows and arrows, brought down the seeds of a tree they had seen in heaven. They planted the seeds in a shell, and the seeds sprouted. Then they planted the seedlings all over the earth, which was barren to that day. The seedlings sown in the dry earth grew into trees. Those that fell on the wetlands became paddy. Those that fell in ponds blossomed as lotuses. Seeds that fell on beaches produced coconut trees. And thus did the Adiya tribe make the entire earth fertile, and are the inventors of agriculture.[70]

Ashoka trees, which are not native to Wayanad, are found all over Thirunelly and in its surrounding areas. The story behind this is connected to Sita's abduction:

> Sita had adorned her hair with Ashoka flowers when Ravana abducted her. He carried her off to Lanka, through these regions. As they passed through the dense forest, the flowers fell down from her hair. From the seeds in the flowers that fell to the ground sprouted Ashoka trees.[71]

Traditional Medicine and the Adivasis

Traditional medicine makes use of the knowledge handed down through generations in Adivasi communities. There is no record of who started the tradition or when it originated, but in general, Adivasi communities are reluctant to share their traditional wisdom about afflictions and their treatments and cures with other communities. There is a belief among the Kurichyas, for instance, that the art of alternative healing was taught to them by Shiva himself. This belief stems from the legend of the Shiva–Arjuna face-off in Poothadi, in the central region of Wayanad. This is the story:

With the intention of testing Arjuna, who was doing tapas, Shiva, accompanied by his army of ghosts, reached Poothadi. Arjuna began a fight with Shiva, who was disguised as a vedan and was hunting wild boars. At the end of the fight, Arjuna recognised Shiva and tendered his apology. After bestowing on him the Pasupathaastra, Shiva left for Kailasa with Parvathy. But he did not take the ghosts along with him. Instead, he instructed them to live in Poothadi. The ghosts found it very difficult to acclimatise to the weather there. They began to perish from diseases such as malaria and small pox. Finally, they decided to return to Kailasa and supplicate for a solution to these afflictions.

A group of ghosts reached Kailasa and informed Shiva about their problem. Shiva said, 'The forests of Wayanad have medicines for all the diseases you are afflicted with now or may be afflicted with in the future.' He also told them about the herbs and plants with medicinal properties. The ghosts committed their names to memory. All the Adivasis of Wayanad who use bows and arrows are the descendants of those ghosts Lord Shiva left behind in Poothadi.

Therefore, the Adivasis believe that the traditional healing methods they use were taught to them by Shiva himself. Whereas it was only much later that Ganapathy, the son of Shiva, taught Dhanwanthary the science of Ayurveda. Hence, traditional medicine and Ayurveda are related, and Ayurveda cannot be considered to be superior. In fact, Ayurveda is believed to have evolved from the ways of healing that Shiva first taught his ghosts.

The Hanuman Monkeys

The monkeys found in the parts surrounding Muthanga in the south-eastern region of Wayanad, are called Hanuman langurs. The story regarding how they came to be known by this name is narrated here:

At Alinkulam near Ponkuzhy, where a lake was formed from Sita's tears, Lava and Kusa imprisoned Hanuman, who had come in pursuit of the Aswamedha yajna horse. Along with Hanuman came the monkey brigade. The monkeys liked this area, which was full of fruits and tubers. After the dispute arising out of the tying up of the horse was settled, Rama and Sita met and resolved the issues between them. Rama took rest for a few days at Rampalli. All this time, Hanuman and the monkey brigade were enjoying themselves in the forest near Alinkulam. For the monkeys, those were days of mirth and revelry. During this time, some monkeys became pregnant and some gave birth. When Rama and his retinue prepared to leave, the monkeys were reluctant to leave the enchanting forest. They continued to stay here. The monkeys seen in Muthanga and surrounding areas are the descendants of the monkeys from Rama's army, and are known as Hanuman langurs in the area. It is believed that Hanuman langurs are found in all those forests of Wayanad where Sita's presence is felt.[72]

The Origin of the Sun and the Stars: The Kurichya Belief

Malakkari is the principal deity of the Kurichyas. They believe that Malakkari came out of the third eye of Shiva, and therefore, the Kurichyas consider Malakkari to be Shiva himself. They hold that Malakkari played a role in the formation of the sun and the stars:

> At the time when Malakkari was born, there was no distinction between day and night. The entire world was engulfed in utter darkness. Moved by the pitiable condition of the world, Malakkari began to weep. The sun was born of the tears that flowed from his right eye. His sweat drops became the stars. Hence, it was Malakkari who created the sun and the stars that lit up the world.[73]

The Adiya Oral Tradition

Traditionally, the Adiya tribe is unlettered. The dialect they speak has no script or alphabet. All their knowledge is communicated orally, from generation to generation. The story among the Adiyas regarding the reason for this lack of literacy, and highlighting their oral tradition goes like this:

> At creation, men were divided into different communities based on their reactions to the appearance of the fierce Mali. Then they were assigned specific trades as well as streams of education. But while instructions regarding these were being given, the first father and mother of the Adiyas were sleeping in their hut. They realised the importance of education only after others had mastered reading and writing. They went to Shiva and Vishnu and begged them to teach them how to read and write. By that time, the stock of papyrus on which writing was taught had been exhausted. Still they continued to implore Shiva and Vishnu to teach them. The two gods rebuked them severely for being oblivious when others were being educated.
>
> The first father and mother persisted in their entreaties. Finally, Shiva and Vishnu took mercy and relented. On the floor were strewn bits and pieces of papyrus left over from the lessons given to others. Shiva and Vishnu collected these and threw them into the fire. They collected the ash and smeared it on the tongues of the first Adiya couple, and then blessed them, 'You have no reading and writing skills. Your knowledge will stay on your tongue.'[74]

The Adiyas ascribe this story as the reason why their language has no script or alphabet. Their songs and stories are transferred orally from generation to generation.

How Kalan Became the God of Death

The Adiyas have a story regarding how Kalan was assigned his powers as the God of death. Some parts of this story have a similar plot as that of the story of their oral tradition. This is the story of Kalan:

> Vishnu and Shiva of the Trimurtis (Brahma, Vishnu and Shiva) jointly created the gods and goddesses. Each God and Goddess was assigned specific roles and powers. While the roles and powers were being assigned, Kalan and his wife were sleeping in their house. When the wife woke up, she found that her husband was still fast asleep. She lay down and closed her eyes. Then from the lane close by, she heard the sound of galloping horses. She opened the window and looked out. She saw the gods galloping on their white horses, returning home after receiving their assignments. She woke up her husband. Cross at having been woken up from sleep, Kalan sprang up. 'What a long sleep! Don't you see the other gods obtaining special powers and returning home? Come on! Hurry up and go get your powers,' the Goddess pleaded with Kalan.
>
> By the time Kalan reached Shiva and Vishnu, the other gods had left with the powers assigned to them. There were no powers left for him. Kalan asked for his share. Shiva and Vishnu said, 'Only a few minor powers are left. If you are satisfied with them, we will grant them to you.' Kalan was not interested in small powers. The words of Shiva and Vishnu made him angrier. He returned home in a huff. Taking his bow, he started shooting arrow after arrow at the sun and the moon. The sun and the moon were frightened. They went and hid behind the clouds. As a result, there were no days and nights on the earth. Shiva and Vishnu were at a loss. The sun and the moon complained to the gods. The gods sent the Goddess Bhagavathy to Shiva and Vishnu. Bhagavathy said to Shiva and Vishnu, 'This is Kalan's doing. You have offended him. Placate him by giving him the powers due to him, otherwise all of us are going to be in trouble.' Shiva and Vishnu authorised Bhagavathy to pacify Kalan. When Bhagavathy reached Kalan, he was still shooting the arrows.

She felt it wasn't proper to speak to him at a time when he was so angry. So she approached Kalan's wife and apprised her of the situation. Together, they managed to pacify Kalan. Kalan then went to Shiva and Vishnu. They transferred to him the two powers they had reserved for themselves: the power of granting death and the power of sprouting seeds. Kalan was pleased. This is how Kalan became the God of death.[75]

Since Kalan is also the God of sprouting seeds, the Adiyas offer Kalan a portion of the fruits and tubers they cultivate. There are many stories related to Kalan among the Adiyas.

The Creation of Cashew: The Kurichya Belief

The cashew apple is considered to a pseudo-fruit by botanists. This is because the flesh of the fruit does not develop out of the floral ovary. The seed (nut) is at the end of the cashew apple. The Kurichyas have a belief regarding how the cashew was created. The story goes such:

> The power of creation belongs to Brahma. Everything was created by him. Once, Saraswathi, Brahma's consort, said in jest, 'You think only you can create. I will show you that I too can create.'
>
> Laughing at that, Brahma said, 'You may also create, if you can.' Saraswathi created a fruit and showed it to Brahma, who examined it closely. It had no seed in it. Brahma said, 'Devi, how can this produce new generations? This has no seed in it.' Saraswathi realised her blunder. When she tried to destroy it, Brahma said, 'Don't destroy what you have created. We can do one thing: we can attach a seed to this fruit.' Saraswathi did as she was told and that is how the seed of the cashew fruit came to be attached to it on the outside.[76]

How the Adiyas Became Slaves

The word Adiya means slave (adima). Once upon a time, the people of this tribe used to work as slaves. But their folk songs and beliefs suggest that in earlier times, they had lived a life of freedom, equality and prosperity. How did they come to be slaves then? There are a number of legends in their culture regarding this. One such legend relates to King Mahabali, the great and benevolent king of Kerala. The Adiyas of today believe that they are his descendants. This is the story of the transformation of the children of King Mahabali into slaves:

> Long ago, the Adiyas were not slaves. In those days, there were no slaves, nor were there any owners. It was the golden age when Maveli (Mahabali) ruled the earth. People lived by farming in lands cleared of forests and by hunting small animals. Maveli Mantu was the guardian of the Adiya society. In those days, there were no divisions among men either. People led prosperous lives. Then, into their midst came three wicked kings. Deceived by their beguiling smiles, Mahabali offered them a hearty welcome. The deceivers waited for their chance and through trickery, brought the land and the mantam (clan territory) into their possession. When the guileless Adiya elder (Mahabali) asked them to return his land, they revealed their true colours. They struck him with a lime-pot. He fell down, wounded, and blood started oozing out of his nose. Soon, he died.
>
> Maveli's subjects were scared and ran helter-skelter. The usurper overlords stopped them and threatened them. They succeeded in dividing the group and fomenting strife among them. The Adiyas were divided into 108 groups, unable to see and interact with each other. The overlords thus tightened their hold over this tribe through the policy of divide and rule. They said, 'This world belongs to the virat purusha (cosmic man). We were born out of the mouth, hands and chest of the virat purusha. You are our slaves. Your job is to

do what we tell you.' But the people ignored these words. They did not sing the praises of the overlords. The wicked lords then brandished their swords and threw their spears. Even then the people were not cowed down. Finally, the overlords brought Mali, the fierce God with a bloody mouth and fiery eyes. They threatened the people and said that those who did not obey them would be eaten up by him. As soon as Mali came, fierce storms began to rage. Thunder roared and lightning flashed. The people were frightened. Shivering with fear, they cried aloud, 'Please save us!' But the overlords did not come to their rescue. The people were sure that Mali would devour them. They ran to the wicked lords and promised to follow their command, and hence turned into slaves.

RAMAYANA CHARACTERS AND THIRUNELLY

Thirunelly, known as the Kashi of the south, is a storehouse of myths. It is the centre of many a belief held by both the Dalits and the Savarna people. These written and oral beliefs and legends have made this place a centre of pilgrimage, in part because the geography and landscape of the region has made it easy to transplant the epics into the soil of Thirunelly.

There are three Ramas among the incarnations of Mahavishnu: Rama, Parasurama and Balarama. The stories prevalent in Thirunelly revolve around the first two incarnations. It is believed that after killing Ravana, following the counsel of the sages, Rama visited the temple at Thirunelly. Hindus believe that on hearing of the demise of King Dasaratha, Rama, Lakshmana and Bharatha offered prayers for the soul of their departed father here.

Parasurama's Journey to Thirunelly

One story tells of how Parasurama, the beloved disciple of Shiva and one of the immortal beings on earth, once visited the Thirunelly temple and took a dip in the Papanasini stream.

The Puranas say that Parasurama, the seventh incarnation of Mahavishnu, armed with the Parasu weapon gifted by Shiva, killed the Kshatriya kings twenty-one times. Their blood flowed like a river. Parasurama dug five lakes in Kurukshetra

(Syamanthaka Panchakam) with his axe, and this blood flowed into these lakes and filled them. Atoning for this sin of great bloodshed, Parasurama gifted the entire earth to the Brahmins. In addition, obeying the command of his father, Parasurama killed his own mother. Weighed down by feelings of guilt, Parasurama made a pilgrimage to several shrines and offered prayers and sacrifices. One of the places he visited was the Thirunelly temple.[77]

Another tradition among the Savarna Hindus in Wayanad has it that when his father was killed, Parasurama came to Thirunelly. The story goes thus:

> Once, the king of Hehaya, Karthaveeryarjuna, while returning from the ashram of Sage Jamadagni after receiving the sage's hospitality, destroyed the trees near the ashram and stole a calf named Surabhi. Infuriated at this, Parasurama killed Karthaveeryarjuna. In retaliation, the sons of Karthaveeryarjuna killed Sage Jamadagni when they couldn't find Parasurama. Parasurama then came to Thirunelly and offered penance in Thirunelly and Papanasini.[78]

Papanasini

Not only the characters depicted in the epics but also the natural phenomena described in them have been transplanted to various sites in Wayanad. The best examples are the Papanasini stream and the Kalindi river in Thirunelly. Papanasini has been accorded the status of the holy river Ganga, and finds several mentions in our epics.

The Papanasini stream can be reached by descending the granite steps built on the western side of the Thirunelly temple and walking half a kilometre through the forest surrounding the temple. It is a stream of crystal-clear water flowing from the Brahmagiri mountain. Hindus believe that, as in the case of the holy river Ganga of Kashi, taking a dip in Papanasini will wash away all one's sins and the sacred rites performed there will take the souls of the departed to heaven.

It is also held that the underground river Saraswathi joins Ganga and emerges as Papanasini. On the southern side, downstream, one can see the sacred rock called Pindappara, to which devotees offer sacrifice. Offering sacrifice here amounts to performing sacred rites for deceased ancestors in other places.

Sri Rama, Parasurama, Sage Jamadagni and sages like Sanaka are thought to have visited Papanasini and offered prayers.

Thirunelly marks the confluence of the seven sacred streams of Papanasini, Panchatheertham, Ramamochini Theertham, Gundika Theertham, Sathabindu, Sahasravindam and Varaham. The most important among these is, of course, Papanasini.[79]

The Tale of Pashanabhedi Turning into Pindappara

Pindappara is the name of a sacred rock in Papanasini. The water of Papanasini falls on it, and offerings for the dead are placed on the stone. There is a story about the origin of this rock:

> Once, Mahavishnu happened to curse an asura named Pashanabhedi. Before being killed, Pashanabhedi asked for a boon. 'Instead of burning me, pray turn me into a rock.'
>
> Vishnu granted the boon. It is believed that Pashanabhedi was transformed into the sacred rock that stretches from Ganga to Thirunelly in Wayanad—his head in Gaya, the middle in river Godavari, and feet at Thirunelly.[80]

Gundika Temple

A little way away from the Panchatheertham stream at Thirunelly is a small temple made of stone, set in the middle of the forest. It is said that this temple, surrounded by gigantic trees, is as old as the Thirunelly temple.

It is customary for all devotees who return after offering prayers for the dead to visit the Gundika temple. The process of worshipping the trinity of Brahma-Vishnu-Mahesh is considered complete only after stopping by the shrine in Gundika. Legend has it that the Shiva idol in this temple was consecrated by Maharishi Agasthya.

Another story claims that this was the abode of the swayambhu, self-manifested, Shiva, and it was from here that Shiva went to Kottiyoor to slay the demon Daksha.[81]

Panchatheertham can be reached by descending the steps of the Thirunelly temple. On the rock in the middle of the Theertham pond, one can see two feet engraved. These are believed to be the imprint of Mahavishnu's feet. There are also reliefs of Lord Vishnu's sacred conch, club and chakra on the rock. According to local belief, it was from this spot that he gave instructions to Brahma.[82]

The head priest of the Thirunelly temple removes the leftovers of the previous pooja and makes arrangements for the next pooja before closing the door of the sanctum sanctorum for the day. The belief underlying this practice is that Brahma, who consecrated this temple, himself comes to perform the pooja at night.

The Conference of the Trimurtis

It is believed that the Trimurtis—Vishnu, Shiva and Brahma—meet daily at Thirunelly temple. Thirunelly Perumal or Mahavishnu is thought to reside in the main temple and Shiva in the Gundika temple, while Brahma is believed to come daily to offer pooja to Mahavishnu in Thirunelly. Thus the Trimurtis meet at the Thirunelly temple, and the local Hindus believe it is the Devaloka (divine abode) on earth.[83]

RAMAYANA TALES IN THE FOLK SONGS OF WAYANAD

Folk songs are a precious part of the lives and cultural legacy of indigenous communities. All communities with oral traditions express their beliefs and practices mostly through songs. These songs give us useful insights into their existence, socio-anthropological identities and consciousness.

Orally transmitted or inherited folk songs are not the creations of any particular individual; rather, they originate in the collective consciousness of communities. Therefore, additions and deletions are normal when songs are handed down from generation to generation. Folklore is a constantly evolving thing. Unlike the written tradition, orally transmitted songs are continuously revised and brought to life.

A song that exists in a particular community might not necessarily be sung by all the members of that community. Different versions of the same song may exist within the same community. Some of these versions are quite modern. The period of the song can be determined on the basis of the theme and the language used in it. Based on the content, these songs have been classified as romantic, epic, folk, magical, supernatural, limerick and so on.

All communities in Wayanad have songs they sing. Most of them are related to religious beliefs and practices. Some, however, are sung purely for entertainment. Folk songs with central themes related to the epics are found among the Adivasi sects of the Adiyas, Kurumas and Kurichyas. The songs sung during the performance of the ritual folk-dances of Kolkali and Vattakali by the Wayanad Chettis, Mandadan Chettis, the Kurumas and the Kurichyas, too, have themes related to the epics. Many of them adhere to the written forms of the epics.

Some songs which have retained the basic themes of the epics are discussed below:

Songs of the Mullukurumas

The Mullukurumas have made abundant use of themes from the Ramayana and Mahabharatha in their folk songs. Most of these songs are sung during the performance of Kolkali and Vattakali. A few of them are described in the next few pages. The songs have been transliterated, and the meaning of the lyrics is given in English.

The first song describes how Ravana abducted Sita, carried her away to Lanka, and prepared a place for her to sit:

> *Pullimaanayivannu*
> *Seethaye Ravan kattu*
> *Kattanganekondupoyi Seethaye Ravanan*
> *Kadalum kadatheettalle kondupoyath*
> *Chembaka vanmaram valiyoru vanmarom*
> *Vanmaram keezhillu kondangiruthi Seethaye*
> *Asure sthreekale kavalum vechu*
> *Agnikond viravalachumketti*
> *Akasham kond pandhalumitt*
> *Nakshatramkond vilakkum vechu*
> *Kottayum kandd, gopurom kandd*
> *Kottaykkal rajavinte varavum kande.*[84]

Disguised as a deer,
Ravana stole away Sita,
And took her to Lanka, across the sea.
He seated her

Under a flowering towering Champak tree
And set Asura women
To watch over Sita.
He made an arch of fire
He set the sky as the pavilion
And made lamps from the stars.
Behold the Fortress!
Behold the tower!
Behold the arrival of the King!

The second song describes the birds Jatayu and Sampathi. Sampathi, while soaring high in the sky, had spotted the place where Sita sat. When Hanuman and his monkeys came in search of Sita, he told them where she was and gave them directions. For this, he received a blessing from Rama:

Chedattum kavunalla uttaravanom
Avvanathingallu randu pakshikalundayi
Jatayuvennum Sampathi ennum
Avvanamppoondu dharbamaanushanmaaray
Belabelangalu thammil pareekshippanayi
Vegam parannithaavar melppottingane
Adityamannelam utbhavichappol
Thalkshanamanujanum theepidichallo
Rakshippan Sampathine pinnilakeenaam
Pakshathayathode Jatayuvum veenu
Vindhyasalathingal Sampatheem veenu
Andanayi moonu dinam kidannanallo
Puthannam chirakippoll varuthavenam
Andanayi kidanooru Sampathithaanum
Praanavedanayode unarnu nokkumbol
Kandeethu thante paksham karinjathu
Ayyo vidhikarmam ennu vicharichu
Appol vidhivasaal angorudikkanu
Seethaye thendivarum markadanmaarum
Agrajanaaya pakshi Sampathi kandu
Seethayirippathum kaatikoduth

Sri Ramadevan thantanughraham kondu
Puthanaam chirakappolavanum vannu
Seethemi ennu cholli parannupoyi
Yudhamathengal chennu maranjaalamma[85]

In the beauteous forest
From the enchanting garden
Two birds,
Jatayu and Sampathi,
Soared into the azure sky
Testing their might against each other
Up and up they rose
And touched the flaming sun.
Their mighty wings caught fire
Down and down they fell
Jatayu and Sampathi
Into the Vindhya mountains
Blinded, bruised and burnt,
For three days, they lay.
Sampathi, opening his eyes in pain,
Saw his burnt wings,
And mused, 'such is fate'.
Seeing the monkeys
In search of Sita
Sampathi, the elder
Showed them where she sat.
And by the blessings of Sri Rama
New wings sprouted on him
And crying 'Oh Sita'
He flew away,
And vanished into the skies.

The third song describes how Sita used her anklet to show where she was being carried away by Ravana:

Kadalinte naduvathan arasante vaanam pol
Avideku vazhiyaarumarivethundo
Avanappol Avaleththan eduthudan tholiletti

Uyarnori kadalmeethe parannanallo
Avalappol Seethadevi ninachu thaan irikkumbol
Ariyathangavaloru puthumacheythu
Theruthera avallu thante kanangalilidunooru
Kanakathe kazhichaval vazhimellitt
Ath kandu Hanumaanum eduthudan nadakond
Baghavante padham vechu vanangikondell.[86]

In the middle of the ocean
Lay the king's palace
No one knew the way there.
Carrying her on his shoulders
Ravana flew over the roaring ocean.
Playing a trick
Sita removed her golden anklet
And threw it down.
Hanuman coming that way
Saw the anklet.
Picking it up
He took it to Rama,
Laid the anklet at his feet,
and prostrated before the Lord.

The next song tells the story of Rama slaying the demoness Tadaka who used to attack the sages in the forest. The event is narrated in a slightly different manner from that found in the *Valmiki Ramayana*.

Vendani poongayil Seethaye kaananju
Kanduvarunna varavathu rakshasan
Kaattathilngaayal pottunathu pole
Potti alari varunnola Tadaka
Tadakanmaarvilorastramayachute
Vanmalapole marinjalo Tadaka
Vanpuzha poleyolikunna chorayum
Choryaum neenthi kadannithu Raghavan
Penkola cheythath aareda Raghava
Penkola cheythath nithyavum njan thava.[87]

Not seeing the beautiful Sita
The demoness comes that way.
Yelling like a tornado
There comes Tadaka.
He sends an arrow to her bosom.
Like a mighty mountain falls Tadaka
Like a mighty river flows her blood
Across that river swims Rama.
Who killed the woman, Rama?
I killed the woman, says Rama.

The Kolkali Songs of the Mandadan Chettis

The Mandadan Chettis are a subgroup of the Chetti community. The Mandadan Chettis living in Wayanad, the Nilgiris district of Tamil Nadu, and other areas adjacent to Wayanad perform Kolkali at functions such as temple festivals and wedding ceremonies.

Bamboo sticks measuring a foot in length are used for Kolkali, a folk art that literally means 'stick-dance' ('kol' means stick and 'kali' means dance). A minimum of twelve people are needed for the game. They either stand in a circle or facing one another. Each of the performers holds a stick and moves in a circle, striking sticks and keeping rhythm to the accompanying music. The circle expands and contracts as the dance progresses. As the music gradually rises in pitch and beat, the pace increases till the performance reaches its climax.

This art form serves to strengthen social bonds and to revive and energise religious beliefs and practices. Characters and episodes from the Ramayana and Mahabharatha lie at the heart of the majority of the songs sung during Kolkali. Many of the stories told through the songs do not permit variations. They are just faithful translations of the *Valmiki Ramayana*. But the storytelling techniques and the embellishments used are close to the folk genre.

The following song, sung at the start of the dance, describes the preparations for the dance, and also describes how Kolkali is performed:

> *Varanamughaneyum vaniyeyum*
> *Krishnaneyum Valmiki muniyeyum Indraneyum thaanum*
> *Shudhamaya komayaneer kondu*
> *Pandhal mezhukittu*
> *Vellivilakkathum vechu*
> *Neyyum pakarnnu*
> *Vedamenna nooleduthu*
> *Thiriyittanthikoluthi*
> *Vendum vannamalangarichaa-*
> *Veriverakolum-*
> *Kayyil pidichudane*
> *Vilakkale valamvechu*
> *Guruve sharanamennangithaa thozhutheen.*

> O Ganapathi, O Saraswathi,
> O Krishna, O Sage Valmiki, O Indra.
> Waxing the floor with pure cowdung
> Placing a silver lamp at the centre
> And pouring in ghee for oil
> And lighting the wicks
> In the gathering darkness.
> Decorating the lamp
> Arranging ourselves
> And circling the lamp
> With sticks in hand,
> Our obeisance to you, Master!

This song is related to the Ramayana story, when Ravana tries to seduce Sita:

> *Uracheythanappol Ravanan*
> *Thaanum tharunimaaril nee vambathi thanne*
> *Kothikunnu baale*
> *Kaalam naalayi*

Hithathoode ninthe
Maaranayuvaan
Mindathe thala thaazhthiyathenthe
Kandaal njanorazhakilalle-baale
Kettitillayo baale nee enne
Komala nayika Ravanan njanum
Vednathokke tharunnathundu njan
Aranjaanam, vala, mothiram, nalkaam
Athineethum kuravilla bhoolokasundari
Uracheythaanaa ...

Thus spoke Ravana
You are incomparable among women
I want to possess you, girl
Long time, have I been longing
To embrace you.
Why is your head down.
Why don't you answer?
Am I not attractive, girl?
Have you not heard of me, girl?
I am the handsome Ravana himself.
I will give whatever you desire
Belt made of gold, bangles, rings
You shall not be in want of anything
Oh you most beautiful on earth!

The next song is sung during the Othukali dance. The song says that Shurpanakha, Ravana's sister, desired to marry Rama. Lakshmana cut off her nose and breasts, and in retaliation for having humiliated his sister, Ravana abducted Sita.

Sri Rama devanum bharyayam Seethayum
Sodharan Lakshmanan
Engane moonupper
Sanyasimaarayi kaatil nadakumbol
Shurpanakha vannu
Ramanodarul cheythu:

Rama, Ramayenne kalyanam cheyyenam
Devanathinethiraakayaal
Kopichu Rakshasi,
Seethayekolluvaan
Bhaavicha nerathu Lakshmanan veganayi
Rakshasithannude mookum mulakalum
Kopicharuthu paranjayacheedinan
Akkaranathaale Ravanan Seethaye
Lankayil kondupoyi thaamasippichathum
Vanara sainyasaha sahaayathaale
Thaamasam koodathe Ramadevan chennu
Ravanane konnu
Seethayekondonnu
Sri Ramadevanum ...

Sri Rama, Sita his wife
His brother Lakshmana.
Thus the three, as mendicants
Wandered in the forest.
Along came Shurpanakha
And spake thus to Rama:
Rama, Rama, you must marry me.
When Rama refused
The demoness raged
And tried to kill Sita.
Lakshmana in anger
Cut off her nose and breasts
And drove her away.
This is why
Ravana abducted Sita
And took her to Lanka.
With the support of the monkey army
Sri Rama at once went over
Slew Ravana
and brought back Sita ...

Songs of the Kurichyas and the Adiyas

There are no indigenous communities that do not have their own songs. A majority of the folk songs are rooted in caste and religious traditions. Their names, Panar pattu, Pulayar pattu, Pulluvar pattu, Mannar pattu, Brahmana pattu, Kaniyan pattu, Velar pattu, Mappila pattu and Kuravar pattu, refer to the the different castes and communities in Wayanad, such as the Panas, Pulayas, Pulluvas and Brahmins ('pattu' means song). In the same fashion, tribal sects such as the Kurichyas, Adiyas, Paniyas and Karimpalas have their own folk-song heritage. These songs are sung at religious festivals and social functions. The themes of these songs are either stories from the epics or paeans dedicated to heroes.

Although there are only a few tribal songs with incidents from the epics as their central theme, references to episodes from them are inserted in many songs as per the communities' discretion. Such songs are found mostly in the oral traditions of the Kurichyas and the Adiyas.

The Kumbhappattu is a set of songs sung by the Kurichyas at the Malakkari festival. The songs refer to Malakkari, who is believed to have originated from the third eye of Paramashiva. These songs sing the praises of Malakkari who fought the demons and harmful creatures wreaking havoc on earth and sent them into the depths of the sea. Incursion of seawater into the land is a sign that those demons are trying to return. But since Malakkari resides in the kavus (sacred groves) on earth, the sea will not succeed in submerging the land.[88]

The Maramayappattu of the Kurichyas concisely describes how Malakkari pushed King Mahabali (Mavothi) into the netherworld:

Athukando Athukando Billan Thaivaannu
Keezhayilam Keeyulokam Thanoyi Daivam

Kattayi Chettiayi Poyoottu Thaivam
Vadakilentta Nattilla Thanoyithaivam
Vadakumbadavatto Pareykkum Chennu
Parammethanallo Nikunne Thaivam
Angane Ninnitt Nokunna Neram
Keeyayilum Vavunna Mavothiyoddu
Moonnadi mannu tharanam enikippo
Athuthaane kettondu Maavothiyalle
Anneram Paranjondo Mavothi kekki
Moonnadi Ningallanolli Kekki
Athu thaane kettondu Billan thaivaanu
Naandadi Alakkuno Billan thaivalle
Eradikku mannu kaanunillalo
Eradikku mannu kaanillath
Onnoodi Kekkano Mavothingallu
Enjjiyedann alakkendiyathippam
Anneram paranjutto Mavothiyalle
Entoode moorthavillu Bellallo kaalu
Chavutti thaaththiyoodannallo Malakkari daivam
Badekkan naadu pidichallo thaivam[89]

See, Oh see the god is descending!
To the lower world, the god himself!
He has come down to the northern land
On a rock he stands and surveys the land.
And then to Mavothi, the ruler of the lower world
The god says: 'You must give me
Three steps of land immediately.'
On hearing it Mavothi replies:
'You can measure out three steps of land.'
The god takes two steps
Was it not god himself?
In two steps the land was covered
The god says, 'two steps are over
Where is the space for the third step?'
At that time Mavothi answers,
'Put your foot on the top of my head'

> The god puts his foot
> On the top of Mavothi's head
> And pushes him down
> Into the netherworld.
> Thus did the god Malakkari
> Conquer the northern part of the land.

Malakkari is the deity of not only the Kurichyas but of the Adiyas as well. However, references to the God Malakkari in the Adiya songs are not as clear as those in the songs of the Kurichyas. For the Adiyas, Malakkari is the God of the bow and arrow. To them, Malakkari is only one among their many gods, including Chuvani, Mallappan, Pookkarimakadaivam, Siddhappan, Vallooramma, Chikkamma and Karichathan. In the Malakkari song of the Adiyas, Shiva takes the form of a savage to test Arjuna. In general, the gods of the Savarna communities do not appear in the songs of the Adiyas. But since the nature and persona of some of their deities is similar to that of the gods of the Savarna societies, such as Shiva and Vishnu (gods of preservation and destruction), they are claimed to be the incarnations of the Savarna gods.

Only very recently were the Adiyas permitted to interact with the members of the Savarna communities and offer worship in their temples. Gradually, the Adiyas began to absorb the Savarna gods into their myths. Therefore, it is only in the modern songs of the Adiyas that the gods of the upper-caste Hindus are featured.

Modern songmakers have a tendency to modernise songs. Some people sing the same song differently on different occasions. This also denotes the evolution of the songs.

Today, there is little chance of references to their traditional gods in their songs being explained to the younger generations. The chances of uninterpretable songs surviving in the oral form are quite bleak now.

WHY WAYANAD RAMAYANAS?

> The Ramayana does not belong to any one moment in history, for it has its own history which lies embedded in the many versions which were woven around the theme at different times and places.
>
> – Romila Thapar, *The Ramayana Syndrome*

The mythological tales that exist in various forms in the Wayanad region are not considered to be the variations of a specific text. The concept of textual variation is alien to the narrator community. This is to say that the communities in Wayanad, including the illiterate Adivasi tribals who have not even heard of Valmiki, Vyasa or the Ramayana and Mahabharatha, believe that these stories are exclusive to their own indigenous culture, religious beliefs and practices.

Since the concept of 'text' or the existence of a canonical text is alien to these people, one story circulating within a community can take on many different forms, interpretations and layers of meaning. It is also not rare for the storyteller to introduce variations when narrating the story on different occasions, or in different situations and contexts. Therefore, it is certain that there are no grand narratives among them that are universally accepted. Nor are there master narratives that are compatible with the religious beliefs, rituals and traditions of all, or that cater to the existential questions of everyone.

The main feature of the mythological tales commonly told among the different communities in Wayanad is their region-specific characteristics. Almost all the Ramayana stories of Wayanad are in perfect harmony with the cultural, social and regional aspects of the area.

Before diving into an analysis of the folk forms of the epics prevalent in Wayanad, we need to seek answers to two questions: What is the underlying reason for the existence and survival of these Ramayana-based mythological stories in Wayanad? How does an existing text take on different versions?

Existence of Ramayana-based Stories in Wayanad: Underlying Causes

The Wayanad region in Kerala is marked by many geographical peculiarities. Surrounded by mountains from all sides, it resembles a grand fortress. This is perhaps one reason for the isolation of this district from the rest of Kerala, as a result of which it has developed a unique culture of its own. The area has had a long history of communities living in its forests. However, the sad fact is that there are no written and reliable records about the Wayanad region. Many historians conveniently begin to trace the history of Wayanad only from the time of the Kottayam dynasty, which ended with the death of Kerala Varma Pazhassi Raja in 1805. Other than a few stories that are a mixture of history and myth, no historical data is available about the Veda dynasty which ruled Wayanad before the Kottayam dynasty assumed the throne. The era prior to that lies in complete oblivion. In the absence of the clear light of history, myths and legends tend to proliferate.[90]

As a result, the folk forms of the Ramayana tales prevalent in Wayanad are commonly believed to be a part of history. Most of the Ramayana-based mythological stories set in Wayanad present their events as believable ones, as having transpired in time and space. The landscape and geography of the region form a sort of tangible backdrop that lends authenticity to the narration. Though the legends are interwoven with the fragments of history available, and deal with events that people believe have taken place, they do not have the same veracity that historical narratives do.[91] The supernatural elements that pop up here and there in these orally narrated tales dissociate the events from history and mark them as matters of belief and fantasy. For those who narrate folk forms of episodes from the epics, the presence of supernatural elements does not lead to the rejection of their faith in the narratives, but only serves to strengthen it.

This mingling of history with fantasy is exemplified by the belief that Wayanad was created by Mayan. As stated earlier in this book, in ancient times Wayanad was known as 'Mayakshetra', meaning the temple of Mayan. Thus, the name 'Wayanad' is locally considered to be the corrupt form of 'Mayanad'. Mayan was the brother-in-law of Ravana, and the master architect who built the sabhathalam, palace, for the Pandavas. In several villages across India, people believe that many of the natural and architectural wonders are the handiwork of Mayan. Indeed, people claim that their areas are associated with Mayan to ensure that they are given importance and recognition. Mayan has not been factually proved to be a historical figure so far. But the folk forms of stories from the epic present Mayan as someone who really existed. Many in Meerut, for instance, believe that Mayan built their city. The story goes that it was Yudhishtira, the Pandava king, who entrusted Mayan with the task of building Meerut.[92]

It is part of the practice of the oral tradition to present Mayan as the creator of architecturally unique and beautiful landscapes. It is therefore easy to understand why Mayan has been accredited with the creation of Wayanad in the oral narratives. In fact, the natural beauty and geographical peculiarities of the region, combined with the similarity of the words 'Mayanad' and 'Wayanad', lend credence to the belief that Mayan is the creator of Wayanad. Thus, the region's associations with Mayan, and his links to the Hindu epics, is one reason why there exist mythological tales and beliefs in Wayanad that are based on the Ramayana.

However, the existence and spread of the Ramayana stories cannot be reduced to just one factor. It is possible that the Ramayana stories reached Wayanad from nearby regions. Wayanad had been largely isolated from the outside world due to its fort-like location in the mountains, coupled with the difficulties created by the dense forests that made the journey through the ghats tough, and the lack of a reason to venture out of the region. It is possible that the people there were at least partially ignorant of the world outside Wayanad. However, the people of Wayanad were familiar with neighbouring areas in Karnataka such as Coorg and Mysore, as well as the Nilgiri areas in Tamil Nadu, because these are all neighbouring hilly regions connected by mountain passes. Tribes in Wayanad might have heard Ramayana stories from their neighbouring tribes in Coorg, Mysore and the Nilgiris, and assimilated them into their own culture and lore. Therefore, one possible cause for the existence of Ramayana stories in Wayanad is the interaction with other tribes from the states of Karnataka and Tamil Nadu.

Another likely reason for the spread of Ramayana tales in Wayanad is the migration of communities from other parts to Wayanad. All the major communities who have assimilated mythological tales into their oral tradition (Kurichyas, Adiyas, Kurumas, Chettis and the Savarna Hindus) are those who migrated into Wayanad in different epochs. It is natural for settlers to connect the names of places to the world of legends and myths in order to establish their settlements as sacred and unique. The change in the names of the places where different communities migrated in different epochs, is an argument in support of this theory.

The large-scale migration of Christians from central Travancore to Wayanad and its nearby regions due to a steep increase in population and the lack of arable land (the Malabar Migrations) during the middle of the twentieth century paved the way for socio-cultural upheavals that were reflected in the cultural behaviour of the tribals and other local people. For instance, Sisumala near Pulpally became Sasimala, and then was transformed into Kurisumala after the arrival of Christian settlers ('sisu' means child, 'kurisu' means cross, 'mala' means hill). There is also proof that when the Christian settlers created new names for places, to counter it, the Hindus created their own new versions and vice versa. For instance, Sitamadi near Pulpally became Sitamount. Many such changes were made—Vincentgiri, Louis Mount, Pallikunnu, are all Christian versions. Such names generated anxiety among a minority of the Hindus, who feared they would lose their local identity to the growing dominance of the settlers' culture. When Christians migrated into Nalloornad near Mananthavady in the northern region of Wayanad in large numbers and started to build churches and schools, a local Hindu leader named his house 'Dwaraka', and later, the locality came to be known by that name, says Karunakaran Cherukara, a teacher and actor from the area. Only in recent times have people started connecting this place with the Krishna–Banasura battle on Banasuramala.

Practically all the dominant communities who migrated to Wayanad during different historical epochs would have created similar names for places and legends.

Existence of Ramayana-based Stories in Wayanad: Linguistic Causes

Language is defined as the ordered use of words and signs. In the opinion of Ferdinand de Saussure and Claude Lévi-Strauss, who laid the foundations for structuralism, structural analysis is based on two concepts: 'langue' and 'parole'. Langue is the totality of all the elements and laws of syntax of a given language. Parole is defined as the form of language used by an individual based on the possibilities of each language. 'Utterance', according to Saussure, is the linguistic expression of the individual. The basic element of utterance is 'sign'. A sign consists of a sound-image and a concept. Claude Lévi-Strauss says that cultural expressions are similar to language structure, and the linguistic model can be applied to the study of traditions, rituals and behaviour.[93]

Structuralism is the study of related structures. Semiology, on the other hand, observes and analyses cultural artefacts as signs transmitting meaning. The Italian semiotician, cultural critic and novelist Umberto Eco was of the view that communication is possible only within a structure of signification. He said signification is based on the function of a signifier that generates an interpretative response in the receiver. It is possible to analyse the prevalence of epic stories in the folk culture of Wayanad in the light of structuralism and semiology.

In the olden days, very few people in Wayanad were literate. The Puranas and Itihasas (epics) were deemed accessible only to the elite. The literate among the Savarna communities might have read and recited from these texts in temples and their homes. The illiterate could only listen. The Adivasis, who fell in the lowest strata of the illiterate, might not have had the opportunity to even listen to such readings. Those who got the chance to listen to the texts must have sought explanations from those who read them. For instance, during the narration of Rama's and Sita's departure from Ayodhya for their fourteen-year exile in the forest, the listeners, who had no knowledge of other places, might have imagined the forests of Wayanad. The terms 'hill' and 'mountain' might have evoked in the minds of the listeners, whether literate or illiterate, first the sign and not the letters. They might have imagined the hills and mountains known to them. Pointing at the nearby forest, those who learnt about the Puranas and Itihasas from their grandmothers' tales might have enquired if these were the places visited by Rama and Sita. To aid their understanding and for the smooth flow of narration, the grandmothers might have answered in the affirmative. The repeated answers registered in the mind and these, in due course, became entrenched beliefs. When such beliefs are transferred from generation to generation, the stories undergo alterations and the theatres of action get transplanted into familiar local settings. The interpretation of these stories is what matters to both the grandmothers and the little listeners. The cultural critic E.D. Hirsch opines that the meaning of a text is the meaning given to it by the interpreter.[94]

The science of hermeneutics deals with the question of whether it is proper to create variations of the written text. Hirsch says that no text has any meaning apart from that given by an interpreter. The text is only an occasion for the creation of meaning. 'We, not our texts, are the makers of the meaning we understand, a text being only an occasion for meaning, in itself an ambiguous form devoid of the consciousness where meaning abides.'[95]

Even in those ancient times when there were no modern means of transportation, the Hindus of Kerala used to undertake pilgrimages to far-off places such as Kashi and Mathura. The ancient pilgrims from Wayanad might have visited spiritual centres and returned to recount their experiences. It is most likely that their narrations were replete with additions and exaggerations. It is possible that the accounts of places such as Ayodhya were highly embellished. These would have naturally inspired among the listeners new interpretations, in keeping with their respective intellectual ability, standard of living and depth of knowledge about the outside world. It is also highly probable that the narrators—back from their travels—adapted their narrations to the capacity of the communities that had lesser exposure to the world outside than them.

The common folk in Wayanad reconstructed the epics and their characters in their own settings, thus making them realistic. This is true not only of Wayanad but of all the places and peoples who have incorporated the epics in their folk stories and beliefs.

Existence of Ramayana-based Stories in Wayanad: Geographical Factors

The geographical features and peculiarities of Wayanad have played a big role in the integration and transformation of tales from the Ramayana in its folk traditions. It has led to the establishment of some locations in the region as the places of action described in the epic. The images of areas full of forests and hills conjured up in the minds of the common folk while listening to the orally transmitted stories might have given birth to such ideas and beliefs. Backward communities have always shown a tendency to posit ghosts, demons and other supernatural beings behind the mysteries they found difficult to solve.

From ancient days, people have been prone to believing that supernatural beings and agencies are behind the mysterious natural phenomena they encounter. There is no room for rational thinking in such belief systems. These irrational beliefs have not only gone unquestioned but have become deeply entrenched in the psyche of the communities.

The natural phenomena and geographical peculiarities of Wayanad have played a significant role in the formation of the folk forms of epic stories in this region. This is quite evident in the legends related to Banasuramala, Muneeswarkoilmala, Brahmagiri, Bhoothathankunnu and Manikunnumala, as well as the names of places such as Wayanad, Ponkuzhy, Althara, Alinkulam, Ashramkolly, Sasimala, Kandathuvayal, Jadayattakavu, Choothupara, Thirunelly, Kanneerthadakom and Sitammakundu. The stories and the beliefs linked to these places have already been discussed in the previous chapters.

The belief that the large rock on top of the Manikunnumala (Kavanappara) was the sling-stone used by Lakshmana during his stay in Wayanad in the company of Sri Rama and Sita might have been generated from the sense of amazement, awe and perplexity that the sight of this huge rock—precariously perched on the hill slope, ready to fall down any moment into the valley below—inspired.

The beliefs about Jadayattakavu near Pulpally are closely related to the geographical uniqueness of the area. In summer, the fields near Jadayattakavu fissure, forming crevices large enough for a cow to disappear into. It is quite likely that people have witnessed the disappearance of such animals into these gorges. This is quite sufficient for them to connect these places with the disappearance of Sita as described in the Ramayana story. Why this place has been linked with the folk versions of the Ramayana story can be well understood in this manner—myths are formed when the conscious merges with the subconscious.

Chains of hills and mountains stretching into infinity are a familiar sight for anyone who surveys their surroundings from the top of the hills in Wayanad. Mountains after mountains, hills after hills, a gigantic fortress. How was this fortress of mountains made? Who made these? The belief that Wayanad was created by Mayan is the result of the local communities reflecting, for generations, on these natural mysteries.

The connection of several legends centred around Thirunelly to the topography of that area is quite evident. This ancient pilgrimage site in the middle of a dense forest, watered by perennial mountain streams, is the ideal location for solitary contemplation. Legend has it that Brahma meditated here. One of the factors attracting pilgrims to Thirunelly is the presence of the Papanasini stream, which originates from the Brahmagiri mountains. People in neighbouring states like Karnataka and Tamil Nadu share the belief that streams emanating from mountaintops are sacred and their water washes away sins. Besides the Thirunelly Papanasini, there are a number of Papanasinis in south India, including Papanasam near Tenkasi, Kuttalam Papanasam in Tamil Nadu, Varkala Papanasam in Kerala and Tiruppathy Papanasam in Andhra Pradesh. All of them are known as holy sites for the performance of the last rites for the souls of the departed. All these beliefs were born around these springs and streams that wash away sins. The Varkala Papanasam is on top of the Sivagiri hill. Devotion to streams is very strong in some areas in Karnataka, like Coorg, which is not far from Thirunelly. The fountains Ramatheertham and Lakshmanatheertham in Coorg district are quite famous.

All these streams have one thing in common: they all originate on mountaintops, and weave their way between the rocks and course through the forest, touching the roots and leaves of different kinds of plants and trees, which renders the water medicinal. It is natural for people to believe that the water in these streams has therapeutic properties. The concept of healing can be easily extended to the concept of 'salvific' or leading to moksha (liberation). The elevated status accorded to such stream would naturally link it in the collective consciousness of a community living in the area, to the divine river Ganga. Such myths and beliefs would recast the nature of the surroundings; rocks and mountains near these sacred streams would get linked to the stories from epics and holy men. Stories about holy men who attained moksha by bathing in these streams would be orally disseminated. These facts are applicable not only to the Papanasini in Thirunelly, but to all the Papanasinis. As has been already mentioned, it is believed that Sage Jamadagni, Sri Rama and Parasurama came to Thirunelly and did penance in the Papanasini stream.

The Papanasini stream flowing through Thirunelly is called the Kalindi river. It acquires the name of Kalindi only once it reaches Thirunelly. This change of name has resulted in the correction of the notion that bathing and performing sacred rites anywhere in the Papanasini stream will lead to moksha. Instead, these rites have to performed at only a particular spot, i.e., Thirunelly, thus enriching its importance and holiness. The Papanasini stream and the river Kalindi, and the association of their name with the Kalindi of the Puranas, has only strengthened the belief of the locals in the sacredness of Papanasini, and its link with the epics.

Existence of Ramayana-based Stories in Wayanad: Historical Aspects

Assuming that the Ramayana has historical roots, what is its timeline? Believers and historians approach this question differently. According to historians, there are no definite answers to this question. Believers, on the other hand, have definite answers. Though the explanations of believers are not historically acknowledged or scientific, they are still relevant to our study.

According to Hindu beliefs and Puranas, there are four epochs or yugas: Krita, Thretha, Dwapara and Kali. Vishnu's incarnations Rama and Krishna are believed to have lived in Thretha Yuga and Dwapara Yuga, respectively. The current age in which we are living is Kali Yuga.

According to calculations based on these yugas, the *Valmiki Ramayana* was composed by Bharadwajan 18,149,115 years ago.[96] Were there human settlements in the Indian subcontinent at that time? Had man reached this stage of evolution at that time? Such questions are quite relevant.

Some Western scholars like the Austrian Indologist Moriz Winternitz put the date of Ramayana in the third century BC; Monier Monier-Williams of the Oxford University places it in the fifth century BC; and Hermann Jacobi, the eminent German Indologist, says it dates back to the sixth century BC. There are some Indian scholars who share the same views. G.V. Veda, the author of the *Riddle of Ramayana* and an honorary fellow of Bombay University, says that Valmiki was a contemporary of Sri Rama in the Thretha Yuga. He believes that the Rama–Ravana battle took place 12,567,101 years before Christ. The sixth edition of the authoritative book *Vedic Sampati*, written by Pandit Raghunandan and published by Prathap Singh Shoorji Vallabha in Mumbai, states that Valmiki composed the Ramayana 1,269,039 years ago. The archaeologist H.D. Sankaliya, during his lecture at the Nagpur University on Ramayana and archaeology, mentioned that the events of Ramayana took place in 1000 BC and that it was composed between 500–700 AD. He also said that, considering tradition and the story, it has a history of 5,000 years.[97]

No concrete evidence has yet emerged which goes to suggest that the events described in the epics took place in those periods in Wayanad. Whatever be the truth, the enquiry whether the events took place in Wayanad 18,149,115 years ago is meaningless in itself. At the same time, recent archaeological and anthropological studies suggest that during the Palaeolithic age, primitive men lived in the forests of Wayanad. Unpolished tools used by them have been recovered from various sites in south India. Dr P. Rajendran has collected artefacts from various sites in Wayanad, Kozhikode, Palakkad, Malappuram, Kollam and Thiruvananthapuram.[98] The tribals in south India, including Kerala, are the descendants of those primitive humans.[99]

In any case, it is obvious that humans lived in parts of Wayanad even before Christ. But it is not possible to determine which communities lived in which areas. The ancient history of Wayanad needs to be studied as part of the history of south India, because this area has close links with the cultural and social history of Karnataka and Tamil Nadu.

In one sense, the invasion of the Aryans was a turning point in the history of India. It led to the eclipsing of the great Indus Valley civilisation and the retreat of the Dravidians to the southern parts of India. The times of Sri Krishna and the Pandavas mark the high point of the Indus Valley civilisation. The Mahabharatha tells the story of the Kurukshetra war waged under the leadership of Sri Krishna and the triumph of morals, and after his time, the decline of that civilisation, which had reached high levels of development, due to internal strife. It was at this juncture in the decadence of the Indus Valley civilisation that the Aryans entered the Indus Valley and established their supremacy. As the Aryan invasion began to destroy the local civilisation and the people there were massacred, the Dravidians fled in large numbers to south India. The sage Nachiniyarkiniyar, in the preface to the famous *Tholkappiyam*, the book of the Dravidians, speaks about this migration, describing how the Dravidians cleared the forests, set up kingdoms and settled in the south. Some scholars have inferred that Agasthya, the Shaivite sage, was a leader of the migrants. He took with him eighteen kings belonging to the decadent Yadukula dynasty. From Dwaraka he led a group of migrants and journeyed southwards. Dwarasamudram near Mysore is one of the kingdoms set up by them. One of the reasons for the large number of legends about Agasthya may be that he was one of the leaders of the migrating people. Some historians place the Dravidan migration between 1750 and 1400 BC.

Ponkuzhy in Wayanad, bordering Karnataka, is only seventy kilometres away from Mysore. Certainly, some of the Dravidians who had settled on the outskirts of Mysore might have crossed over to Wayanad through Ponkuzhy. The names of places from Ponkuzhy to Pulpally, such as Rampally, Ashramkolly, Chethalayalam, related to the Ramayana, point to the possibility of this migration.

It is natural for the invaders and colonisers to exert political, economic, cultural and religious influence on the local population. Dominant communities use beliefs and myths to consolidate their hold and prove their supremacy. When such beliefs and myths are transmitted from generation to generation, they might be passed on to the local communities too. The spread of the epic stories in the soil of Wayanad could be linked to such historical contexts.

Existence of Ramayana-based Stories in Wayanad: Influence of Jainism

Wayanad, the southern belt of the Deccan plateau, has stronger links with Karnataka than with Kerala. Many of the kings of Karnataka had dominion over Wayanad. It is recorded in rock inscriptions dated 1117 at the Parshwanatha Basadhi in

Chamarajanagar near Mysore, that Wayanad and the Nilgiri mountains were among the regions conquered by the Hoysala king Vishnuvardhana. Wayanad was once a prominent centre of Jainism. The Jain temples and the Jains still living in Wayanad are evidence of the fact that Wayanad was once part of the Jain culture. In addition, Wayanad is situated only around a hundred kilometres away from Shravanabelagola in Hassan, Karnataka, which is one of the most important pilgrimage sites of the Jains.

Several cave temples and muniyaras (dolmens) in Wayanad are associated with Jain culture. Thirunelly has cave temples such as Pakshipathalam, Muniyara, Gundika, Basavatheertham and Yogeeswaranpeedham. Sadhu Krishnanda in his book *Thirunelly Puranam* states that in the second century BC, after the reign of Chandragupta, Emperor Samprathi, ruler of the Mauryan dynasty and grandson of Emperor Asoka, extensively and effectively spread Jainism in Wayanad. Emperor Samprathi and King Kharavela, ruler of Kalinga, were followers and proponents of Jainism. They both equally share the credit for having built cave temples for Jain monks. It is also they who introduced the Brahmi script here.[100]

The earliest history of the temples in Thirunelly, Sultan Bathery and Pulpally, which have been described as being related to the Ramayana, is connected to Jainism. Jainism, then, was prevalent in Wayanad before the advent of Savarna Hinduism and the spread of the Ramayana tales. There are a lot of similarities between the structure of extant Jain temples and the architecture of temples where the legends from the epics have spread. This becomes evident when we compare the Kidanganad Basadi near Sultan Bathery with the Sri Rama-Sita temple at Ponkuzhy, both in the south-eastern region of Wayanad. Both are built of gigantic blocks of granite. Both represent the Vijayanagara style of architecture and their structures are similar to other Jain temples. The ruins of Jain temples found in many parts of Wayanad are mute witnesses to the fact that these places were once centres of Jainism. It is possible that with the advent of Shaivism and Vaishnavism, the adherents of Jainism left the place. The few Jains still living in Wayanad may be their descendants. There are many such indicators to prove that Jainism once thrived in the Ponkuzhy area.

The Jain hermits must have chosen the tranquil forests and caves of Wayanad for their meditation and worship. This might explain the presence of several obscure cave temples in Wayanad. When Vaishnavism arrived, it thrived and Jainism declined. Vaishnavite forms of worship are practised now in all temples, including the one at Ponkuzhy. Moreover, Sri Rama is a Vaishnava God.

It is usual for the belief systems and philosophy of invading cultures to dominate the life and culture of the local populations. Cultural domination gets consolidated when the consciousness of the dominating people becomes the consciousness of the dominated. As a result of the domination of Vaishnavism in Wayanad, Vaishnavite myths and legends must have spread by word of mouth and generated textual variations among the local communities. When we closely examine the tribal myths from Wayanad, their songs shed light on the influence of the Goundas (Gaund/Gowda-Jains) and the stories of the Hindu Puranas and Itihasas. A good example is the Pelappattu, which is the ritual song sung by the Adiyas during their funeral ceremony lasting over three days. The song narrates the history of the Adiyas, and entrusts the soul of the dead to their forefathers, whom they believe continue to be slaves of the landlords even in the afterlife. It is usual for oral traditions to present history through myths and songs. The absence of objective knowledge about the world often leads to the formation of myths and beliefs. It is the fertile imagination of the primitive people that gives birth to myths. The Scottish anthropologist James Frazer, in *The Golden Bough*, his book about mythology and religion, maintains that these myths persist even today.[101]

Existence of Ramayana-based Stories in Wayanad: Oral Story Tradition

The oral tradition is the prototype of all language and literature. Folk stories, riddles, folk songs, proverbs, myths and legends are much older than written literature. Much of the ancient literatures, including the Itihasas, were first circulated orally, before being committed to writing. All such forms which spread orally are variegated. These are reconstructed and enriched based on the lifestyle of the local populations and their socio-cultural status. Hence, the same text can have different versions among communities of different castes and tribes. Sometimes, even within the same caste, local variations can be found. Even when an expert storyteller of a particular community narrates a story, additions and deletions are introduced, depending on the nature of the audience and the ambience.

Textual stories often have different oral forms. In course of time, it is natural that variations occur to such oral forms. Sometimes, these oral traditions evolve into forms that have no relation to the original written text, and they end up becoming entirely new stories, with different characters and contexts, embellished and adorned with fanciful trappings.

Kerala, particularly Wayanad, has a rich history of oral traditions. Grandmothers' tales and myths and legends from the epics must have been in circulation from ancient times in these parts. In the days of tribal domination and rule, their songs and art forms must have been widely known and appreciated. After the arrival of Buddhism and Jainism in these parts, stories of Buddhist and Jain origins as well as the *Kathasarithsagara* tales became popular in Wayanad.

Vadakkan Pattukal (Ballads from the North) are folk songs which enjoyed wide popularity in the northern parts of Kerala during the seventeenth century. The main theme of these songs is the exploits of brave fighters. These songs were recorded textually only much later. Rural idioms, direct and clear exposition, rhythms that lend themselves to be sung in quick as well as slow tempos are some of the special features of these songs. Some of the folk songs of the Adivasis of Wayanad have been influenced by the Vadakkan Pattukal. Whether these ballads originated in tribal communities or elsewhere is a valid question. The singing and performing styles of the Kalippattu songs sung by the Mullukurumas during the Kolkali and Vattakali dance are set on the pattern of the Vadakkan Pattukal. Perhaps the similarities may be due to the interaction between the Mullukurumas and the communities in the northern region of Kerala.

Storytelling is an important ritual among the Adiyas in Wayanad. Even today, there are a number of master storyteller elders among them. During my research on the subject, I had many opportunities to observe how children and elders would gather to listen to the storytelling of Mathei Vaidyar, a traditional healer among the Adiyas. More than entertainment, it seemed like a community ritual. Mathei Vaidyar remembers his childhood, when his father used to put him to sleep by telling him stories of Rama and Sita. He says that he never knew how his father's stories ended, as he would fall asleep before they reached their conclusion. P.K. Kalan, another elder of the Adiya community and a Gaddhi artist, also shared such memories. Whether there were storytelling groups several centuries earlier in Wayanad needs to be examined. The *Valmiki Ramayana* has made it clear that its mythological tales were spread by Lava and Kusa, and also by wandering singers. It mentions that Lava and Kusa used to go to the royal court at Ayodhya and recite the Ramayana before Rama. This suggests that the Ramayana story was told orally before being written down as a text. This is to be linked to the fact that Lava and Kusa are prominently portrayed in the folk songs of Wayanad about events from the Ramayana. The prominence given to Rama and Sita (who belong to the Vaishnava tradition) in the legends of Wayanad could be attributed to the influence of storytellers belonging to the Vaishnava tradition on the Adivasi communities that existed in the region before the Vaishnavites arrived.

The mythological tales spread in the Wayanad communities in primarily two forms: simple legends and genesis stories (cosmogonic tales). In simple legends, written mythological tales were recast in the local surroundings of the communities. They referred to the gods of the local people and their communal and social life. The stories were interwoven into their belief system and way of life. These stories had only a tenuous connection with the written forms. More than half the epic stories that gained currency in Wayanad belong to this category.

It can be seen that in some of the genesis stories that are popular among different communities, mythological characters have been accorded the status of the creator. However, it is not essential that they be related to the Puranas and Itihasas. What the genesis stories among such communities describe may well be some natural phenomena that defy explanation.

Both the higher myths (of organized religions, widespread) and the lower myths (of tribals/indigenous communtities, local) contain stories of the origin of the universe and of man. Genesis stories hold an important place in the belief systems of the Adivasis and the Dalits. Creating such myths is an innate characteristic of primitive communities. It is believed that these were formed as an expression of existence and are one way of asserting community identity. The descriptions of natural phenomena and occurrences in these genesis stories are regarded as primitive legends.[102] A number of stories concerning the origin of the universe, genesis of man, origin of castes, and oral traditions in which heroes from the epics are protagonists have been narrated in the earlier chapters of this book.

It is impossible to determine when these genesis stories started to be told. It is likely that it was after the tribal communities were enslaved by the upper castes. The Adiyas, Kurichyas and Mullukurumas, who consider the epics and legends as part of their belief system, were all at one time the slaves or at least dependents of the upper castes. This is borne out by the beliefs and myths popular among them. The famous Malayali folklorist M.V. Vishnu Namboothiri, in his book *Folklore Chinthakal* (*Folklore Thoughts*), records that the Adiyas consider themselves to be bonded labourers of the Thirunelly temple and the Kurichyas hold the belief that they are the bonded labourers of the Kottiyoor Perumal temple.[103]

By adopting and inserting the beliefs and myths of caste superiority from the Savarna castes into their genesis stories, each tribal community tried to establish a higher social status. It is likely that these stories and beliefs emerged from the imagination of the Dalits, based on the stories they had heard from the upper castes when they had been their slaves and dependents.

The genesis stories are not monolithic in structure. Within the same community, there may be multiple versions of the same story. Proliferation of such variants is a characteristic of the oral tradition. Oral variants of stories from the Puranas and Itihasas, as well as the prominence of the epic heroes in genesis stories, are found mostly among the Adiyas. This may be explained by their contact with the communities and castes who performed temple rituals. In Thirunelly and Trissileri, Adiyas were mostly the slaves of the Ambalavasi castes (ranked just below the Brahmin caste, they assisted in temple rituals; 'Ambalavasi' literally means those who dwell in the temple), such as the Chettis, Goundas, Marars, Emprasans, Warriers, Pattans and Namboothiris. The Adiyas are found in several parts of Wayanad, including Mananthavady, Trissileri, Thirunelly, Edappadi, Chelur, Begur, Mottankara, Panamaram, Muthiramala, Vemam, Bavali and Kuppathode, and in certain places in Taliparamba taluk, as well as in areas bordering Mysore in Karnataka. The influence of Karnataka on their lifestyle and linguistic peculiarities suggests that present-day Adiyas may be the descendants the slaves of the Chettis and Brahmins who migrated to Kerala from Karnataka.[104] Wherever they might have been, they eked out their living through slavery for communities whose livelihood was related to temples.

It is but natural for the slave classes to absorb the beliefs, religious rituals and myths of their overlords. It is also natural for these belief systems to be absorbed and then adapted to the lives of those who have been dominated. Domination is complete only when the consciousness of the dominant classes takes over the collective consciousness of those they dominate.

The main reason for the propagation of the stories from the epics among the Adiyas must be their long-standing contact with the above-mentioned Ambalavasi communities. The Adiyas would have witnessed and heard temple discourses as well as dramatic presentations based on the epic stories. They might have overheard the dialogues and discussions between their owners. This was perhaps the route by which the epic stories reached the Adiyas.

The Kurichyas are another Adivasi sect among whom the

mythological tales have propagated. How did the stories reach the Kurichyas? Apart from their regular contact with the caste communities, the prominence they attach to their origin might be part of the reason. The Kurichyas follow a lot of rituals that resemble those of the Savarna Hindus. The places alluded to in their songs are beyond the boundaries of Wayanad. Among the eighteen places mentioned in the Maramayappattu sung by the Kurichyas, which narrates the history of Malakkari, most are in the neighbouring district of Kannur. It is remarkable that the language used by both the Kurichyas and the Savarna Hindus groups differs only in the colloquial expressions. The folk songs Kurichyas sing are full of allusions to the contemporary lifestyle of people in Malabar. In addition, if one analyses their social practices—joint family system, untouchability and craft—it becomes clear that the Kurichyas migrated into Wayanad from some part of Malabar.[105] The Kurichyas prefer to be considered as part of the Hindu fold. They believe that Sri Sankaracharya gave them the name 'Mala Namboothiris' (Hill Brahmins), and that he consecrated the God Malan in the forest for them. They used to practise untouchability with all castes except the Namboothiris. It is possible that the Kurichyas are a sect demoted to a lower status from the highest castes for some unknown reason. All this goes to buttress the argument that the Kurichyas were the warriors of Pazhassi Raja, ruler of the Kottayam kingdom in the Malabar region, who fought against the British East India Company. He was killed in 1805 in a battle with the British. Defeated after the fall of Pazhassi, these formidable fighters were either driven into the interior forests by the British or sought refuge in the forests. Perhaps it is their life in the forests for long periods that reduced them to the status of a marginalised community. Scholars like Kumaran Vayaleri in *Kurichyarude Jeevithavum Samskaravum* (*Life and Culture of the Kurichyas*) and Chacko Kannattumody in *Kurichyarude Lokam (The World of the Kurichyas)* claim the Kurichyas came from Travancore on the request of the Raja of Kurumpanad to fight the Veda king of Wayanad in the seventeenth century. The history of their genesis is steeped in legends and fiction. Whatever may be the historical truth, it is clear that the Kurichyas are a people who migrated to Wayanad from the plains below in recent years. The references to Mahabali in their songs, and the belief that Malakkari is the manifestation of Shiva, point to the caste and social contacts they had centuries ago. But very modern allusions are also seen in their songs—one such reference is the mention of guns. These interpolations may have occurred during the transmission of songs from generation to generation. Hence, the similarities between the beliefs and genesis stories of the Kurichyas with those of the Hindus can be linked to their ancestral roots.

Not many variations are found in the songs sung by the Kurumas during the performance of their ritual dance forms like the Vattakkali, Kolkali and Tappukottikkali. These songs reflect the influence of the *Valmiki Ramayana* and Ezhuthachan's *Adhyatma Ramayana*. The language of these songs is pure Malayalam; therefore, they cannot be called 'ancient' in origin. Many songs refer to the great changes brought about by modern education. But the recurrence of references to Wayanad in the Vadakkan Pattu songs sung in northern Kerala, and the manner of reciting epic stories indicate a textual variation. Many songs reflect the major changes their language underwent after the advent of modern education. Even the elderly people among the Mullukurumas say that they sing the songs they heard their fathers singing. But we must pay attention to the observation that most of their songs have no relation to their way of life.[106] In the few songs that reflect their way of living, the influence of the Puranas and Itihasas is minimal. It can be inferred that the influence of the epics on their songs is due to the Kurumas' contact with mainstream society, the advent of modern education and the group's proximity to Hindu communities.

The Chettis, particularly the Wayanadan Chettis, are a community that have transplanted the epic stories through oral traditions into their culture and made them their own. The cultural world of the Wayanadan Chettis is a social environment built on the firm pillars of beliefs, religious practices and spiritual bonds, with places marked by legends and peopled by Sri Rama, Sita, Lava, Kusa and Valmiki. The Wayanadan Chettis have close links with the places related to the stories from the epics and their oral versions. These people base their identity and existence on them. They think that Wayanad, the land of the Ivarchettis, was the Panchavadi of the Ramayana. They even believe that Lava and Kusa married the daughters of the Areappalli Chetti (mentioned in Chapter 4). The places and legends—relating to the Ramayana—found between Ponkuzhy and Pulpally are part of the belief system of the Chettis. In fact, the Chettis are the real carriers and preservers of this oral tradition. They consider Wayanad as the theatre of the Ramayana story.

The present generation of Chettis are the descendants of those who had migrated to Wayanad. Rao Bahadur C. Gopalan Nair infers in his book *Wayanad-Janangalum Parambaryavum (Wayanad, Its Peoples and Traditions)*, that the Wayanadan Chettis came from Dharapuram near Coimbatore in Tamil Nadu, while the Edanadan Chettis came from Edanad in Coorg in Karnataka and the Mandadan Chettis from Gudallur taluk in the Nilgiri district of Tamil Nadu.[107] In the *Malabar District Gazetteers* published in 1908, W. Francis of the Indian Civil Service says the same. The dialects spoken by these communities and their ways of life give credence to this argument.

The Chettis have always considered themselves a part of Hinduism, and Savarna Hindus have endorsed this concept. There was no practice of untouchability by the Chettis either towards the Savarna Hindus or by the Savarna Hindus towards the Chettis. The Chettis were allowed into Hindu temples. The Chettis have held the custom of inviting Brahmin priests for their religious ceremonies. In recognition of this, other Hindus never considered the Chettis as untouchables. The Chettis also consider the Purana-Itihasa stories as part of their religion. They are well-informed about the *Valmiki Ramayana* as well as the *Adhyatma Ramayana* composed by Ezhuthachan.

There is more than one way for the epic stories to have reached the Chetti communities. The Wayanadan Chettis live in places such as Kidanganad, Nenmeni, Moopianad and Noolpuzha; the Edanadan Chettis in places such as Poothadi, Thirunelly and Amsam; and the Mandadan Chettis in Poothadi, Pulpally and Veliyampam. These areas were already inhabited when the Chettis arrived. Thirunelly, Pulpally and Ponkuzhy are places centred around temples. Vaishnavism had established itself in these regions long ago. It is possible then that the Ramayana was a part of the folk tradition in these places even before the arrival of the Chettis. It may be assumed that what the Chettis did was to further strengthen and fortify these traditions. Many of the epic oral traditions might have been the result of the creation of legends by the migrating people to glorify the areas they were migrating to. It is also possible that this was the result of the attempts of the migrating populations to elevate themselves to the beliefs and social status of the dominant communities in existence at that time.

Another possibility is that the Ramayana stories, already in circulation among the Chettis in oral form in the regions of Tamil Nadu and Karnataka where their forefathers dwelt, were transplanted into the Wayanad soil when they settled in the new areas. This could be the reason why the oral stories have become part of their religious faith, beyond being mere stories. It is usual for the migrants to reconstruct their culture and recalibrate their traditions to their new homeland while incorporating some elements from the area they are settling in and at the same time retaining some of the original elements too. An instance of this residue is the Bammathan daivam (God) of the Wayanadan Chettis. Bammathan is a Kannada God.

If a temple or the name of a place tells legends related to the epics, it is quite natural for the remaining part of the epic to be set in the surrounding areas. A good example of this is the case of the Ponkuzhy temple at Thirunelly. At Ponkuzhy is the pond believed to have been formed by the tears of Sitadevi. Next to it is the pedestal on which Sita sat and wept when she was abandoned by Rama. Valmiki's ashram is not far away. Naturally, the river that flows by the side of the ashram would become the river Thamassa. It is the Noolpuzha River which is is thus transformed into the river Thamassa. It was here that the first verse of the Ramayana took shape in Valmiki's mind, on seeing the heart-rending sight of a bird falling down, struck by the arrow of the savage hunter. The breeze here resonates with the poetic sentiment and compassion which gave birth to the epic poem. It was also here that Valmiki started reciting the poem before committing it to writing. Among the bamboo thickets, quietly flows the Noolpuzha River, unmindful of the passage of centuries. This is the place where Sitadevi bathed and Valmiki did his tapas.[108] Such myths are being created even in modern times.

New names can come into being as a result of colloquialism or due to erosion of syllables on account of prolonged use. An example of this is the changing of 'Shankumeeti' to

'Chankuvetti'. It is not unusual for the names of prominent households to become the names of places, for instance, Erumappally (Areappalli) and Dwaraka. If the new name of the place is related to the Puranas and Itihasas, new etymological stories around it are created shortly after its introduction. Thus, the folk forms of the mythological tales in Wayanad were created in multiple ways.

Time Frame of the Oral Story Tradition

Though there are differing views among scholars on when the written versions of the Ramayana stories originated, they all agree that it was definitely before Christ. As far as the oral traditions are concerned, which are far more in number than the written forms, there is no way to arrive at definite dates. These are phenomena that occur at all places and all times, part of the nature of the evolution of culture. In keeping with the development of civilisations and transformations on social and religious fronts, old forms are renewed and new ones are created. It can be maintained that oral traditions develop based on the exigencies of the times.

Oral traditions are simple in style, form and content, and they can easily be understood by the common man. That is why people connect with these stories. They do not regard them as something that happened thousands of years ago. They look upon them as events that have occurred in their own immediate environment in recent years.

The concept of time in stories from the epic is structured in two ways: the 'once upon a time' of the literate storytellers, who are familiar with the written form of the epic, may refer to a very distant past; whereas the narrations of the illiterate, oral storytellers, with little knowledge about the written versions, may not refer to such a distant past. When the literate narrator tells the story, they include elements of the distant past on purpose to suggest that the events took place a long time ago; the illiterate narrator, on the contrary, for better effect, may include images of modern times. This becomes clear when we compare and contrast the stories told by Mathei Vaidyar in *Adiya Ramayana*, by Kalankandi Ramunny Chetti in *Wayanad Ramayana* and by Balan Puzhamudi in the Wayanad Sitayanam.

The illiterate narrator may not have a proper understanding of the concept of epochs and the peculiarities and complexities of the characters in the story. Hence, there is a greater role for imagination in their storytelling. This is not possible for the literate narrator. While the imagination of the illiterate storyteller spreads its wings wide, the written text creates barriers in the minds of the literate storyteller. Therefore, there is greater scope for variation in the stories of the illiterate narrator. The Ramayana stories told by illiterate storytellers are different from the stories told by the literate storytellers, who believe that the events described took place 18,149,115 years ago. The illiterate storyteller's narration method is abstracted from time. The illiterate share the uncertainties of the new age. They present the sorrows and difficulties they encounter. This is well borne out by the story told by Mathei, the Adiya elder. There are a lot of modern images and idioms in Mathei Vaidyar's narration, including, 'There is a bridge to be crossed before entering Lanka', 'Children are playing marbles in the courtyard', 'Bring also two cans of kerosene', 'Sita would serve coffee as soon as Rama and Lakshmana returned home', and 'They started to shout inquilab'. These reveal the suffering, aspirations, despair and anger of the Dalits, as well as the personal experiences of the narrator. The time of Mathei Vaidyar's narration is not a distant past. This is the case with the tales narrated by other storytellers too. They ensure the participation of their community in many of their stories. For instance, one of the tales mentions Sita's clothes being washed by an Adiya woman in Lanka.

In the toponymic stories, genesis tales, the stories of Sita and Rama and those from the lives of Lava and Kusa, the events described are set in an immediate past. There are two possible explanations for this: either the stories are recent in origin or these are interpolations made by the narrator upon the old story.

Many of these stories may have been formed after the forest-dwelling people, working as slaves, established contact with mainstream society. It is likely that elements from the culture of the mainstream communities were incorporated into their stories. The worldview of the totally illiterate and rustic populations would be quite different from that of the literate and urbanised. The illiterate would have little knowledge about the world outside their environment. Therefore, their knowledge of the locations talked about in the Ramayana and their understanding of Ayodhya and the *Valmiki Ramayana* are bound to be limited to what they have heard. When anecdotes based on hearsay are inserted into their stories, the result could be distorted imitations. Stories thus constructed might, after a few generations, be transformed into something very different. Time as a concept in these stories would thus be a mixture of both the ancient and the modern.

Though attempts are found in the stories narrated by literate storytellers, who have deep knowledge of the Puranas and Itihasas, to anchor the events described in these texts in the ancient age, there are also incidental insertions of contemporaneity. This dual nature of time becomes clear if one analyses the *Wayanad Chetti Ramayana* narrated by Kalankandi Ramunni Chetti. Kalankandi Ramunni Chetti begins his version of the Ramayana with the mention of the

Thretha Yuga. He prefers to travel along the timeline of the written text. But while describing Ayodhya, he does not forget to insert Pulpally.

Another approach in storytelling is to leave the time period vague, as in the statement, 'In those days, when Rama lived in the forest with Sita and Lakshmana, Ravana abducted Sita and took her to Lanka.' The concept of a timeline is unique to the literate community. The illiterate calculate time based on natural phenomena such as storms, floods, rainy seasons, festivals, births, deaths and other events. For the illiterate, time is an elastic, subjective matter. In short, the concept of time for the illiterate is different from the monolithic concept the literate subscribe to, which says the same measure of time is applicable to all. When this is not possible, they have recourse to the usage of 'long long ago'.

In brief, the concept of yugas (epochs) and the calculation of time in the written texts are not found in the oral texts. The concept of time in the written word is a solid entity, while in the oral tradition it is fluid. In the written text, the concept of time is uniform and acceptable to all. In an oral tradition, time is subjective and constantly changing. Each storyteller has their own measure of time. The difference is discernible even in the images that refer to it. In a sense, the oral epic stories either confuse time or play with it.

PART TWO

THE POLYPHONY OF THE RAMAYANA

The Ramayana has influenced the history and culture of not just Hindus, but also the Buddhist, Jain, Muslim, Dalit and Adivasi societies. The body of Ramayana literature is like a great banyan tree that is constantly growing and expanding. Though its roots are Indian in origin, its branches have grown and spread throughout the Asian nations, and have played decisive roles in the formation of the cultures in those regions. Therefore, there exist many kinds of Ramayanas in Asia today. Polyphony refers to multiple voices. In the chapters that follow, the different forms the Ramayana has taken, both outside and within India, will be discussed.

FOREIGN RAMAYANAS

The Ramayana belongs to the Asian commonwealth, and is not solely the inheritance of the Hindus of India alone. It is linked in varied ways to Buddhist, Jain, Islamic and Dalit communities, including Adivasis. As in India, there are several versions of the Ramayana in many other Asian countries. It has been accorded high status in the literature and arts of these nations.

Like the rain that mingles with the colours of the soil that it falls on and then flows with, the Ramayana stories have travelled to different lands, and mingled with their soil. These streams, as they flow, have grown and made up the vast ocean called the Ramayana, and it is this ocean as a whole that is considered when we talk about the plurality of the Ramayana.

In this chapter, the Ramayana traditions of different countries will be introduced, and their variations from the *Valmiki Ramayana* will be explained briefly. This will be followed by a short exposition on how the Buddhist, Jain, Islamic and Adivasi communities have assimilated the Ramayana into their respective societies.

Indonesian Ramayanas

Indonesia is the world's largest island country, comprising the areas of Bali, Java, Sumatra (Sumitra), Kambojam (Cambodia) and Syama (Siam). The Ramayana has existed and thrived in all these places from ancient times. The Indonesian Ramayanas, although closely related to the Indian ones, show many similarities and dissimilarities to the *Valmiki Ramayana*. The Ramayana is not regarded as a religious text in Indonesia, but as a work of literature. Moreover, Indonesia is an Islamic nation and, therefore, Muslims, who form the majority of the population there, are found in the tales about Rama. This is evident in the names of places and persons in the Ramayana stories that exist in Indonesia.

Since the ninth century, a number of literary works have been created in Java and Malaya based on the Ramayana. These include both Ramayana versions close to the *Valmiki Ramayana* as well as modern forms of the Ramayana, very different from the *Valmiki Ramayana*. Prambanan in Yogyakarta, Indonesia, is a temple dedicated to the Trimurti (Vishnu, Shiva and Brahma) that dates back to the ninth century AD. Depictions of the events in the Ramayana are sculpted in stone on the temple's high walls. These are quite close to the events described in the *Valmiki Ramayana*.

The most ancient Ramayana-related literature in Indonesia is *Ramayanakakavina*, considered to have been composed in the tenth century. For long, it was thought that its author was a poet named Yogeeswaran. But recent studies have rejected this assumption and have arrived at the conclusion that the text was composed by an unknown author.[109] The *Ramayanakakavina* diverges from the *Valmiki Ramayana* in a number of ways. For instance:

1. When Hanuman finds where Sita has been taken, she gives the choodamani (jewelled head-dress/crest-jewel) to him to take to Rama as a token. In the *Ramayanakakavina*, in addition to the choodamani, Sita also sends a letter through Hanuman to Rama.
2. When Vishnu takes the form of Varaham (a pig), he

eats the ascetic Sabari's garland and dies. Then Sabari eats his corpse. Telling Rama that it is due to this that her face has darkened, Sabari prays to Rama to remove the blackness of her face.
3. The seven wives of Ravana's son Indrajith fight alongside their husband in the battle with Rama and are killed.
4. Trijada, the rakshasi (demon) who was assigned the duty of guarding Sita in Lanka, is accorded a virtuous status.[110]

In addition to the *Ramayanakakavina*, there are a number of tellings from the Ramayana in Indonesia. The scholar Himamsubhooshana Sarkar mentions three works that exist in ancient Javanese:[111]

1. The *Sumana Santaka Kakavina*
2. *Harisraya Kakavina,*
3. *Arjuna Vijaya*

The main themes of the *Sumana Santaka Kakavina*, dating back to the eleventh century, are the birth of Indumathi, her marriage to Ajana and the birth of their child, Dasaratha. *Harisraya Kakavina*, composed in the thirteenth century, based on the ancient Uttara Kanda, narrates the death of the rakshasas Mali and Malyvan at the hands of Vishnu. The *Arjuna Vijaya*, composed in the fourteenth century, narrates Ravana's defeat in his battle with King Arjuna Sahasrabahu.

A number of other Ramayana variants exist in Indonesia, among others, the *Hikayat Seri Rama*, the *Sri Rama Pathayani Ramayanam*, the *Hikayat Maharaja Ravana*, *Ramakelinga* and the *Serath Kandam*. In addition, many episodes from the epic are to be found in folk stories and folk songs.

The *Hikayat Seri Rama*, composed between the thirteenth and the fifteenth centuries, is a voluminous work that describes the story of Ravana and the reunion of Rama and Sita after her abandonment by Rama. The episode with Ravana's picture is portrayed a little differently in this story:

> Seven months had elapsed since Rama started living in Lanka after killing Ravana. Ravana's daughter had a picture of him that she placed on Sita's bosom while she was asleep. Sita kissed the picture in her sleep. Rama, who entered her chamber at that very moment, was infuriated at the sight. He whipped Sita and chopped off her hair. Then he ordered Lakshmana to kill Sita and bring back her heart as proof of her death.

Note the similarity between this incident and the belief of the Adiyas in Wayanad. Many Ramayana tellings have variations of this episode.

In the remarkable *Sri Rama Pathayani Ramayanam* composed in the fourteenth century, several characters who appeared earlier in the *Seri Rama* are said to be related to a hermit by the name of Mahasiku.[112] There is mention of the four children of Mahasiku: a daughter, Bali, Sugriva and Bilom. The second half of this work relates to the story of Mandoodaki, the foster daughter of Mahasiku. Mandoodaki marries Ravana, and Sita is born to her.

According to the story in the *Hikayat Maharaja Ravana*, Ravana is still alive. At the end of the kalpa (aeon), Ravana makes his appearance as the enemy of Bhagwan, Rama.

There is also another, more popular form of the Ramayana told in Indonesia: the ballet. The dramatic literature of Java is practically based on *Serathukanda* and *Ramakelinga*, two Javanese versions of the Ramayana. Camille Bulcke is of the view that all the cantos in the shadow play *Wayanga Vonga* of Bali are based on scenes from the Ramayana.

Tibetan Ramayana

The Ramayana spread into Tibet in the eighth or ninth century. Manuscripts of tales from the Ramayana, dealing with Ravana's life, Sita's abandonment and the reunion of Rama and Sita, have been recovered from Tibet.[113] The history of Ravana is narrated in detail at the beginning of this version, followed by the news that Vishnu will be born as the son of Dasaratha. Dasaratha has only two wives. The younger wife gives birth to Vishnu and the child is named Rama. After three days, Vishnu's brother is born from the elder wife and is named Lakshmana.

In these works, Sita is said to be the daughter of Ravana. Her horoscope says that she will bring about the destruction of her father and, therefore, she is thrown into the sea. She is rescued and brought up by peasants from India. When Rama, who understands his father's dilemma over which of his two sons should be crowned prince, coerces his father into giving the throne to Lakshmana, and sets out to do tapas, he meets these peasants. They convince him to give up the idea and marry Sita. Afterwards, he ascends the throne.[114]

There are a lot of variations in the story of Sita's abduction, both in its oral and its written forms. According to the *Tibetan Ramayana*, Ravana digs up the earth and makes a tunnel in order to abduct Sita.

In Tibet, which is geographically very close to India, there are naturally more oral versions of the Ramayana than written ones. Thus, we can find episodes in the *Tibetan Ramayana* that have no connection to the *Valmiki Ramayana*. There are several episodes in it that are similar to the *Kathasarithsagara* stories. The *Tibetan Ramayana* is a good example of the extent to which the story of Rama has been restructured by local and religious influences.

Kothan Ramayana

Kothan is the area comprising the eastern parts of old Turkestan. The *Kothan Ramayana* tradition is closely related to the *Tibetan Ramayana*. The period of the composition of this work has been calculated to be the ninth century. Despite several similarities, we cannot conclude that this is an imitation of the *Tibetan Ramayana*. In the *Kothan Ramayana* too, Sita is the daughter of Dasagriva (Ravana). Sita's marriage takes place during her stay in the forest. Perhaps because this text was composed in a region where polyandry was considered normal, both Rama and Lakshmana marry Sita. There is no Uttara Kanda, the last book of the Ramayana that narrates the return of Rama to Ayodhya, his coronation and his banishment of Sita on suspicions of her purity, in this version.

Some other similarities between the *Tibetan Ramayana* and the *Kothan Ramayana* are: Ravana makes Jatayu eat stones drenched in his own blood, a mirror is fixed on the tail of Bali in order to distinguish between him and his brother Sugriva during the Bali–Sugriva battle, and Ravana can be defeated only after he is injured on his weak spot, the navel.

It is Buddha who narrates the story in the *Kothan Ramayana*, just as in the case of the Jataka stories. The narrative begins with a description of the Sakya Muni (Buddha) disseminating Buddhism. The *Kothan Ramayana* states that during the time of Rama, Buddha was Rama and Maitreya was Lakshmana. Jeevaka, the Buddhist physician, is called to treat Sri Rama. Similarly, the wounded Ravana does not die; since Buddha is the apostle of ahimsa (non-violence), when he takes on the form of Rama, he does not kill Ravana, but only wounds him. The wounded Ravana agrees to pay tribute and is spared.

Thai Ramayanas

India had contact with the Laos community, the ancient inhabitants of Thailand, as early as the third century BC. In those days, this region was known as 'suvarna bhoomi', the golden land. Suvarna bhoomi later on became Siam. In 1939, Siam was renamed Thailand by Phibun Songkhram, the then prime minister.

As a result of the interactions carried on between India and Thailand up to the first century AD, Brahminism as well as Buddhism spread in Thailand. The Thai language has similarities with some of the south Indian languages. A lot of Sanskrit and Pali words are found in the Thai language. Also, Buddhism is the state religion of Thailand.

Though the Thais worship the Buddha, their school of Buddhism is closely bound to the Ramayana, Rama, Vishnu, Garuda, the vehicle of Vishnu, and the serpents. Lord Buddha, who fought against the might of Brahminism, is surrounded by these gods and myths in Thailand. The principal deity of the temple in the palace in Bangkok is the Buddha. This idol of the Buddha, made entirely of emerald, is placed on a throne in the form of a chariot conforming to Hindu myths.

The Thais, who believe that Rama is the incarnation of Vishnu, consider their kings the representatives of Rama. They believe that the king is a symbol of the unity and solidarity of the nation. The official name chosen by Phra Phutthayotfa Chulalok, the founder of the currently ruling Chakri dynasty, was Rama I. Their present king, Vajiralongkorn, is Rama X. For about 417 years during the rule of the Chakri dynasty, the capital of Thailand was known as Ayutthaya, a city built on the model of Rama's Ayodhya.[115]

The Ramayana here is known as the *Ramakien* (Rama's Praise). The story of Rama has long held a prominent place in Thai literature, particularly the dramatic form. Although the *Ramakien* has close similarities with the *Valmiki Ramayana*, there are some major differences between the two texts. All the characters in the *Ramakien* are inhabitants of Thailand, and all the events are set in Thailand. Also, the description of the premarital romantic relationship between Rama and Sita found in the *Ramakien* is not present in the *Valmiki Ramayana*.

The *Ramakien* contains certain anecdotes not found anywhere except in Thailand. An example of this is the part where Ravana visits Rama in the guise of a hermit to persuade him, before the construction of the bridge to Lanka, to give up fighting. Following this futile effort, Bemjakaya, Vibhishana's daughter, assumes the form of Sita, and is seen floating in the river near Rama's palace like a corpse. Another episode that is not found in the *Valmiki Ramayana* is Rama calling Brahma for help. When Brahma goes to Lanka and asks Ravana about the recent developments there, Ravana puts the blame on Rama. Brahma calls Rama and Sita and speaks to them. Finally, he orders Ravana to release Sita. Ravana refuses to give her up, and so, Brahma curses him.[116]

A unique feature of the *Ramakien* is that it contains several love plays of Hanuman. Hanuman is found in amorous situations with Mandodari, in addition to Swayamprabha, Bemjakaya, Suvarna Macha, the serpentine damsel, and a monkey damsel in the guise of an apsara. To disrupt the Sanjeevana yaga that Mandodari performs to protect Ravana's life, Hanuman visits her in the guise of Ravana and embraces her. In another scene, he gets into an argument with Rama and says he will fight on Ravana's side. For one day, Hanuman does just that and as reward obtains the entire property that Indrajith and Mandodari have received from Ravana, and ends up spending the night with Mandodari.[117]

The *Rama Jataka* was composed in Lao (the language spoken in the north-eastern regions of Thailand, now Laos) in the sixteenth century.[118] According to this work, too, the entire story of Ramayana takes place in Thailand. Interestingly, Rama and Ravana are cousins in this text. Rama also has a brother named Lakshmana and a sister named Santha. Ravana abducts Santha, and Rama and Lakshmana rescue Santha by defeating Ravana in battle. There is an episode in which Rama marries Bali's widow and becomes Angad's father. This has not been found in any other retelling. The process of adapting the Ramayana story into a Buddhist narrative can also be seen in the *Rama Jataka*. The work suggests that the duos in the *Valmiki Ramayana* and in the *Rama Jataka*—Rama and Buddha, Ravana and Devadatta, Dasaratha and Sudhodana, Lakshmana and Ananda, Sita and Uppalavanna (a mendicant)—are the same persons. Both *Rama Jataka* and *Ramakien* have happy endings.[119]

A number of minor works related to the Ramayana were composed in Thailand from the seventeenth century onwards. The themes of these texts are one or more episodes from the Ramayana. Several poets, including Dhonaburi Futhayothya and Futhale Uthla, have composed great poetic works based on the epic. According to the *Panchathantra* written in Lao, Dasaratha accidentally killed Shravan, the son of a blind hermit couple, and was cursed that he too would experience the loss of a son. Also, Vibhishana, the brother of Ravana, allied with Rama.[120] In addition to these, there are numerous other versions of the epic in Thailand with diverse angles and episodes. The Ramayana has left deep imprints not only on Thai literature, but also on the culture of the Thais.

Burmese Ramayanas

The Ramayana literature of Burma is not ancient, but quite modern.[121] In 1716, Taninganway Min, a powerful Burmese king of the Toungoo dynasty, invaded and destroyed Ayutthaya (Ayodhya), the palace of Siam (now Thailand) in the lower Chao Phraya Valley region. After the destruction of the city, the king took back a number of prisoners with him. They brought the *Ramakien* drama of Siam to Burma. The Burmese poet Yuto composed the *Ramayagan* around AD 1800, which was based on this dramatic version. This is considered the best poetic work of Burma.

A number of works relating to the Rama story are available in modern Burmese literature. The Ramayana's influence can be seen in Burma's dramatic literature too. Sita's abduction is a popular theme among the plays performed here. Moreover, Burma is rich in oral Ramayanas created in the folk tradition.

Malaysian Ramayanas

Malaysia is a country with an old and rich Ramayana-Mahabharatha tradition and literature, both written and oral. The written form of the Mahabharatha is available in Malaysia under the title *Hikayat Yudha*. The culture and language of the country are intimately connected to Indian culture and Sanskrit, and Hinduism has deep roots. The Rama story is a prominent theme not only in Malaysian literature, but also in its performing arts, such as drama and nizhalkoothu (shadow play).

The Ramayana is the theme of the shadow puppet-play *Wayang Kulits*, which is staged at Kedah in north-western Malaysia. The players themselves fashion the episodes out of stories known in literary circles as *Hikayat Seri Rama*. In some improvised plays, Ravana does not die. The story is as follows:

> King Dasaratha had two servants, Kiyavu and Eythong. The king sent both of them to identify a suitable spot in a forest, to build a new palace. After identifying a location, Kiyavu and Eythong started clearing the bamboo thickets there, but in vain. The bamboo stumps grew back as soon as they were cut. This went on for a while. Finally, King Dasaratha himself arrived, and with his sword cut a bamboo tree. Out of the bamboo stump emerged a beautiful maiden named Putheri Bulu Bethong.

Putheri Bulu Bethong means 'daughter of the bamboo forest'. (Notice the similarity between 'putheri' and 'putri', which means daughter in Sanskrit.) King Dasaratha married the girl and gave her a new name: Mandodari. The new palace was named Mandodarinagara. Two sons were born to Mandodari: Seri Rama and Lakshmana. Balidari, another wife of Dasaratha's, also had two sons: Burdan and Chathradan.

Ravana was the king of a country neighbouring Mandodarinagara. He had a wife called Mandodaki. He too had two servants, Aymeng and Aything. When a daughter was born to Ravana and Mandodaki, the soothsayers predicted that the girl would be a curse for the country. They also said that her husband would kill Ravana. Ravana attempted to kill the baby girl by throwing her to the ground, but Mandodaki intervened and stopped him. The child was then put in a box and thrown into the sea. The box was carried by the waves to the shores of a country called Durvathapoorava, ruled by King Maharshikala of the Soorya Bhaktha dynasty. King Maharshikala also had two servants, Aythong and Nunuyi. He asked the servants to pick up the box and take it to the palace. The king decided to bring the baby up as his own daughter and named her Sitadevi.

At the naming ceremony of the child, King Maharshikala planted a pole in the ground and declared, 'Whoever pulls out this pole will be given Sita in marriage.' When the time for the marriage drew near, the king invited all the princes. None of them succeeded in pulling out the pole. Then the king remembered that King Dasaratha's sons had not come. At once, Aythong and Nunuyi reached Mandodarinagara. Dasaratha ordered that Burdan and Chathradan be sent along with them. Aythong and Nunuyi said to the princes, 'There are four routes to reach Durvathapoorva. It will take seventeen days to reach Durvathapoorva via the first route; on the way, there is a demoness called Jegin. The second route will take twenty days; on the way, there is a rhinoceros. Thirty days for the third route, and on the way, there is a dragon. The fourth route will take forty days, but there are no obstacles along the way.' Burdan and Chathradan chose the fourth route. Realising that these were not valiant men, Aythong and Nunuyi approached Dasaratha with the request to send Seri Rama and Lakshmana. Travelling through all the routes, they killed the savage woman, the rhinoceros and the dragon and reached Durvathapoorva at last. Seri Rama pulled out the pole planted in the ground and married Sitadevi. He stayed there for some time.

Finally, Seri Rama left Durvathapoorva with Sita, Lakshmana and the servants Aythong and Nunuyi. On hearing that Burdan had been crowned king in Mandodarinagara in his absence, Seri Rama decided to spend some days in the forest with Sita and the retinue. The sage Asthana Maharshi told them about two enchanted ponds in the forest. He warned them to remember to drink water from the muddy pond; drinking from the clear pond would turn them into monkeys. But one day, they were very thirsty, and forgetting the warning, drank the water in the clear pond. Seri Rama and Sitadevi turned into monkeys. Before long, the female monkey conceived. Lakshmana caught hold of them both and plunged them into the muddy pond. They were restored to their human forms.

But what was to be done about the foetus in Sitadevi's womb, which was still a monkey? Sitadevi vomited it out, and Lakshmana deposited it into the mouth of Anjathidevi, a mermaid who was doing tapas in the sea. The son born as a monkey of Anjathidevi's womb was named Hanuman. In the meantime, Seri Rama and his retinue killed a rakshasa, took possession of his kingdom, and began to rule there.

Ravana had heard of the extraordinary beauty of Sitadevi. He made plans to make her his own. He transformed his servants Aythong and Achmeng into a golden deer and a silver deer, and sent them to lure Sita into the trap laid by him. The rest of the story is similar to the *Valmiki Ramayana*.

Rama and the retinue started their search for Sitadevi. On the way, they made friends with Sugriva, the monkey perched on a tree. Sugriva was hiding in fear of his brother Baliaraja. Seri Rama killed Baliaraja with an arrow. Next, he met Hanuman. When Hanuman revealed that he was Anjathidevi's son, Seri Rama realised that he was his father. He felt guilty, but did not show it. Hanuman insisted that Rama eat from the same plate as him if he wanted his company on the mission in search of Sitadevi. Seri Rama agreed on the condition that Hanuman should have a good bath first.

After reaching the city of Lanka, Hanuman joined the palace servants, and on the pretext of taking water for Sitadevi to bathe, met Sita and gave her Rama's ring and message. Then he set fire to Lanka and returned. Seri Rama, assisted by the monkey contingent, built a bridge and reached Lanka and started a war. Ravana's son Indrajith rained down arrows, hiding in the clouds. Shooting his arrows into the sky, Seri Rama killed him. In the battle that ensued, the Agneya astra was used, as mentioned in Valmiki's Ramayana. But it was only an ordinary arrow with a burning torch tied to it.

When one head of Ravana was cut off, another head would appear in its place. Seri Rama was at a loss. To learn the secret behind this, Hanuman secretly met Sitadevi, who told him Ravana had ten heads, and if an arrow struck the small head behind the right ear, he would surely die. This is how Seri Rama killed Ravana and took Sitadevi back after the fire purification.[122]

Among the Ramayanas of South-east Asia, the above-mentioned story is the one that is the most different from the mainstream Indian tellings.

Chinese and Japanese Ramayanas

In India's neighbour China, the Ramayana tales have existed in many forms since antiquity. Tale 46 of *Liu-tu-chi chin*, a Chinese translation of the Buddhist scriptures by K'an-Seng-Hui, composed in AD 251, Tale 1 of *Tsa-pao-tsang ching* by Chi-chia-yeh in AD 472, and *Xī Yóu Jì*, a novel-like text, believed to have been composed by Wu Cheng'en in the sixteenth century, are the most well-known Ramayana-related literature in China.

Tale 46 in *Liu-tu-chi chin* is a translation of the *Anamaka Jataka* in Chinese, done by the Sogdian monk K'an-Seng-Hui in the third century. Here, Buddha becomes Rama, and it is his maternal uncle who usurps his throne. Rama goes to the forest with his wife, who is abducted by a naga (serpent). With the help of monkeys, Rama gets his wife back and also his throne. (The *Anamaka Jataka* is discussed in detail in the next chapter.)

Tale 1 of *Tsa-pao-tsang ching* is the translation of the *Dasaratha Jataka* by Chi-chia-yeh in the fifth century. Lomo (Rama) is exiled for twelve years along with his younger brother. The events here closely follow the plot of the *Valmiki Ramayana*. However, this version only describes Lomo's stay in the forest, and his third brother refusing to ascend the throne, instead persuading Lomo to return and become the king. Sita's abduction and the war with Ravana are not mentioned. (The *Dasaratha Jataka* is discussed in detail in the next chapter.)

Liu-tu-chi chin's Tale 46 and *Tsa-pao-tsang ching*'s Tale 1 have been translated into English as 'Jataka of an Unnamed King' and 'Nidana of Ten-Luxuries' by Raghu Vira and Chikyo Yamamoto in their book *Ramayana in China* (1955).

Xī Yóu Jì was first translated into English in an abridged form by Arthur Waley in 1942 as *Monkey: A Folk-Tale of China*. The unabridged version has been translated into four volumes as *The Journey to the West* (1977–1983) by Anthony C. Yu, and as *Journey to the West* (1982–1984) by W.J.F. Jenner. This work is about the travels and hardships faced by the Buddhist monk Tang Sanzang during his journey to obtain Buddhist sacred texts from the Indian subcontinent. The major characters are Sun Wukong (a monkey), and Tang Sanzang. In the first part, the many exploits of Sun Wukong are narrated. Sun Wukong is a monkey who was born from a magic stone when the wind blew upon it. Handsome, strong and brave, he is declared as the monkey king by the other monkeys. In addition to his might, he is a quick-witted and happy person who laughs all the time. He also possesses a unique weapon—a rod that can shrink as small a needle, as well as expand to gigantic proportions. Using his powers, he terrorises the demon-kings as well as the gods in heaven who fail to acknowledge his importance. He also steals the fruits of immortality from heaven. The gods try to imprison him in the samadhi fire, but the fire only makes him stronger. The gods finally appeal to Buddha, who is the only one who is able to stop him. Sun Wukong also acquires a new ability—to recognise evil with his gaze. Later, he offers to accompany the monk Tang Sanzang in his journey to retrieve the Buddhist sutras, and protects the monk from various threats during the travels. There can be no hesitation in affirming that Sun Wukong, the monkey king, and Hanuman are the same.

The Ramayana tales in Japan have been inspired by the Chinese Taishō Tripiṭaka canon and the *Ramakien* song-dances of Thailand. *Sambo Ekotoba* (*Notes on the Pictures of the Three Jewels*), a collection of three scrolls of paintings and their explanations, composed by Minamoto Tamenori in 1011 and *Hobutsushu* (*Collection of Treasures*), a collection of stories gathered by Tairano Yasuyori, a monk, in 1179, closely adhere to the Buddhist Jataka stories mentioned above. The character of Hanuman is absent in these versions. In another version called *Bontenkoku*, King Baramon (Ravana) abducts the wife of Tama (Rama).

Bugaku is a Japanese traditional dance mostly performed in the Japanese imperial court, and depicts legendary battles, divine personages and mythical beasts. A popular theme is the fight between Vali and Sugriva from the Ramayana. Gagaku is the music accompanying the Bugaku dance. Fernau Hall, British dance critic, opines that Bugaku and Gagaku are based on Indian classical dances depicting the Ramayana.[123]

How the Ramayana Reached Other Countries

The Ramayana spread to other Asian countries from India in different ways. The Buddhists, Hindus and Jains played the greatest part in this. If some of the foreign Ramayanas are indebted to Valmiki's Ramayana, some others are indebted to the *Anamaka Jataka* and to the *Dasaratha Jataka* of the Buddhists. These Jatakas narrate the previous life of the Buddha as a prince named Rama-pandita. It was the Buddhists who took the Ramayana abroad for the first time. The *Anamaka Jataka* and *Dasaratha Jataka* were translated into Chinese in the third and fifth century AD respectively. After that, another cluster of Rama stories started circulating in the northern regions of Asia. These were based on the *Valmiki Ramayana*. The *Kothan Ramayana* and *Tibetan Ramayana* bear witness to this. *Kothan Ramayana* also bears the imprint of Buddhist influence. In Indonesia, *Valmiki Ramayana* has been popular from ancient times.

Some historians say that in the first century AD, traders from India started to impress their culture upon the Indo-China regions. As a result, the Champa kingdom was established in eastern Indo-China. In a stone inscription discovered in those areas that dates back to the seventh century AD, there is a mention of the genesis of slokas (poetry) in Valmiki's work. The inscription also says that Valmiki is a manifestation of Vishnu.[124]

The Ramayana stories spread abroad through travellers and traders. It is also possible that the propagation of Ramayana stories happened through Buddhist missionaries as well as Brahmin scholars during different periods. They could also have spread through wandering singers, dramatists and other artists. The way the Ramayana reached Burma is an illustration of this. In the eighteenth century AD, the king of Burma destroyed the palace of Siam and took back a number of prisoners with him. They started staging the Ramayana in Burmese theatre. This is how the epic became popular there.

Many people in other countries do not believe that India is the place where the episodes of the Ramayana took place, and that it was later carried to their regions. They believe that the epic originated in their native cultures. They argue that the theatre of those stories is their own country. This trend of falling back on the Ramayana to justify certain customs and practices in a country is seen in many places. For instance, the *Kothan Ramayana* says Sita was married to both Rama and Lakshmana; the Kothan region in south-eastern Turkestan is known to have polyandrous societies.

The Ramayanas in other countries reflect the characteristics of the dominant communities influencing the stories. The Islamic influence on the *Seri Rama* of Indonesia is a good example. In brief, the Ramayana did not travel as mere translation of a foreign work; the local histories and cultures of various countries and societies reconstructed the epic and produced whole new versions of the Ramayana.

BUDDHIST AND JAIN RAMAYANAS

Just as the Ramayana has crossed the boundaries of India and reached many countries, it has also spread across different religious communities, including the subaltern peoples. This has helped in the propagation of the Ramayana beyond the confines of the Indian subcontinent. The integration of the Ramayana into different religious denominations and the transformation it has undergone in their local environments have resulted in diverse readings and interpretations. Religions such as Hinduism, Buddhism and Islam, as well as the tribal communities, have played an important role in the multi-form evolution of the epic. Each religion or community has found ways to fit the Ramayana into its ethos and created its own unique form of the epic. They have also used it to interpret and propagate the beliefs and tenets of their own religions. After the Hindus, it is mainly the Buddhists who have made the Ramayana a large part of their religion.

Buddhist Ramayanas

Buddhism evolved at a time when the moral and spiritual values of Hinduism were on the decline and the inhuman caste system had disillusioned a large part of Indian society. Buddha had the most difficult mission cut out for him: that of restructuring the existing social order. In the course of this mission, the Buddhists might have absorbed the positive elements of the existing traditions while replacing the ones the distressed populations were rejecting.

The Ramayana has had a strong influence on Buddhist literature. However, the epic retold in it is quite different from the *Valmiki Ramayana*. Many of the Ramayana stories from countries that practice Buddhism present the characters in Buddhist attire.

The Jataka stories are about the different avatars Sri Buddha appeared in—both human and animal—in his innumerable previous lives. In these stories, tales from the Ramayana are given prominence. Many scholars are of the view that the original Rama story is embedded within the Buddhist Jataka stories. This is how the Ramayana is told in the *Dasaratha Jataka*; the story was told by the Buddha to a householder living in the Jetavana monastery near the ancient city of Savatthi (present-day Uttar Pradesh) when the householder was overwhelmed by sorrow after the death of his parents:

> Dasaratha, the king of Varanasi, had 16,000 wives. The royal consort bore him two sons and a daughter. The elder son's name was Rishirama and the younger son was called Lakshmana. The princess was named Sita. After some time, when the royal consort died, Dasaratha took another wife as queen. The son born of her was named Bharatha. The new royal consort prayed to Dasaratha that her son Bharatha be given the kingdom, but Dasaratha refused to grant her request. However, as a strategy to keep peace in the palace, he asked Rama and Lakshmana to live in the forest for some time; Rama would ascend the throne only after his demise. Sita accompanied Rama and Lakshmana to the forest. After nine years, unable to bear the pain of separation from his sons, Dasaratha died. Bharatha performed the funeral rites. The citizens of Varanasi did not like Bharatha taking over as king. With the intention of bringing Rama back to the palace, Bharatha went to the forest with his army. He fell at

Rama's feet and informed him of the developments at home. Rama, who was living in a hut, asked Sita and Lakshmana to stand in the middle of a pond, to avoid their falling on the hard ground on account of the shocking news they were going hear. Rama recited this verse thrice:

Sita and Lakshmana, go into the water in this pond
Bharatha says father is dead.

Sita and Lakshmana fell unconscious. The servants brought them ashore and comforted them. Rama reminded Bharatha that their father had instructed them to stay in the forest for twelve years, and so he could not return before finishing twelve years in exile and break the promise made to their father. On hearing Rama's resolve, Bharatha returned to Varanasi with Rama's footwear in his hands. He placed Rama's slippers on the throne and began to rule the country as his deputy. After three years, Rama returned to Varanasi. He ruled the country for many years before ascending to heaven.

After narrating this story, the Buddha said to the householder, 'Dasaratha is King Sudhodana, Mahamaya is Rama's mother, Sita is the mother of Rahula, Bharatha is Ananda, and Lakshmana is the son of Shari. This assembly is the Buddha's assembly. I am Rama.'[125]

Anamaka Jataka is another text related to the Ramayana. The original Indian source-text of this work is not available now. In the third century AD, it was translated into Chinese by Kang-Seng-Hui. According to this work, Rama's story, called the Sarala episode, goes like this:

Once upon a time, Bodhisattva, a righteous king, ruled the country. In the spirit of his four-fold virtue (generosity, politeness, justice and equality), he protected all the living beings of his realm. His uncle was the king of another land, but he was wicked and full of greed, just the opposite of Bodhisattva. He mobilised an army to conquer Bodhisattva's kingdom. Bodhisattva too had his army battle-ready. *I will have to kill many people to secure my interests. If I desist, the entire country will be lost,* he thought. After handing over the charge of the kingdom to his ministers, he left with his queen for the forest. His uncle entered the kingdom and conquered it.

There lived in the sea the most wicked Naga. During Bodhisattva's stay in the forest, the Naga donned the false attire of a hermit, and abducted the queen when the king was away gathering fruits. When Bodhisattva returned, the queen was nowhere to be found. He picked up his bow and arrows and started combing the mountains in search of her. During his search, he met a huge monkey. When Bodhisattva asked him who he was, the monkey replied, 'I was a king. My paternal uncle usurped my kingdom. I am alone and helpless now.'

King Bodhisattva revealed his own predicament, and the giant monkey and he became friends. The monkey ordered his followers to look for the queen. On their way, the monkey contingent came across a wounded bird that informed them that he had seen a Naga abducting the queen.

The king of the monkeys had no means of transporting his army across the sea. Lord Indra arrived, assuming the form of a small monkey, and said, 'Order the monkeys to cut the mountain into pieces and carry it part by part. This way you will be able to build a bridge across the sea and reach the island.' The monkeys did as they were told. Reaching the island, they encircled it. Seeing that his island had been surrounded from all sides, the Naga emitted a poisonous mist, and all the monkeys fell into a faint. The small monkey (Lord Indra) applied a divine medicine to the noses of the monkeys and revived them. Then the Naga hid the sun with storms and clouds. Lightning flashed. Indra told the monkeys that the lightning flash and the Naga were one and the same. So Bodhisattva shot an arrow at the lightning and the Naga fell down from the sky.

The monkeys released the queen. Hearing the news of the death of his uncle, Bodhisattva returned to his kingdom. One day, he said to the queen, 'People will be suspicious about a woman who has returned after being separated from her husband and living in another man's house. According to our tradition, it is not appropriate for me to receive you.'

The queen replied, 'It is true that I lived in the cave of a wicked man. But I am chaste. Let the earth split and testify to my innocence.' The earth split. 'I stand vindicated,' she said.

Concluding this tale, the Buddha said to the mendicants, 'I was the king. Gopa was the queen, Devadatta the uncle, and Maitreya Indra.'[126]

According to the *Kothan Ramayana*, the *Rama Jataka* of Siam, the *Phra Lak Phra Ram* (the national epic of Laos) and its sister-text *Phrômmachak* of Laos, too, the Buddha was indeed Rama in his previous life. There are scholars who have opined that the Ramayana as told in the *Dasaratha Jataka* is the original form of the epic. It was the German Indologist and historian Albrecht Weber who first put forth this view. Another scholar who has supported this view is the Bengali folklorist and scholar Dineṣa-Chandra Sena.[127] But many other scholars argue against this theory and reject it as being absurd.

According to the Buddhist Ramayanas, Varanasi—not Ayodhya—is the capital of Dasaratha's kingdom. Also, the forest in which Rama and Lakshmana were exiled is in the Himalayas, which is a popular setting in Buddhist literature. Besides, the brothers chose forest life because they were afraid of the wicked schemes of their stepmother.

Several scholars maintain that the Pali Tipitaka, or the

Pali canon, the earliest extant collection of scriptures in the Theravada Buddhist tradition, predates the Ramayana, and therefore it is natural for the Ramayana to draw on Buddhism.[128] When the Ramayana was being written, Buddhism had spread right up to Kosala. So, some scholars have pointed out that although Valmiki lived in a Brahmanical environment, he was deeply influenced by Buddhism. There is, however, only one mention of the Buddha in Valmiki's Ramayana. This is in the Jabali episode, where Jabali, a Buddhist priest and advisor of Dasaratha, tries to persuade Rama using rational reasoning to give up his exile. Rama says that the Buddha is a robber and an atheist:

> *Yatha hi chora: sathadha budhastathagatham*
> *Nasthika matra vidhi*
> (Ayodhya Kanda, Sarga 109, Verse 34)

In the opinion of the British historian James Talboys Wheeler, Jabali is the representative of Buddhism. Rama takes the side of Brahmanism that was opposed to Buddhism. But Jabali, without defending Buddhism, speaks about the Lokayatha vision.[129]

Dineṣa-Chandra Sena, the Bengali folklorist and scholar, has observed that Valmiki developed the Sarala episode of the *Anamaka Jataka* that was discussed earlier with a special end in mind. In depicting the meditation of the Buddha and his life as a mendicant, Valmiki, the first poet, is presenting the allure of the Hindu grihastha (married life) in the Ramayana. When we compare Valmiki's Ramayana with the Buddhist Jataka, we realise how skilfully the master poet has refined and transformed the Buddhist version into the gem of a poem that is the Ramayana.[130]

The historian Albrecht Weber, while finding the prototype of the Ramayana in the Buddhist *Dasaratha Jataka*,[131] infers that the seed of the story of Sita's abduction is the abduction of Helen by Paris in the Illiad by Homer, and the basis for the description of the war in Lanka is the invasion of Troy by the Greek army.[132] Many scholars have rejected this interpretation.[133] The only similarity between the works of Homer and Valmiki's epic poem is the abduction of a woman and the use of bows and arrows. These were common occurrences. In Homer's work, ships are given importance. If Valmiki was familiar with Homer's work, he would not have taken recourse to the construction of a bridge across the sea to Lanka; he would have introduced ships. Hence, the argument that Valmiki was influenced by Homer is not tenable.

In short, the Buddhist versions of the Ramayana cannot be overlooked in any serious discussion on the origin and evolution of the epic.

Jain Ramayanas

The Jains, who have made lasting contributions to Indian history and culture, link the Ramayana with the foundations of their faith. The literary works produced by Jainism have accorded prominence to characters from the Ramayana. Rama (Padma in Jain texts), Lakshmana and Ravana are introduced as followers of Jainism, and are included among the Trishashti men, who the Jains consider venerable. Most important among the Trishastis are the twenty-four Tirthankaras, the great teachers of dharma. The other great personalities include twelve emperors, nine Baladevas, nine Vasudevas and nine Prathivasudevas. The stories about these personages are considered legends in Jainism. Rama, Lakshmana and Ravana are the eighth Baladeva, Vasudeva and Prathivasudeva, respectively.[134]

It was Vimala Suri, a Jain monk, who tried to adapt the Ramayana to the tenets of Jainism by writing *Paumacariyam*.[135]

This work was composed after the *Valmiki Ramayana* was written. *Paumacariyam* rejects Valmiki's narrative and presents an alternative one. In fact, Vimala Suri wrote in the introduction to the *Paumacariyam* that it was composed to rectify the contradictions and absurdities in the *Valmiki Ramayana*.[136] In a sense, this is a counter-Ramayana.[137] Based on the language used in the work, scholars such as Hermann Jacobi think that the *Paumacariyam* belongs to the third or fourth century AD.[138] Composed in the Prakrit language, this work was translated into Sanskrit by Ravi Sena Acharya in 660 AD as the *Padma Purana*.

Let us examine how the *Paumacariyam* differs from the *Valmiki Ramayana*: Yama, Indra, Varuna and the like are not gods in *Paumacariyam*; they are ordinary kings. Ravana is a cowardly Jain who undertakes the renovation of Jain temples and objects to the performance of animal sacrifice. It is a distinguishing feature of the Jain versions of the Ramayana that episodes based on the material world, such as the descriptions of Rama's hunting, Ravana's cannibalism, Kumbhakarna's six-month long sleep, Ravana as a rakshasa, and Sugriva as a monkey, are omitted. Hanuman is portrayed as follows:

> Pavanjaya, the prince of Adityapura, married Princess Anjana of Mahendrapura. Before the marriage, he had heard from the princess's maid that she despised him. Therefore, for twenty-two years he showed no interest in her. Afterwards, he joined Ravana's army and fought against Varuna. One evening, overcome by great love for his wife, Pavanjaya returned to Adityapura and slept with her. The same night, he returned to wage war. As a result of this secret visit, Anjana became pregnant. This pregnancy in the apparent 'absence' of her husband led to the expulsion of Princess Anjana and her maid Vasanthamala from both the house of her husband and the house of her mother. But the

underlying cause of this expulsion was that in her previous life, Anjana had taken out the Jain idol of the co-wife and put it outside the house. She gave birth to a son in a cave. Later, Anjana's uncle Prathisooryakan took her and the baby to Hanuroohapura. On the way, her little son, Baka, leapt from her lap and fell on a rock in the mountain. Due to the impact of the fall, the mountain below was shattered to dust. This is why he was given the name Srisailan. Pavanjaya returned after the war and testified to Anjana's faithfulness. Following this, Princess Anjana returned to her husband's home with little Baka. On account of his stay in Hanuroohapura, Baka came to be known as Hanuman.[139]

There are several such stories about the birth of Hanuman.

According to Vimala Suri, the following events led to the abduction of Sita:

Shambuka, a shudra, did tapas for twelve years to obtain the Suryahasa sword. He succeeded in obtaining the sword. When Lakshmana passed that way and saw the sword, he took it and cut a bamboo tree nearby and then the head of Shambuka. Pained at the death of her son, Chandrananakha began to roam the forests, weeping. She met Rama and Lakshmana, and requested them to marry her. Since her request was not granted, she returned to her husband and informed him about their son's death. Ravana too was informed about the matter. Lakshmana single-handedly stopped the army of Khathadooshana. Hearing of this, Ravana arrived and became enamoured of Sita. Using his *avalokani vidya*, his secret power, Ravana came to know that whenever Lakshmana wanted to call Rama, he would roar like a lion. Ravana imitated the lion's roar and Rama went out to meet Lakshmana. Ravana then swooped in and abducted Sita.[140]

In the canto on the war with Ravana, too, there are several differences between the *Valmiki Ramayana* and *Paumacariyam*.

Another Jain text on Rama's story is the *Uttarapurana* composed by Gunabhadra. Gunabhadra was a disciple of Jeenasena, and he hailed from Karnataka. In the *Uttarapurana*, Sita is said to be the daughter of Ravana and Mandodari. (In the Ramayanas of Tibet, Khothan, East Turkestan, Indonesia and Siam, too, Sita is introduced as the daughter of Ravana.) Gunabhadra's version of the epic contains no mention of building the bridge. It is Lakshmana who kills Ravana with the chakra (wheel). However, for killing Ravana, Lakshmana is afflicted by a horrible disease, and he dies and goes to hell. Rama receives Sita without demanding a chastity test. After that, Lakshmana, with the help of Rama, remotely conducts the Aswamedha yajna for forty-two years. He then returns to Ayodhya and rules as Rama's deputy. The two brothers are crowned together. It is said that Lakshmana has 16,000 wives, and Rama, 8,000 wives. After a few years, Rama and Lakshmana hand over the reins of the kingdom to their brothers Bharatha and Shatrughna, and go to Varanasi. Sita gives birth to eight sons, the eldest being Vijayaraman. Rama anoints Lakshmana's son Prithvi Chandra as king and Sita's youngest son Ajitham Jayan as prince, and along with 500 kings, including Sugriva, Hanuman and Vibhishana, and 180 sons, leaves to perform tapas. After 395 years, Rama attains enlightenment. Sita, along with many other co-queens, takes to ascetic life. After this, Gunabhadra mentions the attainment of liberation by Rama and Hanuman, and Sita reaches heaven.[141]

On which text might Gunabhadra have based his work? The Jain scholar Nathuram Premi says, 'My inference is that long before Gunabhadra, another master like Vimala Suri may have composed his own independent and logically sound text, in keeping with the tenets of Jainism, and Gunabhadra may have gained access to it through his tirthankaras.'[142]

Paumacariyam by Vimala Suri is only one of a number of

works related to the Ramayana in the Jain folk tradition. Other major works include *Ramalakhanacariyam* by Sheelacharya, *Ramayana of Kahavala* by Bhadreswara, *Siyacariya* and *Ramalakhanacariya* by Bhuvanathungasoori. These are composed in Prakrit. Among the works in Sanskrit are *Padmacharitham* by Ravisen, *Jain Ramayana* and *Sitaravana Kadhanakom* by Hemachandra, *Ramadeva Purana* by Jidasa, *Ramacharitha* by Vijayagani, *Ramacharitha* by Somasena, *Lakutrivashti Salaka Purusha Carita* by Somaprabhacharya and *Meghvijaya Ganivara, Uttarapurana* by Gunabhadra and *Ramayana Kadhanakom* by Harishena. In addition to these, there have been works composed in many regional languages, including Malayalam, based on the Jain Ramayanas.

MUSLIMS AND THE RAMAYANA

Islam, which originated in the Arabian subcontinent, reached India during the time of Mohammed. Belief in one God is its basic tenet. The Muslims believe that all the great prophets who lived in different historical epochs preached the faith of Islam.

The Quran mentions twenty-five prophets. However, Muslims believe that whenever righteousness is threatened and society suffers moral and spiritual decay, prophets make their appearance in different parts of the world. They also believe that more than 124,000 prophets have been born on earth until now. According to the Quran:

> And for every nation is a messenger. So when their messenger comes, it will be judged between them in justice, and they will not be wronged.
> (10:47 Sahih International)[143]
>
> O Prophet, indeed We have sent you as a witness and a bringer of good tidings and a warner.
> (33:45 Sahih International)[144]
>
> Indeed, We have sent you with the truth as a bringer of good tidings and a warner. And there was no nation but that there had passed within it a warner.
> (35:24 Sahih International)[145]
>
> And certainly We sent messengers before you: there are some of them that We have mentioned to you and there are others whom We have not mentioned to you, and it was not

meet for a messenger that he should bring a sign except with Allah's permission, but when the command of Allah came, judgment was given with truth, and those who treated (it) as a lie were lost.

(40:78 Shakir)[146]

Giving equal respect and paying equal homage to all the prophets who have appeared in different times, places and communities is part of the Islamic faith. Muslims also believe that all these prophets are mere men, and not God or sons of God. Attributing divine origin to men is against the basic tenets of Islam.

As Islam spread from Arabia to other lands and nations, cultural exchanges became possible among communities. Islam's belief in one God influenced other communities even as the belief systems and practices of other communities started influencing Muslims. Many of the communities which converted to Islam continued to more or less maintain their previous religious beliefs and practices.

Though Islam belongs to the family of Semitic religions, its links with the Brahmanic religion are almost on par as with Judeo-Christian religions. For example, namaz (prostration) is a compulsory religious practice that each Muslim is supposed to perform five times a day. Sri Sri Ravishankar compares the prostration of the Muslims and the vajrasana of the Hindus thus:

> Prostration (namaz/namaskar) includes all the elements of vajrasana. Hindus offer morning prayers facing the east and evening prayers facing the west. Muslims, during their namaz, sit facing the Kaaba at Mecca, which lies in the west. The cleansing of hands, face and feet before prayer by the Hindus and the *vulu* (ablution) by Muslims have close similarities. While the Muslims offer prayers five times a day: morning, noon, afternoon, evening, and night, the Vedas

prescribe prayers for the Hindus at dawn, noon and dusk. In the temples, poojas are performed five times: pre-dawn, dawn, noon, evening and night. While Friday is sacred for the Muslims, for the devotees among the Hindus of the Divine Mother, Friday is a special day. The thirty-day fast during the Ramadan month is among the five compulsory practices prescribed by Islam. The Hindus have the Mandalapooja. Muslims undertake Haj, wearing seamless white clothes. This is also the dress of the Hindus during pilgrimage. This practice is not found among the Judeo-Christians. Killing any living thing is forbidden at Mecca during the Haj. The same is true of the pilgrimages of the Hindus.[147]

Thus, there are a lot of similarities between Islam and Hinduism. The Kaaba was founded by Ibrahim (Abraham), whose wife was called Sara. According to Hindu belief, Brahma is the creator. His consort is Saraswathi. Sri Sri Ravishankar has alluded to the similarity between the names Brahma and Abraham and Saraswathi and Sara.[148] An in-depth study of the similarities between Hinduism and Islam is warranted.

There has also been a cultural give and take between Hinduism and Islam in India. The Bhakti movement and Sufism strengthened this blending of traditions. The mystic poet Kabir Das's teacher was Ramanand who accepted Muslims and Dalits as avatars. It is said that some Muslims worship Vishnu. They link the 'bism' in 'bismillah' with Vishnu. Moreover, they acknowledge that Vishnu is pure and everlasting, formless and spiritual.[149]

Muslims use 'Rahman' in the sense of 'Ishwar'. The Sanskrit-Malayalam scholar Balarama Panicker's view on the relation between the names Rahman and Rama is noteworthy. He opines that the Ramayana was a great epic written in relation to the practice of sun-worship in ancient Egypt, or roughly in that region. He argues that the word Ramayana means the path of Rama's life and, etymologically speaking, it has its roots in the word referring to 'sun-worship'. He says the word 'Rabbi', which is Arabian for God, is indeed the word 'Ravi', which means the sun, and that the word 'Rahman', which is used in Arab nations for God, is in fact another form of 'Rama' the way we chant it.[150]

M. Venkata Ratnam, the renowned scholar and former principal of the Rajahmundry Government Training College, in his book *Rama, The Greatest Pharaoh of Egypt* (1934),[151] claims that Dasaratha was Tushratta, king of Mitanni in Syria, and Rama was Rameses II, the ruler of Egypt till 1292 BC.

It was during the reign of the Mughals in India that most of the socio-cultural and intellectual exchange between Muslims and Hindus came about. Indian mythologies and the Upanishads were translated into Persian. There were multiple attempts to foster and strengthen brotherhood between Hindus and Muslims. Akbar considered the exchange of ideas and concepts an effective tool for creating a syncretic atmosphere. Many of the Mughal rulers who succeeded him followed the same principle.

Akbar's Ramayana

Emperor Akbar was a great man who tried his best to foster brotherhood between Hindus and Muslims. For that, he established the Din-i-Ilahi faith. He saw that it was the lack of mutual understanding that posed a hindrance to brotherhood between the two faiths. He put to use the Brahmanical text of the *Valmiki Ramayana* as a bridge to mutual understanding, but changed certain parts. This modified text is called the *Akbar Ramayana*.

Emperor Akbar had the *Valmiki Ramayana* translated first into Awadhi and then into Persian. It was Badayuni (Abd al-Qādir al-Badāyūni) who translated it into Persian in verse form between AD 1584–1589. The original text of the *Akbar Ramayana* is lost, and only the copy created by Abdur Rahim-e-Khana is now available, which is currently exhibited at the Freer Art Gallery in Washington.

Akbar's court painters also made changes of their own. In the paintings they made to illustrate the epic, Rama and Sita were dressed in Mughal fashion. Hanuman, who came to see Sita, was, except for his jaw, not a monkey. Instead, he was a hairless man wearing a crown. Sita was depicted as a Muslim princess on a terrace built in Persian style.

Similarly, Dasaratha's final moments on his deathbed is depicted in Mughal miniature paintings with an extraordinary restraint that is almost poetic. While in the *Valmiki Ramayana*, Sita lived under an Ashoka tree in the forest in Lanka, in the pictures drawn at Akbar's court, Sita was an inmate of the zenana. The loneliness of the woman who has been abducted evokes the same emotion in all circumstances, across all cultures. It is this expression that is foremost in the depiction in the Mughal manuscripts. Most of these paintings were done by Hindu artists.

The *Akbar Ramayana* is a testament to an emperor's wisdom, who used art as a great diplomatic measure. The plants, flowers, birds, mountains, animals and people of the exotic and beautiful country that is India were all delightful subjects for the delicate, naturalist paintings of the Persian school of art. The paintings exemplified the Orientalist eroticism of the Mughals gazing at an 'other' (Indian) culture. Strange as it may seem, many of the Hindu painters who lived in Akbar's palace, like Kesu, Lal, Miskin and Basavan, had to take part artistically in this curious gaze. They knew how to incorporate Islamic details into their art and condense multiple perspectives onto the same page. Thus, like other illustrated books such as the *Hamzanama* (illustration of heroic deeds) and the *Razmnama* (illustration of the Mahabharatha), the *Akbar Ramayana* has the beauty of having been established as an administrative strategy, instead of highlighting the otherness between Hindus and Muslims.[152]

Giridhar Das, a contemporary of Tulsidas during the time of Jahangir, condensed and translated the *Valmiki Ramayana* into Persian as a poem. It was also during Jahangir's reign that Mulla Sadaullah Masihi composed the *Ramayan-e-Masih* in Persian. It was published by Naval Kishor Press, Lucknow, in AD 1898. A Persian translation of the *Valmiki Ramayana* published during Shah Jahan's time was called *Ramayana Faizi*. In the nineteenth century, Devidas translated Tulsidas's *Ramcharitmanas* into Persian from the Hindi. Rayi Munshi Parameshwarisahayan and Lalchand Amalchand also composed a condensed Persian translation of *Ramcharitmanas* in verse.

Indonesian and Malaysian Ramayanas

After India, the country with the highest propagation and acceptance of the Ramayana is Indonesia, which is also the nation with the largest Muslim population in the world. The Ramayana has been popular in this region from ancient times. Though there are many similarities between the Indonesian Ramayana and the Indian Ramayanas, Muslims, which form the majority of the population of Indonesia, feature prominently in the Ramayana existing there. In the *Hikayat Seri Rama*, which is the Ramayana in Indonesia, the names are listed in this order: Prophet Adam, his son Dasaratharama, his son Emperor Dasarata, and his son Dasarata Maharaja, and his son Seri Rama.[153] According to Islamic belief, Adam was the first man and the first prophet.

There is not much difference between the *Serathu Kandam* of Java and the *Hikayat Seri Rama*. In the wide canvas of the *Seri Rama*, tales about Prophet Mohammed and Prophet Adam are also found.[154] There is also a description of Ravana's penance in the *Hikayat Seri Rama*: Reaching the island of Sinhala after attaining enlightenment, Ravana performs penance for twelve years. At last, at the insistence of Prophet Adam and Prophet Mohammed, Allah grants Ravana sovereignty over the four realms (Heaven, Earth, Hell, Ocean), on the condition that he rule with justice and without sin.[155] The Ramayana in Indonesia is frequently performed as puppet-plays. There are numerous Muslim artists who lead such performances. The famous Indonesian theatre actor Sardono Kusumo is a Muslim. He has staged numerous Ramayana-themed plays in many parts of India. Characters with long beards, dressed in the traditional Muslim clothing of the region, play the roles of Rama and Lakshmana in these plays.

Just as Valmiki is regarded as the first poet—Adikavi—in Sanskrit literature, there is a first poet in Java as well: Adiwali. (Sufi saints are called 'wali'). The name of the Javanese Adiwali is Sunan Kalijaga. He was a preacher of Islam. Numerous similarities can be seen between the lives of Valmiki (Adikavi) and Kalijaga (Adiwali). Kalijaga was a gambler and a robber. He was very skilled, and cunning enough to rob an entire population. He was said to be the son of King Tuba. One day, he robbed a hermit named Sunan Bonang, who was a teacher of Islamic philosophy. Bonang taught the robber Kalijaga the principles of Islam, and thereby he was transformed. He began to follow Sufism. It is believed that Islam was propagated in Indonesia by Kalijaga. Islam was spread throughout Indonesia by nine walis (Sufi saints).

The Muslims of Malaysia too have a deep connection with the Ramayana and Mahabharatha. There are Muslims there who read the Ramayana regularly. In an interview, Anwar Ibrahim, the former deputy prime minister of Malaysia, had said, 'I am a Muslim who prays five times a day. In our culture, your Ramayana and Mahabharatha have played decisive roles. There are Muslims in most parts of Malaysia who regularly recite them. Our Mahabharatha and Ramayana may perhaps not be the same as those you see in India. I am given to think that they may have been "Islamically" rewritten in Malaysia. The fact is, within our limitations, we have inculcated these myths as a part of our culture ... '[156]

The *Maharadia Lawana* of the Philippines

The Ramayana stories have plenty of roots in the Philippines, and traditional beliefs based on the Ramayana still exist among the Maranao community in the southern region of this country.[157]

It is in the *Maharadia Lawana*, discovered by Juan R. Francisco in 1968, that a large number of Islamic icons are seen. In this text, Ravana is called Maharadia Lawana. The story goes as follows:

> Lawana was the son of the Sultan of the Pulu Bandiar lineage. Unable to bear the arrogance and aggression of his son Lawana, the Sultan exiled him to an island near the city of Pulu. In Pulu Nagara, Lawana gathered leaves and wood, ignited these, and climbed a tree over the fire. He cried that the world was chained. Diabarail (Angel Gabriel), hearing this, appeared before the Lord (Tohen), and informed the latter that Maharadia Lawana was crying because the world was in chains. The Lord (Tohen) instructed Diabarail to tell Maharadia Lawana to desist sacrificing himself, because nothing could cause his death, except being cut by a tool (knife, sword, and so on) sharpened upon a whetstone kept in heart of the palace of Pulu Bandiarmas.[158]

The *Hikayat Maharaja Ravana* is another variant from the Philippines that has close similarities with the *Valmiki Ramayana*. Scholars say the inspiration for this work would have been the *Valmiki Ramayana* itself. The text begins with the exile of Ravana. He does penance by placing his head on an altar of fire night and day. After twelve years, Allah delegates Adam to find out what Ravana wants. Ravana expresses his desire to be lord of the four worlds: Heaven, Hell, Earth and Sea. He also tells Adam that if he is granted this wish, he will henceforth not be angry at anything in the universe.

There are numerous such instances in the Ramayanas available in the Philippines where Allah, Adam, Diabarail (Jibreel/Gabriel) and others from Islamic texts and faith figure in the tales. They assume the positions of Brahma, Vishnu and other deities of the Hindu faith. The Philippines is a region where Hinduism and Buddhism reached before Islam. These texts are proof of the symbiosis between the three cultures.

Umar Pulavar and the *Kamba Ramayana*

Tamil Nadu in India, the land of the *Kamba Ramayana*, is another region where there is a strong link between the Ramayana and Muslim society. Many Muslim scholars in Tamil Nadu studied the *Kamba Ramayana* centuries ago. Prominent among them is Umar Pulavar, who lived in the seventeenth century. (The word 'pulavar' means poet.)

The *Cira Purana* composed by Umar Pulavar, based on the life of Prophet Muhammad, has been written in the style of the *Kamba Ramayana*. The use of the word 'Purana' in the title is itself suggestive of the influence of Hindu texts.

Many episodes and dialogues from the *Kamba Ramayana* have been transplanted in an Arabian setting in the *Cira Purana*. For instance, in the *Kamba Ramayana*, a passage describes the plentiful rains that bless the land and cause the rivers to overflow. The land is so rich and prosperous that precious jewels and valuable wood float in the swelling waters:

> Carrying the pearls, gold, peacock feathers,
> beautiful white ivory from an elephant, aromatic akil wood,
> sandalwood, matchless in fragrance,
> the floods looked like the merchants (bearing precious goods)[159]

In the *Cira Purana*, Umar Pulavar describes Arabia in the following manner, which closely resembles the lines in the *Kamba Ramayana*:

> Carrying the fallen sandalwood
> branches from the dark akil tree,
> pearls from the broken elephants' horn, white ivory,
> more precious than these, red rubies, radiant in three ways,
> carrying these all towards the sea,
> the stream, laden with rich bamboo, looked like a merchant (bearing precious goods)[160]

Umar Pulavar had never visited Arabia, but what he describes as Arabia in the *Cira Purana*, is drawn on the descriptions of Tamil Nadu as given in the *Kamba Ramayana*. In fact, the actual landscape and the flora and fauna of Arabia is strikingly different from that described by Pulavar.

There are also other Tamil Muslims, in addition to Umar Pulavar, who have been inspired by the *Kamba Ramayana*. Such scholars are invited to participate in the festival of Kamban, the Kamban Thirunal, which is held annually in Chennai. Presentations on the contributions of Umar Pulavar are quite common at this conference.

Prominent among the Muslim scholars who have studied the *Kamba Ramayana* in the twentieth century, is the former chief justice of the Madras High Court M.M. Ismail. He was born in Nagur near Nagapattinam in Tamil Nadu. He has delivered hundreds of talks about the *Kamba Ramayana* in Tamil Nadu and in places where Tamilians live in large numbers. His book *Moondru Vinaakkal (Three Questions)* about the killing of Vali, the monkey king of Kishkinda, by Rama, is very famous. A voluminous work stretching to over 400 pages, it discusses three issues: One, why was Vali killed by Rama? Two, was the method of execution justified? Three, did this result in the denting of the image of Rama? M.M. Ismail also has in-depth knowledge of the *Valmiki Ramayana* and the *Ramacharitamanas* of Tulsidas, in addition to the *Kamba Ramayana*. He has written about the literary merits of Umar Pulavar's *Cira Purana* and its connections with the *Kamba Ramayana*. Notable among his writings is his study on how the *Kamba Ramayana* differs from the *Valmiki Ramayana*.

Mappila Ramayana

The Mappilapattu are folk songs sung by the Mappila Muslims of the Malabar region in northern Kerala. There are specific tunes, similar to the ragas in Indian classical music but with a distinct influence of Arabic folk music, called ishals, to which the lyrics of these songs are set. The *Mappila Ramayana* is a lyrical text very similar to the conversational style of these Mappila songs. It comprises 148 lines, which can be categorised into five songs. In the 1930s, eminent Kerala folklorist T.H. Kunhiraman Nambiar, as a teenager, followed a wandering mendicant and memorised the lines of a folk song that is now known as the *Mappila Ramayana*. In 1976, he sang these lines from memory to the Malayalam academician and writer M.N. Karassery who was researching the Mappila songs. Karassery recorded these lines. It is uncertain who composed this epic poem that then spread via the oral tradition. Nambiar informed Karassery that he was unaware of anyone else who knew these songs and that he did not know of Muslims who sang the *Mappila Ramayana*.

Dr M.N. Karaserry also states in his article 'Mappila Ramayanam Kandethiya Kissa' (The Legend of the Discovery of the Mappila Ramayana) that the *Mappila Ramayana* was received in the various ishals (tunes) of the Mappilapattu, and that verses from it have been included in many Mappila folk songs. He records the conversation between him and T.H. Kunhiraman Nambiar in the article:

> 'Who wrote this?'
> 'These are all folk songs. No one wrote them. It's the creation of the people. The creation of their society.'
> 'Who gave this name to it?'
> 'I don't know. When I heard this song, it was called thus …'
> 'Whom did you hear it from?'
> 'Oh … in my childhood, many people where I lived used to sing this. I heard and learnt it from many different people. I did not foresee that someone would come and ask me such questions …'
> 'Can you name someone else who knows this song …?'
> 'No.'
> 'Who were the people who sang this song? Were they Muslims or non-Muslims?'
> 'I have not seen Muslims singing the *Mappila Ramayana*. We were the ones who used to sing it.'

Before Kunhiraman Nambiar sang the *Mappila Ramayana*, there is no recorded evidence of this song having been sung among the Mappila communities. However, John Richardson Freeman who translated these songs into English, writes that a young boy had memorised the songs sung by a person referred to as Hassankutty. In the book *Ramayana Stories in Modern South India: An Anthology,* edited by Paula Richman, the *Mappila Ramayana* translated by Freeman has been included, with the following note:

> *Mappila Ramayana* of Hassankutty ('The Mad')
> Collected by M.N. Karassery from T.H. Kunhiraman Nambiar

Then, Hassankutty is introduced thus:

> There is a distinctive metre and style that characterises the folk songs (called Mappilapattu) sung by the indigenous Muslims of Kerala. Since the Ramayana sung by Hassankutty resembled the Mappilapattu in language and metre, it came to be widely known as the *Mappila Ramayana*. Hassankutty was eccentric to the point of earning himself the nickname 'piranthan' (crazy), but his audience was so appreciative that one among them, a fifteen-year-old Hindu boy, committed a part of the work to memory.[161]

Therefore, we can surmise that it would have been the *Mappila Ramayana* sung by Hassankutty that Kunhiraman Nambiar learnt by heart when he was a child. In these verses, Rama, Ravana, Sita, Lakshmana and Shurpanakha are very much entrenched in the ethos of the Mappila Muslims of Kerala. When, after asking Rama to marry her, Shurpanakha realises that he is already married to Sita, she says:

> So what if a man takes four or five wives. There is no problem.
> But the Sharia says, it's not the same for a woman.

Rejecting Shurpanakha's advances, Rama replies thus:

> Why do I need a nikah[162] and a woman over and over?
> My young brother, that flitting parrot, wants a woman and a nikah. You'll suit him. And can he refuse
> after seeing your eyes, nose, bosom, and your thighs!

Though it is uncertain as to who authored the *Mappila Ramayana* procured by T.H. Kunhiraman Nambiar, there is no doubt that it was a poet of north Malabar. And yet, it cannot be said that this work that gives a Mappila colour to the Ramayana is entirely free from the influence of the northern ballads (*Vaddakan Pattu*).[163]

The *Mappila Ramayana* is replete with images and

expressions alluding to the Muslim way of life, and words borrowed from both Arabic and Sanskrit. The references to *kozhi* (chicken) biriyani, *beevi* (lady), *bappanadu* (father-land), Shariath, Sultan, *mayyathayi* (die), *cheeni* (a wind instrument), *Pengalumma* (elder sister), *auliya* (Saint), *lasalasan* (King of kings), *mowth* (death), *oulu* (her), *beedar* (wife), *anuzan* (younger brother) are only a few of the instances. An introduction to the *Mappila Ramayana* can be found in the poem itself. Some of the terms are retained as such in the English translation below:

> Prelude
> This song that was sung by the bearded ouli[164] long ago
> This song that we saw not, this Lamayana[165] story
> This song that we waited to sing in Karkidakam[166]
> This song that we will intone, plugging our ears with our fingers[167]
> This song about Dasaratha having taken in nikah[168] three women
> This song about their household chaos, and their barrenness
> This song about the three eating the payasam,[169] and birthing four[170]
> This song about Lama, the precious gem of the four
> This song about breaking the bow of the poison-drinking god[171]
> This song about taking the hand of the little golden-girl[172]
> This song about the angry Parashu-Lama[173] blocking his way
> This song about Lama returning to his native land
> This song about the father preparing Lama to rule the land
> This song about his stepmother heeding the hunchback's[174] lies
> This song about Lama being sent away for fourteen years to the forest
> This song about his wife and his younger brother going along for company

This song about the father writhing in agony at the loss of his children
This song about that king of kings stuttering and stammering as he died
This song about Varatha[175] who came rushing out from his mother's palace
This song about him going to bring back Lama ...

Valmiki is the person who is being referred to as 'ouliya' here, a term used for Muslim Sufi mystics. It is hinted at right from the start that this song has been sung long ago and that the singer has not seen these incidents first-hand. The verses also mention that this is sung during the Malayalam month of Karkidakam, and that it is sung by covering one's ears, as is the tradition in the aazan, the Muslim call to prayer. The above introduction further states that the lines touch upon the various incidents in the Ramayana.

Another peculiar feature of the *Mappila Ramayana* is that the conversation between Rama and Shurpanakha takes place in the Malabar dialect of Malayalam, such as when she proposes to him.

When she saw the handsome Lama
Clad in a leather cloak,
Spreading grass and arranging flowers,
She felt a great desire for him.
Precious, golden Beevi[176] Shurpanakha
With eyes full of yearning, murmured to Lama:
'Who are you, young man, what's your name?
That woman with you, is she from your house?
Don't you have children, or in-laws?
That girl with flowers in her locks, has she borne children yet?

To this question Rama replies thus:

> I am Lama, Sita is my wife, and she has not given birth yet.
> My younger brother over there,
> Lakshmana, is also here with us.
> My father-land, the Kosala-land, is a gossip-land,
> That's the reason we came to this forest.
> Who are you, Umma?[177]

Shurpanakha answers thus:

> I am the alluring, exquisite, tender younger sister
> Of King Lavana the ruler of Lanka.
> Oh golden cuckoo of the garden, come away with me to Lanka!
> Won't you like a brother-in-law who is a king?

Rejecting Shurpanakha's invitation to come to Lanka, Rama lists out his reasons and quotes from the Sharia:

> A woman for a man, and a man for a woman, that is the Sharia law.
> It's dangerous, my lady, to suck from a different breast.
> If you like the oil you massage with, why should you change it?
> Lioness of Lanka, be on your way, and leave us alone!

Shurpanakha counters Rama's objections by citing the same Sharia law. She also lays bare her heart and makes seductive promises:

> So what if a man takes four or five wives. There is no problem.
> But the Sharia says, it's not the same for a woman.
> Oh the desire of my heart, my gold, my precious gem,
> My hellish[178] Kadamba,[179] my flower, my milk, my sugar
> Of the the Queen-Mother's sons, three are here
> Having power, grandeur and pride in ten nations,
> And there is a seven-storied octagonal mansion for us!
> So you need not worry about the preparations for the nikah.

Finally, Rama makes it clear that he is not interested in another marriage. At the same time, he says he has a brother who is looking for a wife, and her extraordinary beauty will certainly ensnare him:

> Why do I need a nikah and a woman over and over?
> My young brother, that flitting sparrow,
> Wants a woman and a nikah.
> You'll suit him. And can he refuse
> When he sees your eyes, nose, bosom, and your thighs?

As are Shurpanakha's romantic overtures to Rama, so are Ravana's overtures to Sita, the theme of another song in the *Mappila Ramayana*. Ravana's yearning for Sita and his vanity are beautifully depicted in these lines:

> Lama Lama, Lama Lama; Lama Lama, Lama Lama!
> Lama Lama, Lama Lama; Lama Lama, Lama Lama!
> To the golden, lotus-honeyed Sita whom brother Lama,
> The beloved son of King Dasharatha, with desire, had made his bride—
> The king of Lanka, the ten-nosed Lavana,
> Boldly called out to her, that gem of femininity,
> 'My precious jewel, how many days have passed since I brought you to Lanka,
> My pearl, my blazing flower bouquet!
> Upon my two eyes, I swear, my golden one,
> That I desired to see you and tell you:
> You are the flower-goddess ruling my heart!
> So that I could see you,
> I left the eminent one of my own household.
> My soul! Am I not especially overjoyed
> That we are now in the same land together?
> Numberless days has my heart longed, my pearl, to see you
> Whose flower-like body makes the lotus-buds to droop in shame

It was not out of fear, my golden one, that I took you out of Lama's sight
But out of desire, my girl, that I carried you off in my chariot.
It's now almost a year from the day I brought you here,
When will I get to know your pristine self?
Is it because we haven't yet been together in the bridal chamber?
Why do you glare thus? Am I not manly enough?
There are four elephants, decked with caparisons,
And I will arrive heralded by Chinese drums,
Jangling tambourines and rhythmic Djembe-drums.
And a thousand maidens will accompany you.
Fine robes for a garment and lace veil you will have,
And your ears will be with earrings like,
And the ministers will adorn you with earrings like the champak[180] blossoms.
Lotus-bangles that will reach up to your shoulders are being made,
Four measures of gold being is melted and hammered on the roof of your chamber,
A fine flower necklace, and pendants for your forehead,
I bought and kept these for you four months ago.
With chicken biriyani and rice-pancakes
To be served four times.
All who come to the fort of Lanka
Must stay at the garden of bliss.
Why, in Allah's name, did you have to marry that pig Lama!
Two days ago, I came to know of a secret,
That Lama got bored and took another girl.
What's the use of waiting for a dead cow?
Buy and rear a better cow when your grief fades.
Two months ago, that traitor Lama abandoned you, girl,
And wed another, and sailed away on a ship somewhere.
If you hear the sound of the falling showers, by the grace of Allah,

Won't your dark clouds lift, my dear, my golden-lotus-parrot?[181]

Hanuman's travel to Lanka, the sights he sees and the encounters he has with the rakshasas are portrayed thus:

> While the dark lord of Death, Lavana
> Was having his ten beards shaved,
> The tailed-Anuman[182] leapt across to Lanka,
> And alighted on a goodly branch.
> Like skinned chickens, five ladies
> Lay fast asleep, hands over their privates.
> With rings in the ears and bangles on the arms:
> A dancer in a palm-leaf skirt.
> Another with protruding minaret-teeth and nostrils like burrows,
> And snoring like the chirping of the crickets.
> One with a twisted nose and a triangular butt,
> Dark and muddy like a mongoose.
> One was cross-eyed and with a flat nose,
> And a belly as large as a granary.
> Another with vertical legs and perpendicular arms,
> And sores on the knees and leech-bites long as a snake.
> One with thighs like the pillars of bridges
> And her skirts slipped off
> With no garment on the body, no blanket to cover,
> Her nipples standing erect.
> The tailed-one prostrated himself
> Spotting that golden flower-bud maiden Sita,
> As she took off the glittering ornaments from her hair.
> Seeing that angelic girl start to change,
> He reached that parrot's flower bower.
> The very instant he entered, the guards
> Stabbed at him and beat him
> And started to fight
> With bricks and blocks, clubs, rods and spears,
> And whatever they could get their hands upon.

And the tailed-one hit back with his tail,
With blows to their stomachs, blows to their chests
Circling and circling them, he rushed in,
Locked in his embrace, and long bitten by his sharp teeth
Those who received his blows fell dead.
With no legs, no hands, no eyes, no nose.
No man was left to guard that flower bower.

In another song, the fifty-six-year-old Shurpanakha gets decked up in the likeness of a sixteen-year-old as she sets off to see Rama:

Scrambling across the mountain and hills,
Panting and groaning all the way,
Came a beauty, the sister of Lavana
Beevi Shurpanakha, the shining golden apple-of-the-eye of
The Sultan of the great, golden Hades,
Who died of misfortune.
But the vulgar woman, she still wanted a husband.
She made her desire known to King Lavana, her brother
Who gave his consent in case she found a man to wed.
If her age were to be counted since the day of her birth,
It would be fifty-six.
But if she tried, it wouldn't seem over forty.
She put coal and honey on each white hair
Of her greying head to dye them black,
Sent for Fatima from the nearby house,
Quoted a sufficient fee and had her hair done.
Her round sunken eyes, like dried up cisterns,
She fortified with a wall of eye-shadow all around.
She pulled out her long chin-hairs,
She massaged the gums over her buck teeth,
She picked her nose with a palm-leaf and cleaned it out,
And mixed jaggery with red-powder and smeared it on the lips,
And scrubbed her ears, this side and that,

And donning ivory earrings, she shook her ears.
She put supports under her sagging breasts to make them firm,
And on top tender mangoes to stand out in her sheer garment.
She opened the trunk of the long-buried Queen-mother,
And grabbed the gold and jewellery within.
She pleated her sheer garment to puff it up,
And wore a waist-chain over it.
Above and below her ten bangles,
She wore a pair of bracelets set with precious stones.
Glittering with gold and sparkling stone, draping a crisp waist-cloth,
She wore a jiggling locket as big as a mirror.
Gathering her garments and the drapes, she took flight.
Scrambling across the mountain and hills,
Panting and groaning all the way,
Came a beauty, the sister of Lavana.

It can be said that there are no other songs in Malayalam which transplant the Ramayana story into another social and communal milieu so exquisitely.

There have been several narrations in the vanishing Arabic-Malayalam literature related to mythologies such as the Ramayana and Mahabharatha. Most of these are no longer extant. The *Naveena Ramayana*, composed in 1937 by the Islamic scholar K.V. Karuman Gurukkal in Malayalam, is very famous. The foreword to this poem that spans over 720 pages was written by Vadavannur Vadakkepattu Narayan Nair, a Sanskrit scholar in Kerala.[183] This work is a notable modern-day attempt by a Muslim scholar to retell the Ramayana story.

Ishal Ramayana

The *Ishal Ramayana* is a poem in Malayalam composed by the lyricist Ottamaliyekkal Muthukoya Thangal, otherwise known as O.M. Karuvarakundu in 2017. It faithfully renders the *Valmiki Ramayana* in the nature of the Mappila ballads, the Mappilapattu. The composition of this work marked a new chapter in the history of the Mappilapattu tradition.

One of the many unique features that the Mappilapattu has exclusive claim to is its tunes, its ishals. Most of the well-known ishals—the *Kombu, Kummiadi, Chinth, Padam, Muhibunoor, Akashabhoomi, Aaramba, Pookainar, Oppanachaayal, Poomakalane, Arambam Thulumbum, Thombal, Param Enikkathal, Undenum Mishkathil, Vanthullameghathil, Oyyathikkund, Hagana, Kazhuth, Vambutta Hamsa, Kandara Kadummal, Maranabi Aayisha, Badrul Huda, Khatabin Rahmamathude, Thamarappoonkavanathil, Urathya Moulan, Bismiyum Hamdum* and *Kothi Khalbil*—have been used in the *Ishal Ramayana*.

Bharatha, on coming to know that Kaikeyi, egged on by Manthara, plots to send Rama into exile and make her own son Bharatha reign in his stead, is overcome with grief. This scene has been depicted thus in the *Ishal Ramayana*:

> As soon as he heard the words 'hail',
> Bharatha burst out:
> 'No, nothing doing, this is not my wish.
> The title of the king,' he confessed,
> 'Is this not the reason that my father
> Would die, drowning in sorrow?
> I will not come forth to rule,
> By sending my worthy elder-brother to the forest.'

This song is arranged to the ishal of *Vambutta Hamsa*. The song that depicts Sita's swayamvaram is set in the ishal called *Oppanachayal*, and a portion of it goes thus:

> Wearing the kasavu cloth, nibbling its edges with delight
> Shyly, shyly the princess dreamed of the bridal chamber

Knowing this mighty archer was worthy of being her groom,
While her father invited King Dasaratha.
With his folk and his kinsmen, the king reached Mithilapura
There was gold, there was silver, and an abundance of pearls and gems
And chariots and chariots laden with all kinds of gifts.

Whereas the fight between Ravana's son Atikaya and Lakshmana is set to the *Chadichamarakkalam* ishal, and described thus:

> The two wrestlers came face-to-face
> And the fight stretched out for long hours
> The battleground blazed with sharp arrows
> The armours, the great arrows became futile
> Atikaya began to leap and jump.

A song arranged to the *Poomakalaane* ishal goes thus:

> The very instant he heard this,
> The elder brother offered his sandals
> Bharatha with the sandals as witnesses said,
> 'I will rule for you, my elder brother.
> Then awaiting Sree Rama's return,
> I will sit for fourteen years.
> If on the day after this, you fail to come,
> I will embrace death for sure.'
> His word was sure and sharp,
> Its power made the earth tremble and quiver.
> The instant Bharatha started to leave,
> His wish remaining unfulfilled,
> Thus spake Sree Rama:
> 'Son, don't hurt your mother even a little bit.
> That our father's soul may rest in peace,
> You must fulfil his commands, my dear.'
> Honouring Sree Rama's wish, Bharatha said adieu:
> 'Without gaining the satisfaction of a son,

I will fulfil my duty,
Joining the wise sage Vasishta.'
The guards moved back, and Rama spoke:
'We should not stand here any longer,
We should not stay here any longer
If we are here, many will come in search,
They will sway your mind with tales.
The bliss of the forest will vanish.
Listen, my Lakshmana, they will sway your heart'.
Obeying the elder brother's word,
To leave this place soon,
Lakshmana along with Rama and Sita
Is searching for another shelter.

O.M. Karuvarakundu aimed at fostering religious unity and friendship through the performance of the Ramayana as a Mappila song. Therefore, he crafted each line with the utmost care. Though the Ramayana has been performed in various art forms, its presentation in the form of Mappila songs is novel indeed.[184]

The Arab Ramayana

The noted Egyptian writer Kamel Kilani Ibrahim Kilani's (1897–1957)[185] most famous creation is *Fe Gabathishwayathwin* (*In the Great Jungle of Devils*). This is a work of children's literature and runs into about eighty pages. It narrates the Ramayana in very simple language that can be easily understood by children.

In the Great Jungle of Devils is based on an English version of the Ramayana. *The Arab Ramayana* is quite different from the *Valmiki Ramayana*. The major differences between the two are as follows:

1. In *In the Great Jungle of Devils*, the story ends with Sri Rama who, upon returning to Ayodhya after killing Ravana and rescuing Sita, reigns for a long time,

keeping the welfare of his subjects foremost. Sita's abandonment is absent from this work. In the *Valmiki Ramayana*, when Rama meets Sita after Ravana is killed, he speaks brusquely to her because she's lived in a stranger's house for many months. He even goes on to say he doesn't need her. Overcome with grief, Sita jumps into the fire. Rama takes her back when she emerges unharmed from the trial by fire. This incident hasn't been talked about *In the Great Jungle of Devils*.

2. The killing of Bali is narrated differently. In Kilani's Ramayana, the true ruler of Kishkinda is Sugriva. His brother Bali tries various methods to usurp the throne. Sugriva, losing his mind, abandons the throne. This is how Bali becomes the king. Rama throws in his lot with Sugriva and kills Bali to restore Kishkinda to its rightful ruler.

3. The character Shurpanakha does not appear in *In the Great Jungle of Devils*.

4. Sita commands Lakshmana to run to the aid of Rama who has gone in pursuit of Maricha, who magically took on the form of a golden deer. In *In the Great Jungle of Devils*, Sita does not doubt that Lakshmana desires her, and she does not speak any harsh words to him. Instead, she persuades Lakshmana to go to Rama by goading him: 'Are you a coward?' Unable to bear this aspersion, Lakshmana rushes out in search of Rama.

Kilani's Ramayana presents a king who is an ideal in all respects. Rama is not a deity or an avatar. Even so, he does not do anything untoward, be it great or small. Kilani frees Rama from even the aspersions cast by Maharishi Valmiki—the test of Sita, the killing of Bali, the slaying of Shambu and other incidents that even die-hard devotees of Rama are unable to justify—and erases them from the history of Rama.[186]

THE ADIVASIS OF INDIA AND THE RAMAYANA STORY

The Adivasis are communities which have followed their original way of life based on nature, and have not been subjected and adapted to 'external' cultural influences. They have for long stayed away and also been alienated from the mainstream, retaining, as a result, their own unique ethos. There are no definite written documents about the history of these people who have been oppressed, subjugated and marginalised by the upper castes. To mainstream societies, the history of these communities is a mix of legends and myths in which they have often even been depicted as savages.

To a great extent, the Adivasis have themselves taken refuge in legends and myths to establish and protect their identity and to overcome existential risks and challenges. They constitute 7.76 per cent of the national population. It is estimated that there are 450 Adivasi groups in India. They have their own languages and cultures, and their own deities too. Recently, some communities have started worshipping Hindu gods along with their traditional deities. Several Adivasi groups lay claim to the Ramayana tradition. Some regard the characters in the Ramayana as their own ancestors. This may be read together with the scholarly opinion that in the Ramayana and the Mahabharatha, those who were called 'vanaras' (monkey-like humanoids), 'rishans' and 'rakshasas' (giant humanoid demons) were the non-Aryan Adivasi sub-tribes of the Vindhya regions and central India. Though Valmiki refers to the Adivasis as vanaras and rishans, it is evident from numerous verses in the first epic, the *Adikavya,* that they were earlier considered humans. The vanaras in Valmiki's Ramayana have been described to be as intelligent as humans. They speak the language of men, wear clothes, stay in houses, respect the traditions of marriage, and dwell under the rule of kings. From this, it is evident that they were not mere monkey-like humanoids in the poet's imagination. In fact, vanaras, rishans and the such were actually human tribes.[187]

In India, there are numerous tribes with names that mean 'monkey'. Among the Oraons and the Mundas of the Chota Nagpur region, there are tribes called Tigga, Haleman, Bajrang and Gaddi. The meaning of all these names is 'monkey'. Similarly, among the Raddi, Barai, Basor, Baira and Khangar castes in the north and central regions of India, there are derivations of the vanara tribes. There are also those who claim to be the descendants of Ravana and Hanuman. The Bhuiya tribe of Singbhum in the state of Jharkhand claim to be the descendants of Hanuman.[188] They call themselves the 'pure clan'. The Gonds in Madhya Pradesh believe they belong to Ravana's clan. The Oraons, too, trace their lineage to Ravana.[189]

There are numerous other indigenous groups who connect the characters and events from the Ramayana to their own tribes in a similar fashion. The vanara-risha-gedhas in the Ramayana were actually Adivasis of the Vanara, Risha and Gedha tribes. What can be understood from this is that either the Adivasis were deeply influenced by the Ramayana or they had some role to play in the events of the Ramayana.

Valmiki and Vyasa were not from the upper classes of society. Valmiki's Ramayana says that before he became an ascetic, Valmiki used to be a woodsman and a robber, and

Vyasa, the author of the Mahabharatha, was the son of a fisherwoman. Moreover, Valmiki is the name of a caste as well.

There are numerous Adivasi groups who claim a connection with episodes in Ramayana. In many Adivasi groups, there are legends about Shabari. However, they are quite different from those recorded in the *Valmiki Ramayana*. The Kols are a tribe in present-day Uttar Pradesh and Madhya Pradesh who migrated from Chota Nagpur in the central region of India. This tribe considers itself to be the descendant of Shabari. Walter Griffiths has collected their beliefs in his book *The Kol Tribe of Central India* (1946). The legend they believe in is briefly summarised:

> Once, Rama, Lakshmana and Sita were in the forest during their exile, and were hungry and in need of help. Shabari (Savari/Sheori), who also lived in the forest, at once began to serve them, and satisfied their hunger with a jungle plum called ber (jujube). After that, she would gather and save the plums for the guests. One day, lost in her thoughts, she unwittingly took a bite from each plum as she picked it, and gathered them in her basket. When she reached home and looked into the basket, she remembered what she had done. She hesitated to offer the half-eaten plums to Rama. However, Rama insisted on having the plums, and both he and Sita ate them. Lakshmana refused to touch the food which had the saliva of an Adivasi on it. Then suddenly he was struck down by an arrow and was revived only when he ate those plums. When they were leaving Shabari's ashram, Rama asked her to choose between a kingdom and a family as a boon. Shabari asked for a family, and asked that her descendants might never starve or lack for clothes. Rama immediately granted her the boons.[190]

Camille Bulcke has recorded a tale about the burning of Lanka in circulation among the Adivasis of the Asur tribe in north India:

An Asur warrior and his wife were smelting iron. Hanuman, who was nearby, saw the reddish iron and felt like eating it. The Asur couple tried very hard to drive him away, but Hanuman sat near the forge and constantly disturbed them, and made himself a nuisance. Finally, the Asur man surreptitiously tied cotton around Hanuman's tail. His wife poured oil on it and set it on fire. Hanuman began to run and jump around. He leapt and landed in Lanka and burnt Lanka to ashes, and then, finally, rubbing his tail against a tree, he managed to douse the fire.[191]

The Santhals

The Santhals are a prominent Adivasi people in India who live in parts of Bihar, Jharkhand and Bengal, and have a culture and language of their own. Among them, the Ramayana story exists in a very different form. Some of the unique features of their version are noteworthy, and are summarised as follows:

1. Dasaratha obtains four mangoes from a yogi and gives them to his wives to eat. As a result, all three of them become pregnant.
2. Bharatha and Shatrughna come from the womb of Kaikeyi.
3. Rama, after killing Ravana, comes to live in the land of the Santhals. He and Sita build a Shiva temple there and pray there daily.
4. Once, Hanuman is guarding some watermelons. Lakshmana, who comes along that way, wants to have some of them. The two begin to fight and a duel ensues. After this bitter encounter, Lakshmana and Hanuman recognise each other. Finally, Hanuman gives the watermelons to Rama and Lakshmana.
5. When Hanuman is leaving for Lanka, he sits on the tip of Rama's arrow. Rama shoots the arrow into the middle of the ocean.

Among the Santhals, the episode centred around the search for Sita also differs from how it has been described in Valmiki's Ramayana. In the middle of the search, Rama spots a squirrel sitting on a tree-top and sobbing bitterly. When he asks the squirrel if it has any news of Sita, it replies: 'That is why I am crying. Ravana ravished Sita. He passed along this way.' Comforting the squirrel, Rama says, 'From whatever height you fall, you will not be hurt.'[192]

Another tale is related to the jujube tree. Rama sees an old cloth hanging on a jujube tree. The tree says to Rama: 'Ravana has taken Sita along this path. I tried to free her. But I was unable to do anything except grab this piece of her sari.' Rama blesses the jujube tree and says, 'However much you are chopped down, you cannot be destroyed.'

The Birhors

The Birhors are a prominent Adivasi tribe in Bihar. They are nomadic or semi-nomadic groups who make a living by hunting. Among them too, there are folktales relating to the Ramayana. These find mention in the book *The Birhors: A Little-known Jungle Tribe of Chota Nagpur* (1925) by Sarat Chandra Roy. In this book, tales from Rama's birth to the slaying of Ravana and Kumbhakarna have been collected. A few features in which the *Birhor Ramayana* differs from the *Valmiki Ramayana* are as follows:

1. Dasaratha is portrayed in the Birhor version as having seven wives.
2. In an open space where King Janaka offers sacrifice is a gigantic and heavy bow, the bow of Shiva, which nobody is able to move. When Sita goes to clean the yard and plaster it with cow-dung for the sacrifice, she takes this bow in her hand as if it were an ordinary bow

with no weight, cleans the place and keeps the bow in its former place. On learning that Sita has lifted it, the king declares that she will be given in marriage only to the suitor who can lift the bow.

3. Before the abduction of Sita, while going to the aid of Rama, Lakshmana gives some magic seeds to Sita saying: 'Keep these, and throw them at any outsider approaching the kumba (small leaf-hut). If you cast one of these seeds at any person, he will fall unconscious for an hour and then revive. If you cast two seeds, he will stay unconscious for two hours ...' When Ravana comes, Sita flings one magic seed at him and he lies dead for an hour. Then she throws a second seed and he lies dead for another hour, and so on, till finally Ravana tells her, 'Why take all this trouble? Why not throw all the seeds at once so that I may die forever?' Sita takes him at his word and throws all the seeds at him. Ravana dies. His body bursts into flames and is reduced to ashes. But out of the ashes, Ravana springs to life again, and catching Sita by the hair, carries her off in his chariot.

4. There is a different version among the Birhors of how Rama and Lakshmana cross the ocean and reach Lanka. In the *Valmiki Ramayana*, the monkeys build a bridge of stones so that Rama and Lakshmana can cross over to Lanka. In the Birhor version, Hanuman stretches out his tail, and Rama and Lakshmana sit on it and cross the ocean using it as a bridge.

The conversation that Rama has with the jujube tree and the boon he grants it are recorded as a legend among both the Birhors and Santhals, with only slight differences between the two tellings. In the Birhor version, the jujube tree does not try to save Sita. It only catches hold of a piece of Sita's sari and gains the boon of immortality. This story exists among the Munda tribe as well. In the Birhor version, Hanuman enters Lanka assuming the form of a suga bird (parrot). Also, it is Lakshmana, and not Rama, who slays Ravana.

Just as the Santhals have the tale of Rama's conversation with the jujube tree, the Birhors have the tale about a stork. The story is recorded in both the works *The Birhors: A Little-known Jungle Tribe of Chota Nagpur* (1925) by Sarat Chandra Roy and *Myths of Middle India* (1949) by the British anthropologist Verrier Elwin: when Rama inquires of the stork about Sita, it replies, 'What do I care for your Sita or Fita? I am engrossed with the thought of my own belly.' Annoyed at such a rude reply, Rama tells Lakshmana, 'Seize hold of the bird.' Lakshmana catches the stork and pulls it by the neck, and since then all storks have long necks.[193] This tale about the stork exists among the Asur tribe as well.[194]

There is also a unique tale about Hanuman during the search for Sita. When Sita is abducted, Hanuman is still in the womb of his mother. He sees Rama and Lakshmana from the womb while the brothers are combing the forest in search of Sita. He recognises them and cries out: 'Wait, Dada (elder brother), I shall also accompany you.' Hanuman forthwith takes birth and accompanies Rama and Lakshmana.[195] (Scholarly works tend to agree that Hanuman was an Adivasi belonging to the Vanara tribe, and later, along with the other Adivasis in the Ramayana, was considered a vanara.)

The Birhors believe that Sita, on reaching Lanka, in a bid to escape Ravana's assault, caused repulsive sores to appear all over her body with a magic spell. There are numerous such oral tales among the Birhors. Some of them can be found among other Adivasi tribes as well.

The Pardhans and the Bhumiya-Baigas

The Pardhan tribe lives in the upper Narmada. One of the Ramayana tales existing among them goes like this:

> Once, Lakshmana went to live in a temple, and did not see Sita and Rama for twelve years. At last, he went to Jainpur to visit them. Sita said to Lakshmana, 'I saw in a dream that you were fighting a battle against the king of Kalasapur, and winning it.' Lakshmana set off for Kalasapur to test the truth of this dream. Worried that she had sent Lakshmana to the brink of death, Sita left the palace and went in search of Lakshmana to try and stop him. She turned into a female fox, a fig tree and a flood, and when touched by Lakshmana, she returned to her original form. Paying no heed to Sita's persuasion, Lakshmana continued on his way to Kalasapur. Sita returned to her palace in despair. She dreamt that Lakshmana had been killed at Kalasapur. When she told Rama about her dream, he went there and revived Lakshmana.[196]

According to the belief prevailing among the Bhumiya-Baiga tribe in Madhya Pradesh, Sita is the Goddess of farming. The story recorded by Stephen Fuchs, Austrian anthropologist, in his book *The Gond and Bhumia of Eastern Mandla* (1960), goes that Janki mata, as Sita was also known, had six fingers on one hand. She cut off the sixth and planted it in the ground. After some time, a bamboo tree grew out of this finger, with many knots between the hollow tubes. In the hollow tubes were all kinds of seeds.

Another folktale collected by Fuchs is the Bhumiya-Baiga belief about the birth of Hanuman:

> When Bhagwan (the supreme being) took the form of Parvati and tempted Mahadeo (Shiva), Mahadeo was filled with love and began to ejaculate. A few drops of his semen fell into a hollow bamboo. Bhagwan gave Bhimsen, one of the

Pandavas, the bamboo. Bhimsen took it to a mountain in the jungle, where there was a locked palace in which a woman named Kariandni lived. Because it was locked, he could not get inside, nor could she come out. She put her ear to the hole of the door and asked Bhimsen to blow Mahadeo's semen into her ear. He did so. After nine months, Kariandni gave birth to Hanuman.[197]

In short, the Bhumiya-Baigas believe Hanuman was born from Shiva's semen. This is just one of the numerous legends about the birth of Hanuman that exist among various tribes in India.

The Agariyas

The Agariyas are an Adivasi group living in Madhya Pradesh. There are many tales and beliefs related to the Ramayana among them. The famous Indian anthropologist from Maharashtra T.B. Naik, has collected many of these. The story of Sita killing the thousand-headed Ravana is a popular one among them:

After the killing of Ravana, Sita informed Rama that a sahasra-kanda (thousand-headed) Ravana was dwelling in hell. Rama shot an arrow to hell and wounded the sahasra-kanda Ravana. But Ravana took Rama's arrow out of his foot and commanded it, 'Go back to the person who sent you and kill him instead.' On being hit by the arrow, Rama lost consciousness and slumped to the ground. Then Sita went to King Logundi and asked for a vessel of coals. She also requested that he accompany her. When the king agreed, Sita took the vessel of coals in one hand and a sword in the other, and they set off. Due to the soot flying up from the coals, Sita turned black. She went near Ravana and cut off his head, and Agyasur, the Agariya God of fire, and Lohasur, the Agariya God of iron, drank up his blood.[198]

According to a story in Braj literature (Braj bhasha is one of the western Hindi languages), after killing the thousand-headed

Ravana, Sita turned into the Ma Kali who has a temple in Calcutta.[199]

If some of the Ramayana tales existing among the Adivasis are ancient, some of them are quite modern too. The British anthropologist Verrier Elwin, in his book *Myths of the North-East Frontier of India* (1958), has collected many myths from the region. A very peculiar story goes thus:

> The Khampti Raja had a swelling on his hand. Soon the swelling cracked open and a girl emerged from the crack. She grew to be so beautiful that a demon with eight heads kidnapped her. The Khampti king went in search of her and slayed the demon. However, the girl was kidnapped again by another demon who took her across the sea. The king went in search of her, but could not find her. In the end, he went to the king of the monkeys (the vanaras) for help. When the monkey king arrived at the demon's palace, the demon set fire to his tail. The monkey king ran around the village and set fire to the houses there. In the chaos that ensued, he rescued the Khampti king's daughter and took her back to her father. As a reward, the Khampti king gifted the monkey king a fine palace made of gold and silver. As soon as the monkey king entered the palace, his hair fell out, his skin turned white, and he became the first Englishman.[200]

There are numerous traditions and beliefs associated with Sita among the Adivasis of Kerala too. The Manavalan Theyyam performed in the Kasargode district in northern Kerala is one such example. Manavalan and Manavatti are Theyyams, ritual dances, performed in places such as Madiyankulam and Srirama Vilyakazhakam. The deities worshipped there are modelled on Sri Rama and Sita. These Theyyams are staged by people of the Vannan (washermen) caste. They recite parts of the Ramayana during the ritual dances.

The Irulas

The Irulas, also known as Iruliga, are an Adivasi tribe inhabiting the Indian states of Tamil Nadu, Kerala and Karnataka. 'Irular' means dark people in Tamil and Malayalam. They are the second largest Adivasi tribe in Kerala, living in Palakkad district. The Adivasis in the regions of Varagambadi and Uthukuzhi, believe that Maharishi Valmiki, after composing the Ramayana, entrusted it to the Adivasis in person. It is also their belief that Valmiki wrote the Ramayana in Tamil. The art form *Sreerama Kushalava Natak* was started among them five generations ago when Songa Moopa ruled over them. From then on, this art form has been performed without fail. There are some differences between their version of the Ramayana and the *Valmiki Ramayana*. This play begins with Sri Rama sleeping and seeing a dream:

> Sita is five months pregnant. It is at this time that she is sent away (abandoned) into the forest. Inside the forest, Maharishi Valmiki offers her sanctuary. She gives birth to Lava and Kusha at the Maharishi's ashram. When Lava and Kusha come of age, they destroy seventy of Sri Rama's soldiers.
>
> When he wakes up, Sri Rama is worried that the events he saw in the dream might actually come true. He immediately sends Lakshmana to find out if Sita is pregnant. Lakshmana asks his mother (Kausalya) and she confirms that Sita is indeed pregnant, and asks him to make the required arrangements for her care. By this time, Sri Rama has visited Sage Vasishtha to seek his counsel about the dream and its interpretation. Vasishtha tells Rama that things will unfold exactly as he saw in the dream. He also hands Rama the muhurtha, the auspicious time to perform the various rituals.
>
> Sri Rama goes to Sita and says, 'I thought you would not bear children for 9,000 years. But now, after asking

Vasishtha and Mother (Kausalya), I am convinced. So, what wishes of yours do you want me to fulfil?'

Sita expresses her desire to go to the Dandakaranya (Dandak forest) where they had lived earlier. Rama tries to dissuade her by listing out the difficulties of living there. But Sita remains firm in her wish. At this, Rama decides to send Sita alone to the forest, and orders Lakshmana to take her there. At the same time, he delegates four messengers to gather news from his country.

A Vannar (washerman) sends his wife to deliver washed clothes to the houses and to get rice in return. Though she does exactly as he tells her, the wife returns home late. The furious Vannar beats and kicks his wife, and she runs away. The Vannar's mother blames him and asks him to bring her back. But he rejects the proposition saying only those like Sri Rama take their wives back.

The four messengers return and report this incident to Sri Rama. On hearing this, Rama is furious. He tells Lakshmana to take Sita to the middle of the forest and abandon her. But Kausalya forbids them to take Sita to the forest. However, Sita says now that Rama does not want her, the forest will be her refuge. Lakshmana takes Sita to the forest. On their way, they see ill omens such as a crow, a snake and a man with a pot of oil on his head. Lakshmana leaves Sita in the middle of the forest and returns to Rama. Sita undergoes many hardships there. At last, she meets Valmiki. At his ashram, she gives birth to Kusha.

Valmiki asks Sita to fetch water for the naming ceremony of the child. Sita leaves the child in the garden and goes to fetch water. When she sees the monkeys in the forest holding their young ones close to their chests, she begins to miss her own baby, and decides to go back to the ashram. She returns and takes Kusha with her to the stream.

Valmiki sees that the child has gone missing, and quickly creates another child exactly like Kusha, from haifa leaves.

(Here, too, we see a deviation from Valmiki's Ramayana.) When Sita returns, Valmiki tells her how he lost Kusha and gifts Lava to her. After that, the naming ceremony is performed. Lava and Kusha grow up in the ashram, and Valmiki becomes the boys' teacher.

At this time, Sri Rama performs the Aswamedha yajna. Kusha and Lava are out hunting, and Lava captures the horse. Shatrughna ties up Lava in his chariot and takes him away. Kusha is unaware of this incident. The maids who witness this rush to inform Sita. Kusha arrives at this point, and after hearing that Lava has been captured, takes leave of his mother and goes to fight with his bow and arrow. In the battle that ensues, he kills everyone, including Lakshmana, Bharatha and Shatrughna. Sri Rama arrives, but seeing all his loved ones dead, he faints. Lava and Kusha tie up Hanuman and the others who are still alive but unconscious, and take them prisoners. They take the prisoners to Sita. Sita recognises them, and requests Valmiki to revive all of them, or else she will end her life. Valmiki brings everyone back to life. Then Sri Rama asks Valmiki who all these people are, and Valmiki makes the proper introductions. Thus Sri Rama recognises Sita and his sons Lava and Kusha. He agrees to take them back after a cleansing by fire. Lava is burnt in the fire, but the rest survive. Kusha is given the throne, but Sita is not willing to go back with Rama. She says she cannot bear more shame, and that she will go back to her mother. The earth opens up and Sita descends into it.

The Irulas perform this play while retaining their own style. The performance is interspersed with songs and sayings. A background choir with accompanying instruments such as the harmonium, mridangam and kanjira sings the songs in the play. The first to enter the stage is Vinayakar (Ganapathi). He wears masks made of wood and saffron cloth that suit the character. After a prayer is offered to Ganapathi, he withdraws behind the curtain. Then the clown, wearing a conical crown, and who plays only a minor role, exits and disappears. A female dancer enters singing *'nadiya penkal mantare'* (the dancing girl has come) and exits. Finally, the minister Kattiyakkaran comes announcing the arrival of the king and exhorts everybody to be prepared to receive him. The play begins at this point.[201]

This play not only has numerous differences from the *Valmiki Ramayana*, but the Adivasi perspective on life is also presented in these performances. The storyline of the play is a good example of their social awareness, and their relationship with the forest is an important part of the play. This art form of the mountain people of Attappadi is traditionally performed over the three nights before Shivaratri.

These mythical tales are known and told across the length and breadth of Kerala. The Malayalam poet M. Govindan says in a poem that in the paddy fields of Ponnani (a coastal region in northern Kerala), the Ramayana grows along with the paddy. This is true not only of Kerala, but of every Indian village:

> *Ororo karichaaliloro nurikumbil Ororo chiruthayundirippoo chirichoodi*
> *Janakanmaarum koodeppadunnu Ramanmaarum*
> *Janakeeyamaayi manju Maithili mahakavyam*
>
> In each furrow, in each clod of soil
> There are smiling Sitas
> The Janakas and the Ramas sing along
> How beautiful is this popular poem on Sita!

Nomadic Literature

Among the numerous downtrodden communities of India, independent interpretations of mythological tales exist as songs, stories, ritual forms and so on. They are mostly linked to the social structure and identity of these groups. Among the folksinger communities, the mythical tales are freely interpreted and reinterpreted, and new lines are added to enhance the effect of songs, thus resulting in newer versions of stories. Because they are a part of the oral tradition, each poet and each singer creates many versions of the same song.

The character most loved by these folk singers is Sita. She is the representative of all women; the emotions, thoughts and feelings of every woman is reflected in Sita. Many things left unsaid by Valmiki are manifested in these folk songs. For instance, in a Kannada folk song collected in *Janapada Ramayana* (*Folk Ramayanas*) by Rame Gowda, P.K. Rajasekara and S. Basavaiah in 1973, Sita is Ravana's daughter. But it is not Mandodari who carries Sita in her womb, but Ravana himself! Ravana, overcome with greed, eats a magical mango given by Shiva for Mandodari so that she will be blessed with a child. The folk song talks about the gradual growth of Ravana's belly, the nine months of pain and shame, the child born from a sneeze, and the astonishment of the midwives. By presenting Ravana as a father who, through a twist of fate, begins to lust after his own daughter, this story becomes a tragedy. However, the important thing here is that, in the folk songs about the Ramayana, the centrepiece of events can be toppled at will, and the emotions and the feelings of both the narrator and the listener can be respected.[202]

The study by the academician Velcheru Narayana Rao on the Telugu oral tradition of the Ramayana[203] is remarkable. He shows us how the themes of female experience and interests predominate the folk songs in Telugu. Events which are left untold in male-centric versions of the mythology, including Kausalya's pregnancy, her morning sickness, details of the delivery, the lullaby she sings for Rama, bathing of the child Rama, Sita's wedding, Sita's journey to her mother-in-law's house, Sita's puberty, and the games Rama and Sita play, find their voice here. Such tellings that depict the female experience are present among both the Brahmin (where the women are totally dependent on their husbands, and are forced to live a sheltered life) and non-Brahmin communities (especially the lower castes, where women do agricultural labour, earn wages, live relatively less sheltered and controlled lives).[204] Velcheru Narayana Rao illustrates the differences between the Ramayana songs sung by the women of both communities. While the themes are women-centric, the songs sung by the Brahmin women elaborately describe rituals, clothes and ornaments, allude to sexuality and the games played by husband and wife. On the other hand, the songs sung by the non-Brahmin women (particularly the Mala caste) describe work such as cooking, sprinkling cow dung in the yard, and digging the fields.[205]

In the *Chitravarna Ravana* composed in Kannada by Helavanakatte Giriyamma, a Haridasa mystic poetess from Karnataka who lived in the eighteenth century, there is a folktale about Shurpanakha which goes much further than the *Valmiki Ramayana*. Shurpanakha is a favourite heroine of the folk singers. In this tale, after all the events have ended well, Shurpanakha is brought back. In the traditional narrative of the Ramayana, Shurpanakha's presence is limited to the Panchavati grove where she encounters Rama and proposes a union with him. When she realises Rama is beyond her reach, she desires Lakshmana. And when that too does not happen, she becomes violent. In the argument that ensues, her nose, ears and breasts are cut off. She goes and complains to Khara and Dushana, who launch an attack on Rama, and are subsequently killed. She then goes to Lanka and complains to her brother Ravana, also informing him that her enemy's wife is exceedingly beautiful. The plot gains momentum with the establishment of the twin motives of revenge and lust. Seeking treatment for her wounds, Shurpanakha disappears from the scene. From this point onwards, she is invisible. However, in the *Chitravarna Ravana*, Shurpanakha stages a return. The desire for Rama is still burning within her, and her thirst for revenge on Sita is yet unquenched. Shurpanakha reaches the palace in Ayodhya disguised as a sanyasin (female hermit). There, she cunningly tricks Sita into drawing a picture of Ravana's toenail. While living in the Ashoka Vatika forest in Lanka, Sita had seen only the toes of Ravana, who kept coming to either appease or threaten her. So, she draws only the toenails. Shurpanakha then completes the picture. Then she prays to the Creator, Brahma, that the picture may be made to come to life so that she can see her brother alive once again. Brahma grants her wish. The picture of Ravana comes to life. Ravana exhorts Sita to return to Lanka. Sita threatens to burn the picture, but does not do so. At this point, Rama comes in and begins to doubt Sita's fidelity. Refusing to heed the pleas by Urmila, Mandavi and Shrutakirti, Rama orders that Sita be banished to the forest.

This tale inspired the writer Chaduranga to pen the Kannada drama titled *Bimba* in 1990. The play depicts Sita and Shurpanakha as characters who submit to innate human emotions. This work does away with many of the values imposed by an androcentric world.[206] Indeed, such folktales and cultures are able to delve deep within the recesses of human emotions and bring them to light.

So, as water flowing through different lands mingles with the colour of the soils along the way, our legends and myths too, as they travel across lands and communities, mingle with their environs and sensibilities. Time will create newer and newer Ramayanas, because society is endlessly conversing with, debating on and sometimes even quarrelling with the Ramayana. All these conversations and conflicts serve to enrich the canon of Ramayana literature. Just as unity in society is a product of its diversity, mythological tales too represent such diversity and unity. This will surely lead to the evolution of a new culture based on pluralism.

THE MANY VERSIONS AND VARIATIONS OF THE RAMAYANA

The literal meaning of Ramayana is 'Rama's Way'. However, the Ramayana is not only Rama's way, it is also Sitayana, that is, Sita's way. And since Ravana is the anti-hero, the epic is also the story of Ravana.

Though Valmiki is known as the author of this epic, it existed in the oral tradition of many communities even before the time of Valmiki. This fact is borne out by the concise story of the Ramayana in the Drona Parva and Shanti Parva of the Mahabharatha, considered to have been composed before the Ramayana.[207]

No reliable data is available regarding the history of Valmiki. There is no reference to the sage except in the Yuddh Kanda, the war canto, of the *Valmiki Ramayana*. But it is recognised in the Mahabharatha and in the Bala Kanda, the childhood canto, of the *Valmiki Ramayana* that Valmiki is the author of the Ramayana. He is not just a prominent character in the epic itself, but the events narrated in it occurred during his time.

The origin of the Ramayana is talked about at the beginning of the Bala Kanda in the *Valmiki Ramayana*. Valmiki, the sage and hermit, hears the gist of the Ramayana from Narada. Following Brahma's instructions, Valmiki sets into verse the story of Rama, and teaches his two disciples the poem he has composed. These disciples go about reciting the Ramayana. Once, they recite the epic poem in front of Rama and his brothers in the palace at Ayodhya.[208]

Lakshmana leaves the abandoned Sita in the precincts of Valmiki's ashram, telling her to take refuge there. He also mentions that Valmiki is a Brahmin and a friend of Dasaratha.[209]

Sita gives birth to Lava and Kusha in Valmiki's ashram. The boys learn the Ramayana from Valmiki and, on his instructions, recite it at the venue of Rama's Aswamedha yajna. After hearing the poem, Rama sends for Sita and she is brought by Valmiki, who testifies to her faithfulness. At this juncture, introducing himself, Valmiki states that he is the son of the tenth Pracetas.[210] Pracetas is one of the Prajapatis (the Hindu God of creation and protection, sometimes identified as Brahma) and an ancient sage and law-giver. He also makes it clear that he has never sinned: '*Manasa karmana vacha bootha poorvam na kilbisham*' (no impurity has touched me either in thought or deed).[211]

According to some narratives and traditions, Valmiki had been a robber before becoming a sage. After many years of penance, he became competent enough to compose the Ramayana. In the Ayodhya Kanda of the *Adhyatma Ramayana* the account of this is as follows:

> Rama, Lakshmana and Sita started from Ayodhya and reached the area near Chitrakoot. They sought Valmiki's advice before deciding where they would live.
>
> After praising Rama, Valmiki recited his story to show the greatness of the name Rama. 'Earlier, I lived with the savages and was immersed in the deeds of a Shudra, hence I was a Brahmin only by birth. I had many sons from a Shudra woman. In the company of thugs, I too became a thug and always carried a bow and arrow. One day, I saw seven hermits passing by. I stopped them in the middle of the dense forest with the intention of robbing their clothes and other belongings.
>
> 'The hermits said, "The family for which you are amassing sins, ask them if they are willing to share your

guilt." I put this question to the members of my family and they said, "Your sins are yours alone, we only want your wealth." Hearing this, I felt detached from everything and hence joined the hermits.

'O Rama, the hermits consulted among themselves and, inverting the letters of your name, said, "Sit here and mentally recite the word mara." I did so. I sat so still on the ground while chanting the word mara that termites made their mound around me. After the passage of a thousand yugas, the hermits returned. Instructing me to come out, they said. "Oh great hermit, henceforth you will be known as Valmiki. You have emerged from the Valmikam (termite mound), hence you have been born a second time."'[212]

This incident finds mention in Tulsidas's *Ramacharitamanas* and other works like the Rajya Kanda of the *Ananda Ramayana*, the *Skanda Purana* (a collection of eighteen Hindu religious texts attributed to the sage Vyasa), *Krittivasi Ramayan* (composed in Bengali in the fifteenth century by Krittibas Ojha) and the *Adhyathma Ramayanam* (composed by Ezhuthachan in Malayalam in the seventeenth century).

There are other texts dealing with the life of Valmiki. According to the *Odia Mahabharatha*, composed by Sarala Das in the fifteenth century, the birth of Valmiki came about this way:

> One day, a Brahmin went to a place called Manumeghala in the Gangetic riverbed to do tapas. Seeing eight goddesses emerging from the river after a bath, he ejaculated involuntarily. He threw a part of the semen on Mount Meru. Merusila Rishi was born out of that. The remaining part of the semen he deposited on the banks of the river and Valmiki was born from it.[213]

There are many such stories about Valmiki among the Dalit communities too.[214] A story from the Bhangi (scavengers'/

sweepers') community, collected by the British Orientalist William Crooke in *Tribes and Castes of the North Western India*, is about Parmeswar (the supreme God) sending Guru Nanak to meet Valmiki. At the insistence of Guru Nanak, Valmiki asked his wife, 'Are you willing to give up your life for me?' On hearing her answer in the negative, Valmiki started doing tapas; he became a hermit, and began to live in the mountains of Chandal Ghat (Chunar in Uttar Pradesh). Later, that place became a pilgrimage site for the Bhangis. These people, who are devotees of Valmiki, solemnly observe Valmiki Jayanti (the birth anniversary of Valmiki) in Kolkata on Ashwini Poornima, the day of ritual bathing during the month of Karthika. Crooke cites another story from Punjab, where, until the inhabitants of Benaras city learned to look at the faces of the Bhangis, Valmiki's dead body was seen every day at different parts of the city, inside houses, so the inhabitants had to call the scavengers inside their houses to remove the body.[215]

Several texts ascribe the authorship of the Ramayana to Hanuman. It is believed that after completing the composition of the Ramayana, Hanuman threw down the manuscript from the top of a mountain. Valmiki only did the work of collecting its torn fragments.[216]

Another story says that Hanuman was deeply pained when Sita was abducted. He could not bear the grief of having to witness the suffering of Rama. During those days of intense suffering, Hanuman inscribed the *Ramacharita* on the rocks on the hillsides. One day, Valmiki chanced to pass that way, and he read the story written on the rocks. Valmiki told Hanuman that he would compile this touching tale in book form. On hearing this, Hanuman collected all the rocks on which he had etched Rama's story, and hurled them into the depths of the ocean. Hanuman could not bear handing over to someone else what he had written about his beloved Rama.[217]

A large number of ancient Ramayanas contain stories different from those in the *Valmiki Ramayana*. Camille Bulcke cites Ramdas Gaud's Sanskrit work *Hindutva*, in which summaries of nineteen Ramayanas are mentioned. The structures of all these nineteen Ramayana tales are different from that of the *Valmiki Ramayana*. Many of these works are voluminous. Their origins have been attributed to the maharishis (sages), and the period of the composition of most of these works are unknown. These Ramayanas exist in textual form in Sanskrit. The special features and the number of verses in these works are given below:

1. *Maha Ramayana* (350,000 verses): This describes the Rasalila (amorous dances/love-play) of Rama. Rama in this work is a man of fertile imagination. The text, whose author is unknown, is composed in the form of a dialogue between Shiva and Parvathy.
2. *Samvrutha Ramayana* (24,000 verses): It is believed that Sage Narada, the singer-storyteller and messenger to the gods, and a devotee of Vishnu, composed this version. Narada is also a universal character in the Puranas. In this version, Manu and Shatrupa (the first humans according to the Vedas), see a divine vision of Rama, and are granted the boon to have Rama as their son. In their next birth, Manu and Shatrupa appear as Dasaratha and Kausalya.
3. *Lomasa Ramayana* (32,000 verses): This was composed by Sage Lomasa, an ardent devotee of Vishnu, who was granted the boon of a long life in order to worship Vishnu. (Lomasa has been referred to as a storyteller in the Puranas. It can be seen from the *Laghu Purana Nighandu* (*Concise Encyclopaedia of the Purana*) that many of the episodes in the Puranas were related in

different stages by Lomasa.[218]) In this work, King Kumuda (the grandson of Manu) and Queen Viramati are reborn as Dasaratha and Kausalya.
4. *Agasthya Ramayana* (16,000 verses): It is believed that Agasthya, a revered scholar and sage, wrote this version. Agasthya is one of the Saptarishis (seven great sages). Here, Bhanupratap and Animardan become Ravana and Khumbakarna, and King Kuntala and Queen Sindhumathi are re-birthed as Dasaratha and Kausalya. (Tolkāppiyam, the most ancient grammar text of Tamil literature was written by Tholkappiyar, who was a disciple of Agasthya.[219])
5. *Manjula Ramayana* (120,000 verses): It is believed to be authored by Sage Sutikshna who saw a vision of Rama, and on opening his eyes, saw the same Rama standing in front of him. In this version too, Bhanupratap and Animardan become Ravana and Khumbakarna. The *Valmiki Ramayana* mentions that Rama and Lakshmana visited Sage Sutikshna's ashram during their exile. Therefore, it can be supposed that he was a contemporary of Valmiki.
6. *Saupadhma Ramayana* (62,000 verses): This was written by Sage Atri, prominently mentioned in the *Rigveda*. (The *Ugveda* is said to have been written by Maharishi Atri, who was a scholar of the fifth mandala [Book 5] of the *Rigveda*.[220]) Atri is one of Brahma's sons, and one of the Saptarishis. In this version, Rama and Sita first meet in the pushp vatika (garden) at Mithila.
7. *Mahamala Ramayana* (56,000 verses): This Ramayana is in the form of a dialogue between Shiva and Parvathy. In it, the Sage Kakbhushundi, who had been granted the boon of a thousand lives due to his devotion for Rama, narrates to Garuda that he has visited multiple

universes and has seen the Ramayana taking place in all those universes. The author is unknown.

8. *Sauhardha Ramayana* (40,000 verses): This work was composed by Sage Sharabhanga, who was visited by Rama during his journey through the Dandaka forest. A special feature of this telling is that Rama and Lakshmana try to learn the language of the vanaras (monkeys).

9. *Maniratna Ramayana* (36,000 verses): This version is a conversation between Sage Vasishtha and his wife Arundhati. Vasishtha was the oldest and most revered of the sages in the Vedas, one of the Saptarishis, and also the teacher of Rama. This version mentions, here varying from the *Valmiki Ramayana*, that Rama celebrates Vasantotsava (spring festival) and other festivals at Mithila and Ayodhya along with Sita. The originator of this work is unknown.

10. *Saurya Ramayana* (62,000 verses): The special features of this text are the dialogue between Hanuman and Surya (the sun God). It also covers the story of Suka and the abandonment of Sita, where Suka becomes the rajaka (washerman) who proves to be a catalyst in Rama's abandonment of Sita. The composer of this version is unknown.

11. *Candra Ramayana* (75,000 verses): This Ramayana is composed in the form of a dialogue between Hanuman and Chandra, the moon God. The story of Kewat, the boatman who helped Rama, Sita and Lakshmana cross the river Ganges while they were exiled, and his previous birth is told here. In his previous birth, Kewat was a tortoise. The authorship is unknown.

12. *Mainda Ramayana* (52,000 verses): This Ramayana is a dialogue between Mainda, a mighty vanara warrior in

Hanuman's army, and Kaurava. Rama and Sita's first meeting in the pushp vatika (flower garden) and their falling in love is described here.

13. *Swayambhuva Ramayana* (18,000 verses): This version of the epic has a dialogue between Brahma and Sage Narada. Manu and Shatrupa appear as Dasaratha and Kausalya. Dasaratha has 700 wives, and Sita is born of Mandodari's womb. The originator of this version is unknown.
14. *Subrahma Ramayana* (32,000 verses): Written in the form of slokas, the *Subrahma Ramayana* features Brahma and Sage Narada engaging in a debate. The composer is unknown.
15. *Suvarchasa Ramayana* (15,000 verses): This is a dialogue between Sugriva and Tara, the queen of Kishkinda who later becomes his wife after the death of his brother, King Vali. The creator of this version is unknown.
16. *Deva Ramayana* (100,000 verses): This is a dialogue between Indra and his son Jayanta. The composer is unknown.
17. *Sravana Ramayana* (125,000 verses): This is a dialogue between Indra and King Janaka. The originator of this version is unknown.
18. *Duranta Ramayana* (61,000 verses): This is a dialogue between Sage Vasishtha and King Janaka. A special feature is the description of the greatness of Bharatha, the younger half-brother of Rama. The composer is unknown.
19. *Champu Ramayana* (15,000 verses): This is a dialogue between Shiva and Narada. It mentions that Sita's swayamvara was held in the palace of King Seelanidhi, who was the ruler of the grand Silanidhi city built by Vishnu's maya. The originator of this version is unknown.

It is possible that in addition to these versions of the Ramayana, there were many others that did not stand the test of time. There would have been multiple Ramayana texts based on the adi (source) Ramayana.

The *Valmiki Ramayana*: Period of Composition

It is believed that Rama lived on earth towards the end of the Thretha Yuga. Philosophers are of the opinion that the Thretha Yuga came nearly 862,100 years before Christ. The *Valmiki Ramayana* mentions that Rama ruled for 11,000 years:

Dasha varsha sahasrani dashavarsha shatani cha
Ramo majyamupasithwa brahmalokam prayasyathi

(*Valmiki Ramayana*, Balakanda, Sarga 1, Verse 97)

The *Valmiki Ramayana* notes that Rama was forty years old when he became the king of Ayodhya. Valmiki started composing the Ramayana only after the birth of Lava and Kusha. Based on these assumptions, some believe that the Ramayana was composed about 878,000 BC. However, this hypothesis, which is based on belief and not on objective evidence, has been rejected by several scholars of both Occidental and Oriental origins. It is doubtful whether the human race had even evolved at this point of time. Different researchers put the date of composition of the *Valmiki Ramayana* as follows:

1. Hermann Jacobi, German Indologist: between the sixth and the eighth century BC[221]
2. August Wilhelm Schlegel, Sanskrit scholar and translator: eleventh century BC[222]
3. Gaspare Gorresio, Italian Indologist: approximately twelfth century BC[223]
4. Chintaman Vinayak (C.V.) Vaidya, Marathi historian: second century BC[224]

5. Arthur Berriedale Keith, Scottish Indologist: before fourth century BC[225]
6. Camille Bulcke, Belgian Ramayana scholar: before 300 BC[226]

Most scholars who have studied the time of composition of Ramayana agree that it could not have been composed later than the seventh century BC. Some studies have suggested that the Ramayana was composed around the time of the Buddha. In any case, the faith-based argument that the Ramayana was composed 878,000 years ago is not tenable.

Textual Variations of the Ramayana

The *Valmiki Ramayana* contains references that suggest the Rama story was first propagated orally through songs and other art forms. Both the Bala Kanda and the Uttara Kanda mention that after teaching his disciples the Ramayana, Maharishi Valmiki instructed them to go around reciting it before kings, sages and ordinary people.

> *Chirtsanam ramayanam kavyam gayatam paramudha*
> *Rishivadeshu punyeshu brahmanavasadeshtacha*
> *Radhyasu rajamargeshupardhivanam griheshucha*
>
> (Uttara Kanda, Sarga 3, Verse 5,6)

> Go, and with great enthusiasm sing the Epic Ramayana, cheerfully and carefully, in the sacred enclosures of the Rishis, the dwellings of the brahmins, along the roads and highways and in the residence of princes, and especially it should be sung at the gate of Rama's pavilion, where the sacrifice is taking place and also before the priests.
>
> (trans. Hari Prasad Shastri)

This proves that the *Valmiki Ramayana* was propagated throughout the country by way of songs and recitation. Groups like the Sūtas, Debgurus, Devgunias, Mailaris, Kalavants, and so on that eke out their living from singing songs have always been present in India. Even today, there are religious orders like the Bauls, who live as mystic minstrels.

Apparently, the *Valmiki Ramayana* was learnt by heart by Valmiki's disciples, including Lava and Kusha. They might have passed it on to their children, and might have observed the interest shown by those who listened. The singers, who were well versed in the art of poetry, would have developed the parts that were pleasing to the audiences, thus extending the ambit of the original story. They would have made their own contributions to the popular parts of the epic poem by way of improvisation, adding elements of suspense, drama and pathos. Such episodes would have become more and more popular as time went by. Later on, these embellished versions would have been written down. So, the so-called interpolations might be such additions, first introduced in oral presentations and later on written down and documented. When these written texts reached a whole new set of listeners in oral form, naturally each group would have constructed their own textual variations. Their next generation would have gone on to create newer forms, and this must have turned into an ever-evolving cycle of storytelling as far as the variations in our epics are concerned.

The *Valmiki Ramayana* is itself not a single, unified text. It has three recensions, according to scholars such as Hermann Jacobi[227] and Camille Bulcke:

1. Southern recension: the Baroda Edition (BE)
2. North-eastern (Bengal) recension: the Gauda/Gorresio Edition (GE)
3. North-western recension (NW)

Each of these three recensions has verses that are not present in the other two. In fact, the southern recension and the Bengal recension have only one-third of their verses in common. Even the structures of the verses in the three recensions are not similar. In many places, their sequence of verses is different, according to the Ramayana scholar and German Indologist Hermann Jacobi.

The southern recension is generally considered to be the most original. This view is enhanced by the fact that the concise Ramayana tales in the Mahabharatha are most similar to that of the southern recension. Moreover, the grammar and style of the southern recension is crude, pointing to the oral ballads from which the Ramayana took form. August Wilhelm Schlegel, Sanskrit scholar and translator, says that the grammarians of Bengal edited the crude text, deleting obsolete words and syntactical regularities in the north-eastern recension, which is also called as the Bengal recension.[228] Indeed, the Bengal recension is smoother to read, the grammar accurate, and the language refined. The north-eastern/Bengal recension is also called the Goressio edition, as Gaspare Gorresio, the Italian Indologist, used this recension to translate the *Valmiki Ramayana* into Italian in 1843.[229] The north-western recension is similar in style to the southern recension, and both these recensions contain matter which is not found in the north-eastern recension. Camille Bulcke is of the opinion that the north-western recension is a corrupted form of the southern recension. In fact, the idioms and the wording of the text are less obscure in the north-western recension than in the southern recension, which is more conservative with regard to textual alterations. Therefore, it is regarded that the southern recension is the closest to the original archetype of the *Valmiki Ramayana*, and the north-eastern recension exhibits the greatest divergence.

There have been numerous narrations of the Ramayana story in India as well as abroad. As a result, the epic has become imprinted in peoples' imagination, both as an art form and in the form of faith. The Ramayana has been imbibed in societies not just as a book, but as a great culture and tradition.

Outside India, the epic has generated reinterpretations in all Asian countries. In India, it exists in myriad forms in all our official languages. There are Ramayanas in languages such as Tulu, which has not received much recognition, and in tribal languages such as Bhili and Santhali. There are Ramayanas in Assamese, Chinese, Balinese, Cambodian, Japanese, Lao, Malaysian, Thai and Tibetan languages too. In Sanskrit alone, there are more than twenty-five notable variant texts. We can affirm that in world literature, there has been no poet who has had so extensive an influence on literature that came after their time as Valmiki, who is referred to as the Adikavi (first poet) of India.

In the eyes of Valmiki, Rama is the epitome of nobility. For many poets in other languages, Rama is a deity. Examples are provided in the *Kamba Ramayana* by Kambar and the *Adhyatma Ramayana* by Ezhuthachan. Kambar incorporated elements from folk texts and the *Valmiki Ramayana* in his work. There have also been rare instances of exquisite poetic treatment, where other poets have outshone Valmiki in the matter of poetic imagination and diction. The poetic quality of the lines by Kambar in the *Kamba Ramayana* while describing Indra's seduction of Ahalya is unmatched in its subtlety and dramatic description. This episode from the *Kamba Ramayana*, translated into English by P. Sundaram, is rendered thus:

> ... once in days gone by, the God of Thunder saw the sage's doe-eyed wife and was smitten. Pierced by her spear-like eyes and Madan's shafts, he sought, his senses lost, a healing balm in her arms. Tricking the sage away, he entered the hut in a guileless guise.
>
> She knew who he was, but inebriate with unfamiliar feelings induced by his ingress, she didn't desist—so low she'd sunk.

When her lofty husband hurried home and saw what he saw, he became a second Siva.

An arrow might have been thwarted, but not his curse or blessing. She knew this and stood trembling, a figure now of everlasting shame, while the rattled god tried to flee in the guise of a cat.[230]

All the poets mentioned above tried to present the Rama story in tune with their imagination and the requirements of their times. During the Bhakti movement, when people had moved away from truth and righteousness and were interested only in material comforts, the Bhakti poets elevated the Ramayana to the level of devotion and godliness. This was another case of textual reconstruction.

There have also been instances where a written text has silenced many other texts. The wide reception of the televised version of the Ramayana made by Ramanand Sagar, which presented a visual text of Tulsidas's Ramayana, is an instance of how one rendition can capture the popular imagination and establish itself as an 'authentic' or 'definitive' version. We cannot give the stamp of authenticity to any single text. All the texts are authentic. Also, there is no greater or lesser variant among the existing texts. The epic cannot be reduced to be that of a particular locality or community. Romila Thapar, in her article 'The Ramayana Syndrome', which critiques the television series on the Ramayana by Ramanand Sagar, says, 'The Ramayana does not belong to any one moment in history for it has its own history which lies embedded in the many versions which were woven around the theme at different times and places… The appropriation of the story by a multiplicity of groups meant a multiplicity of versions through which the social aspirations and ideological concerns of each group were articulated.'[231] The domination of one text over the other numerous versions only serves to limit the vast expanse and the unlimited scope of the Rama story.

Ramayana Versions in the Major Indian Languages

In the following paragraphs, a list of various versions and works, including poems and plays based on the Ramayana that exist in the various major languages of India such as Malayalam, Tamil, Telugu, Kannada, Bengali, Urdu, Persian, Kashmiri, Assamese, Odia, Gujarati, Marathi and Punjabi are enunciated. A brief description of the major works in each of these languages is also added.

Malayalam

The Ramayana has had a profound influence on literature across language territories in India. There have been a large number of works in Malayalam related to the Ramyana, including the *Rama Charitham* by Cheerama, the oldest work discovered so far; *Kannassa Ramayanam* by Kannassa Panicker; *Ramakathappattu* by Ayyappilli Asan; *Ramayana Champu*, thought to be the work of Punam Namboothiri; *Adhyatma Ramayanam* by Ezhuthachan; *Kerala Varma Ramayanam by* Kerala Varma Valiyakoyi Thampuran; *Ramachandra Vilasom* by Azhakathu Padmanabha Kurup; *Ramanattam* by Kottarakkara Thampuran, *Ramayanam Manjari* by Oduvil Sankarankutty Menon; *Bhasha Ramayana Champu* by Kadathanattu Krishna Varrier; *Ramayanam Attakatha* by Mannanthala Neelakandan Moos; *Ramayanam Thullalkathakal* by Nalukettil Krishna Menon; and *Balaramayanam* by Kumaranasan. Besides these exist the translation of *Kamba Ramayana* by S.K. Nayar; the translation of Tulsidas's Ramayana by Vennikulam; adaptations of *Abhisheka Natakom* and *Prathima Natakom* by Bhasa; *Ramayanam Prabantham*, which comprises eight Thullal works based on the Ramayana, by Kunchan Nambiar; translations of works by Shakthi Bhadra, Dignatha, Rama Bhadra Deekshithar, Bhavabhoothi, and Murari; and performing arts based on the Ramayana such as Vanchippattu (a poetic metre with a rhythm similar to the rowing of a boat), Tholppavakkoothu (shadow-puppet play), and Pathakom (a dramatic exposition of the Puranas).

A large number of plays based on the Ramayana exist in Malayalam. These include *Sita Swayamvaram* by Kodungalloor Kunjikuttan Thampuran, *Mandodari* by Sirdar K.M. Panikkar, *Adbhutha Ramayanam* by M. Neelakandan Moos, *Sitaharanam* by N. Sankaran Nair, *Bhasha Ramayanam* by A. Govinda Pilla Chattampi, *Ravana Putran* by Pallathu Raman, *Lankam Ravana Palitham* by Madassery Madhava Varier, *Rama Rajabhishekam* by E.V. Krishna Pillai, *Pushpavrishti* by Thikkodiyan, and *Kanchana Sita, Lanka Lakshmi* and *Saketham* by C.N. Sreekandhan Nair.

All the major Malayalam poets of the twentieth century have written on themes, characters and events from the epic. These works include *Chinthavishtayaya Sita* by Kumaranasan, *Sitadevi* by P. Kunjiraman Nair, *Innathe Sandhya* by Sugathakumari, *Samarpanam* by Punaloor Balan, *Thamasa Kanangalil* by Pala, *Lakshmanan* by Vishnu Narayanan Namboothiri, *Vibheeshanan* by Balamani Amma, *Ravana Putri* by Vayalar Ramavarma, *Sabari* by Ayyappa Panicker, *Ahalya* and *Janaki Poru* by K. Satchidanandan.

Tamil

The *Kamba Ramayana* (also called *Ramavataram*), composed in the twelfth century by the poet Kambar, is the oldest version of the Ramayana—not only in Tamil but in all the south Indian languages. It is similar to the southern recension of the *Valmiki Ramayana*. Kambar portrays Rama as both as a man and as a

God. Even today, scenes from the Ramayana are enacted in Tamil Nadu in the form of puppet plays called pavakoothu. The pavakoothu performers are known as pulavar.

Telugu

The oldest known Ramayana in Telugu is the *Nirvachanothara Ramayana* composed by Thikkanna in the thirteenth century. Another ancient Telugu work is the *Dwipada Ramayana* by the poet Ranganatha (Gona Budda Reddy), which is also called the *Ranganatha Ramayanamu*. It was composed in the fourteenth century, in the form of couplets. It is based on the Uttara Kanda of the *Valmiki Ramayana*. There is another Telugu text based on the Uttara Kanda called the *Uthara Ramayanam Champu*. It was written by Kakadipapa Raju in the eighteenth century.

The *Bhaskara Ramayanam* is a prominent work on the epic in Telugu, by Hulukki Bhaskara . Composed in the fourteenth century, it is inspired by the *Ranganatha Ramayana* and *Valmiki Ramayana*. The *Molla Ramayanam* by the early female poet Atukuri Molla is a text that has become more popular than the others, due to its simple language. It was composed in the early sixteenth century, and has close similarities with the *Valmiki Ramayana. It is* is devotional in nature.

The *Sri Ramayanamu* (also called the *Dwipada Ramayana*), composed by Katta Varada Raju in the seventeenth century, is a voluminous poetic work in couplet form and is based entirely on the *Valmiki Ramayana*. In addition to these, the works *Ekoji Ramayanam* (composed in the late seventeenth century by Raja Vyankoji Bhonsle, the ruler of Thanjavur Maratha kingdom), *Achatelugu Ramayanam* by Kuchimanchi Timma Kavi, composed in pure Telugu and *Gopinatha Ramayanam* by Venkata kavi, following the Champu style, where verses are interspersed among prose passages, are also noteworthy.

An ancient pictorial version of the Ramayana, the *Chitra*

Ramayana, too, has been discovered in the Telugu language, but its author or artist, and its date are unknown.

Kannada

Works based on the Ramayana began to be produced in Kannada around the eleventh century. The first known text was the *Pampa Ramayanam* created by Abhinava Pampan, also known as Nagachandran.

Karnataka being a region deeply influenced by Jainism, Ramayanas with a Jain background deserve special mention. The prominent works among these are Kunudenthu's Ramayana, composed in the sixteenth century; *Ramavijaya Charitham* by Devappa; *Ramakathavatharam*, composed by Devachandra in the eighteenth century; and the *Jina Ramayanam* by Chandrasagara, from the nineteenth century. These tellings of the epic are different in many respects from the *Valmiki Ramayana*. The Jain Ramayanas lay emphasis on the principle of non-violence. Hence, the war between Rama and Ravana has been described as inappropriate in the Jain texts.

The *Thorave Ramayanam* and *Mairavanakalaga*, composed by Narahari in the sixteenth century, on the contrary, highlight the importance of the battle between Rama and Ravana in the true spirit of the *Valmiki Ramayana*. The *Jaimini Bharatham*, composed in the sixteenth century by Lakshmeesha, is a popular telling in Kannada, in which Sita is given prominence over Rama.

Bengali

The most popular and ancient Ramayana of Bengal is the *Krittivasi Ramayan* (also known as the *Sriram Pacali*), composed in the fifteenth century by the poet Krittibas Ojha. This work mentions that even the rakshasas (demons) were devoted to Rama. The current version of this text is very different from its original, as a lot of interpolations have corrupted this work. The current version shares similarities with the north-eastern (Bengal) recension of the *Valmiki Ramayana*.

Translations of the *Adbhutha Ramayana* (a brief account of the Rama story, attributed to Valmiki) are popular in Bengal. Prominent among these are the *Adbhutha Ramayana* (also known as *Ascharya Ramayana*) by Badu Nityanand Acharya, *Adbhutha Ramayana* by Rameswara Datta and *Ramayana Gatha* by Chandravathi. Some texts based on the *Adhyatma Ramayana*, too, have been produced in Bengali. The most prominent among them is the *Sri Rama Panchali* by Dwijavanee Natha.

In addition, in modern times, a number of works based on the epic have enriched Bengali literature. Many fresh translations of the *Valmiki Ramayana* were produced in the twentieth century. Prominent among the creative texts written during this time are the *Ramarasayanam* by Reghunandana Goswami, *Ramayanam* by Jaganmohan, *Valmiki Ramayanam* (prose) by Rajasekhara Bose, and *Meghanatha Vadha* by Michael Madhusudan Dutt. The *Meghanatha Vadha* is a counter-Ramayana, where Ravana and his son Indrajit (Meghnath) are portrayed sympathetically, but without any change or distortion from the original plot.

Urdu and Persian

Retellings of the Ramayana are abundant in Urdu. *Ramayana Khusthar*, composed by Munshi Jagannatha Khusthar (printed in 1860), *Ramayan Manzum* by Hakim Vicerai Wahmi, *Ramayana Bahara* by Bankebi Harilal Bahara and *Yak-Qafiya Ramayan* by Ufaq (published in 1914) stand out for their excellence. Acharya Narendra Bhooshan, Indian linguist and

Vedic scholar, is of the view that though these three texts might have drawn on the *Ramacharitha Manas, Adhyatma Ramayana* and *Valmiki Ramayana,* they exhibit signs of originality and can be considered independent creations in their own right.[232]

It was only in the nineteenth century that writings related to the Ramayana gained popularity in Urdu. In recent times, a number of poetic works and studies related to the Ramayana have emerged in Urdu. Interestingly, the exploration of the Ramayana gathered force in Urdu only after the decline of the Persian language. Earlier, there were a large number of poems about and interpretations of stories from the Ramayana in Persian, and the best of them were produced during the Mughal period. The first work in Persian on the Ramayana was the translation of the *Valmiki Ramayana* in verse by Abdul Qadir Badayuni. It was commissioned by Akbar the Great.

During the reign of Emperor Jahangir, two Ramayanas were written in Persian. These were the *Ramayan-e-Masih,* composed by Mulla Shaikh Sadullah Kairana (pen-name Masih Panipati), and the abridged *Valmiki Ramayana,* written by Giridhar Das in verse as *Ramayan.* Giridhar Das's poem is in the form of a heroic tale. He adheres closely to the *Valmiki Ramayana.*

Ramayan-e-Masih was published in 1899 by Munshi Naval Kishor Press, Lucknow. Masih wrote the Ramayana in the form of a poetic romance, using the trope of a lover who has to face numerous obstacles before he can take the hand of his beloved. *Ramayan-e-Masih* diverges from the *Valmiki Ramayana,* and treats the characters freely. Interestingly, Camille Bulcke is of the opinion that the composer of the *Ramayan-e-Masih* might have been a Christian. In several places in the text, Biblical characters such as Jesus (Issa) and Mary (Mariam) are introduced by way of comparison and in parables. An example is where Trijata consoles Sita, who is mourning the death of

Rama after a false report, by saying that Rama is as immortal as Issa (Christ). Moreover, Masih, the pen-name of the composer Mulla Shaikh Sadullah Kairanavi, is a term used in Christian scriptures for Christ (Messiah).

Other notable works in Persian are the prose piece *Ramayana Faizi*, composed during the time of Shahjahan; the *Tharjuma-thu-Ramayan* by Gopal; the translation in verse and prose by Chandrabhan Bedi; *Ramayana Amar Prakash* by Lala Amar Simha; and the translation of Valmiki's Ramayana in prose by Amanath Rai Lalpuri.

Kashmiri

The most notable work based on the Ramayana in Kashmiri is the *Ramavathar Charitha* by Prakash Ram Kuryagrami. Written wholly in verse, it was composed in the eighteenth century. There are several variations from the *Valmiki Ramayana* in it. It narrates various incidents, from the birth of Rama to his ascension to heaven, in ways very different from the *Valmiki Ramayana*. The entire poem is set in the form of dialogue between Shiva and Parvathy.

Assamese

The *Saptakanda Ramayana*, written in the fourteenth century by Madhava Kandali, is a popular work in Assamese. It predates Ezhuthachan's *Adhyatma Ramayana*. In this text, Dasaratha has more than 700 wives. Madhava Kanadali has made a lot of interpolations in his narration of the *Valmiki Ramayana*. Rama and Sita are not portrayed as heroes, but as persons with both human weaknesses and extraordinary qualities.

The other Ramayana versions in the Assamese language are *Lava-Kushar Yudha* by Harihara Vipra (fourteenth century); *Geethi Ramayanam* and *Maheeravana Vadham* by Durgabar

Kayastha (sixteenth century); *Jeevastuthi Ramayanam, Pathalakhanda Ramayanam* and *Sitara Pathala Pravesana Natakam* by Ananta Kandali (sixteenth century); *Ramavijay Nat* by Sankardeva, who is also the author of *Uthara Ramayanam* (sixteenth century); *Ramabhavana Natak* by Madhavadeva (sixteenth century); *Sree Rama Keerthanam* by Ananthatakur Atha; *Ganaka Charita* by Dhananjaya (eighteenth century); *Sita Banabas* by Gangaram Das (eighteenth century); *Nagaksha Yuddha* by Bhavaveda Bipra (eighteenth century); *Patalikanda Ramayana* by Dwij Panchanan (nineteenth century) and *Seetaharan Kavya* by Bholanath Das (nineteenth century).

In the *Uttarakanda Ramayana*, Sankaradeva takes the side of Sita, while adhering to the *Valmiki Ramayana*. The author adopts a tone of anger as well as compassion when describing the suffering of Sita, who has been abandoned by Rama in the forest, even after her purity is proved by the test of fire. Sankaradeva says that Rama's action was not only abandoning her, but also, essentially, her murder. Later, overcome with guilt, Rama sends messengers to Sita, who are shocked on seeing her condition. Living in the forest, surviving on roots and fruits, Sita is emaciated, her clothes soiled, and her body pale. The messengers ask forgiveness from her, but she says that to her Rama seems like the heartless God of death. When Valmiki asks Sita to forgive Rama, she does not reply, but only weeps. When she is brought before Rama, she does not speak to him, but calls on Mother Earth to take her. Then, before disappearing into the earth, she looks at Rama so fiercely that he trembles.

Odia

The most ancient Ramayana storyteller in Odia was Sidheswara Parida (later known as Sarala Dasa), who was the author of *Chandipurana* and *Mahabharatha*. Though the period of his life is not determined, he is believed to have been an early fifteenth-century poet. In Parida's work, the Rama story appears as an episode within the Mahabharatha. In this text, Sita is Draupadi, Anjana is Kunti, Sugriva is Arjuna, Bali is Karna, Lakshmana is Balarama and Bali is Bhima. This text has close similarities with the *Krithivasa Ramayana* in Bengali.

The most famous Ramayana in Odia is the *Jagamohana (Dandi) Ramayana* composed in the fifteenth century by Balarama Dasa. The story is told in the form of a dialogue between Shiva and Parvathy. Balarama Dasa also composed two messenger poems based on the Ramayana, *Kanta Koili* and *Kaka Koili*. In *Kanta Koili*, Sita sends a koel (cuckoo) as her messenger from the Ashoka Vatika (garden) in Lanka, whereas in *Kaka Koili*, it is a crow that carries the written message about Sita's sufferings in the Ashoka Vatika.

Other notable Ramayana versions in Odia include the *Tika Ramayana* by Neelambaradasa; *Reghunatha Bilasom* by Dhananjaya; *Baramsi Koili* (which describes the pangs of separation felt by Kausalya when Rama is exiled) by Sankaradasa; *Tika Ramayana* by Maheswara; *Ramarasamrutha Sindhu* by Kanhudasa; the translation of *Adhyatma Ramayana* by Haladhara Das; *Vilanka Ramayana* by Siddhesvara Dasa (written in the seventeenth century); and *Angada Padi* by Vipra Laksmidhar (composed in the eighteenth century).

Many literary works based on the Ramayana were composed in Odia in the eighteenth century. Notable among them is the *Baidehisa Bilasa* by the poet Upendra Bhanja, which is a highly erotic treatment of the love-plays of Rama and Sita. Each line in the work begins with the letter Ba. Bhanja made use of complex poetic devices.

In addition, in the nineteenth century came major works such as *Ramayanam* by Krishnacharan Pattanaik, *Seetesa Vilasom* by Bhuvaneswara Kavichandra, *Nritya Ramayanam* (also known as *Kesava Ramayanam*) by Kesava Harichandra Patnaik, and *Poorna Ramayanam* by Kesava Tripathi.

Besides these, several folk versions exist in Odia. The *Haliya Ramayanam* is one of them; it is sung during the ploughing of fields. It tells the story of Ahalya's release. According to the *Valmiki Ramayana*, Ahalya, the most beautiful creation of Brahma, was given to Sage Gautama as wife. However, Indra desired her, and disguised as Gautama, he seduced her. Sage Gautama found them together, and flew into a terrible rage. He cursed Indra to be covered with a thousand vaginas all over his body, and Ahalya to be turned to a stone. Indra performed penance, and the vaginas all over his body were turned into eyes, giving him the name 'thousand-eyed God'. Ahalya was cursed to be a rock until Rama's foot touched it. Centuries later, when Rama entered the hermitage, his feet brushed against this stone, and Ahalya was liberated.

Gujarati

In Gujarati, odes to Krishna are more prominent than stories about Rama. Nevertheless, in the fourteenth century and later, a number of works based on the Ramayana were composed in Gujarat. Most notable among them are the *Ramaleenapada* by Asayeethi (fourteenth century), *Ramavivaham* and *Ramabalacharitha* of Bhanala (fifteenth century), *Sitaharana* by Mantrakarmana, *Ramaleelanapado* by Bhim, *Ramayana* by Mandanabandasa, *Sita Hanuman Samvada* by Udhav (sixteenth century) *Ravana Mandodari Samvada* by Lavanyasamay, *Lavakusakhyanam* by Nagaru, *Ranayanjam* by Premanand (seventeenth century), *Sita Viraham* by Haridas, *Ramayanam* by Giridharadas (nineteenth century, and it is as popular as Ezhuthachan's *Adhyatma Ramayanam* in Malayalam), and *Ramayana* by Udhava and Vishnudasa, the sons of Bhalana (sixteenth century). Besides these, several translations exist of Tulsidas's *Ramacharithamanasa* and the *Yoga Vasistha* (discourse of Sage Vasistha to Prince Rama).

Marathi

The oldest Ramayana in Marathi is the *Bhavartha Ramayana* composed by Ekanatha in the sixteenth century. It is largely based on the *Valmiki Ramayana* and *Adhyatma Ramayana*, but has parts based on the *Ananda Ramayana* that vary from the *Valmiki Ramayana*. These include Ravana's participation in Sita's swayamvara, the testing of Rama by Parvathy wherein she takes on the form of Sita, the pilgrimages undertaken by Rama in his boyhood, Ravana's beard catching fire during the burning of Lanka, and Lakshmana killing Shurpanakha's daughter. It also tells the tale of Hanuman's birth from the payasam (a sweet dish) prepared for the Putrakameshti yajna conducted by Dasaratha in order to have a son born to him.

Sita's swayamvara was a favourite theme of many remarkable Marathi poets, like Bidha Renukanandan, Janardanan, Ramdas, Jayasamaswami, Vamana, Venavay, Vadagavkar, Anandathanay, Gosawinandan, Nagesh and Bidhal, who lived between the sixteenth and eighteenth centuries.

The major Marathi tellings based on the Ramayana include the *Yudhakanda* by Krishndasa Mugala; *Salaghu Ramayana, Sundara Kanda and Yudhakanda* by Samartha Ramdas; *Samkshepa Ramayana* and *Ahamahi Ravanavadham* by Multheswara; two Ramayana texts by Madhavadas; and the Ramayana by Venabayi. The most popular among the works that were produced in later years is the *Ramavijaya* by Sreedhara, composed in 1703. It is quite similar to *Bhavartha Ramayana* in its themes and narration. Moreshwar Ramchandra Paradkar (popularly known in Maharashtra as Moropant) wrote seventy-four texts based on the Ramayana in the late 1700s. Amritharavu Oka's *Sathamukharavana Vadha*, composed in the nineteenth century, and about the killing of Ravana, is also very famous. As in other Indian languages, literature related to the Ramayana is popular in Marathi even today.

Punjabi

The Ramayana has been a favourite theme of writers in Punjabi. There are many Ramayanas in the language that are quite different from the *Valmiki Ramayana*. The most popular among them is the *Govinda Ramayana*, believed to have been composed in 1698 by Guru Gobind Singh, the last guru of the Sikhs. According to this text, Rama and Sita know each other prior to their marriage, Valmiki creates a son and gifts him to Sita, Rama doubts Sita's fidelity due to Ravana's picture, and Sita goes down into the earth as a result.

Another work of great worth in this epic's Punjabi tradition is the *Adiramayana*. This was written by Sodhi Meherban in the sixteenth century in a language that is a mixture of Hindi and Punjabi. The description of hermitages and the life of the ascetics find prominence in this work.

Written works based on the Ramayana have been composed not only in the major languages of India but in all the Indian languages having a script. Some languages have produced more literature than others. These texts have imbibed the essence of the belief systems, and borrowed elements from the ways of life, of the people amidst whom they were created. Even a cursory reading of these works will reveal the way in which the Ramayana, over centuries, has continually adapted itself to the nature of the times, the people and the culture in which it has been produced.

CONCLUSION

This book, as evident in its name *Living Ramayanas*, is an attempt to present the Ramayana as a living text that is perpetually growing and evolving. The Ramayana versions of the Adivasi/tribal communities of Kerala have hitherto been unexplored. They are narrated in detail in the first section of this book, which presents the versions of the Ramayana that exist among the often overlooked forest and tribal regions of Wayanad in Kerala, India.

The second part of this book deals with the versions of Ramayana that exist both within and outside India. Different nations, cultures and communities have different versions of the Ramayana that vary in their theme, characters and narration. In this section, a brief outline of the many versions of the Ramayana is laid out.

The concept of polyphony, as put forward by the Russian thinker Mikhail Bakhtin, who borrowed the idea from music theory, refers to multiple voices. Bakhtin affirms that polyphonic works are made up of 'a plurality of independent and unmerged voices and consciousnesses, a genuine polyphony of fully valid voices', where the characters are, 'by the very nature of his creative design, not only objects of authorial discourse but also subjects of their own directly signifying discourse'.[233] This holds true for the Ramayana as well. The Ramayana is not a stagnant text but, rather, a living text that accommodates many different and diverse voices that are unblended into a single dominating perspective. Nor are they subordinated to a monologic control of one author. Each differing voice has its own perspective, its own validity, its own narrative significance and its own ideology. Just as a living being constantly interacts, engages with, modifies and is, in turn, modified by the environment around it, the Ramayana, as a living text, continues to transform and be transformed by the social worlds in which it exists, and in which it will continue to exist.

NOTES

1. Iruppu is a place in the Kodagu (Coorg) district of Karnataka adjoining Wayanad.
2. Narrator: Balan Puzhamudi, Kalpetta.
3. Narrator: Prabhakaran, Ashramkolly. Caretaker of the Valmiki Ashram. Member of the Ezhava community.
4. Refer to the Hindu Minority and Guardianship Act, 1956.
5. Narrator: Raman Chetti, Areapally.
6. Joseph Munjad, 'Wayanadan Chettimar', in *Jeevithavum Samskaravum*, M.V. Vishnu Namboothiry (ed.), Kannur: Kerala Folklore Academy, 2003, p. 130.
7. Chummar Choondal, *Karutha Kalakal*, Thrissur: Kerala Folklore Akademi, 1991, p. 53.
8. Narrator: Evoor Narayanan, Sulthan Bathery.
9. O.K. Johnny, *Wayanadan Rekhakal*, Calicut: Olive Publications, 2001, p. 102.
10. *Mangalam Daily*, 12 April 2004.
11. Narrator: Peethambaran, Manikkavu.
12. Narrator: Kunjananthan Master, retired headmaster, Muttil.
13. Narrator: Narayanan, poojari of the Irappa Rameswaram temple.
14. Narrator: Evoor Narayanan, Sulthan Bathery.
15. K.C. Radhakrishnan, 'Pithrukarmmasayujyam', *Mathrubhumi Weekend Edition*, 23 July 2006.
16. Narrator: K.K. Annan, Kammana.
17. Ibid.
18. Ibid.
19. M.R. Pankajakshan, *Wayanattile Adivasikalude Pattukal*, Thrissur: Kerala Sahitya Akademi, 1989, p. 19.

20 Narrator: Karunakaran Master, Cherukara, Wayanad (theatre actor).
21 *Madras Manual Of Administration*, Vol. 3, p. 1025.
22 O.K. Johnny, *Wayanadan Rekhakal,* Calicut: Olive Publications, 2001, p. 102.
23 Joseph Moonjad, 'Vayanadan Chettimar', in *Jeevithavum Samskaravum*, Vol. 3, M.V. Vishnu Nampoothiri (ed.), p. 30.
24 Babu Kattayad, 'Alinkulavum Kannuneerthadakavum', *Indian Labor Rashtreeya Vartha Masika*, p. 20; *Punaprathishta Mahotsava Supplement*, Ponkuzhy Sri Rama Kshektra Samuchayam, 2004.
25 Evoor Narayanan, 'Ponkuzhy temple and Indian thought', in *Indian Labor Rashtreeya Vartha Masika*, p. 2; *Punaprathishta Mahotsava Supplement*, Ponkuzhy Sri Rama Kshektra Samuchayam, 2004.
26 Babu Kattayad, 'Alinkulavum Kannuneer Thadakavum', *Indian Labor Rashtreeya Vartha Masika*, p. 20.
27 Narrator: Evoor Narayanan, Sulthan Bathery.
28 Narrator: Kalankandi Ravunni Chetti, Muthanga.
29 Narrator: Prabhakaran, Ashramkolly.
30 Narrator: Jayaraj, Pariyaram.
31 Narrator: Prabhakaran, Ashramkolly.
32 P.K.K. Nair Cherukattor, 'Wayanadan Malamadakukalile Kshetrasamskarapolima', *KSSPU Smaranika*, 2005.
33 Narrator: Kalankandi Ravunni Chetti.
34 Sudharshanan, 'Ente Deshamenna Column', *Mathrubhumi Daily*, 28 December 1999.
35 T.P. Balakrishna Pillai and Kalankandi Ravunni Chetti in *Ponkuzhy Kshektra Smaranika*, 2004.
36 Narrator: Prabhakaran, Ashramkolly.
37 T.P. Balakrishna Pilla, 'Wayanad Adi Kavyathintte Urava', in Ponkuzhy Sri Rama Kshektra Samuchayam, 2004, p. 577; Narrator: Prabhakaran, Ashramkolly.
38 Narrator: Balan Puzhamudy, Kalpetta.
39 Narrator: Balan Puzhamudy, Kalpetta.
40 Narrator: K.K. Annan (former MLA), elder of the Kurichya community.

41 E.A. Karunakaran Nair, *Pazhashiyude Priyabhoomi*, Kottayam: Current Books, 2005.
42 Narrator: Kunjananthan Master, retired teacher, Muttil.
43 'Sitadevi Kshektram', published by Pulpally Devasom in the *Punaprathishta Mahotsava Supplement* by the Ponkuzhy Sri Rama Kshektra Samuchayam, 2004; Narrator: Kalankandi Ravunni Chetti.
44 P.K.K. Nair, 'Malamadakukalile Kshetra Samskara Polima', *KSSPU Smaranika*, p. 99.
45 *Thirunelly Mahatmyam*, Thirunelly Devaswom, p. 7.
46 Ibid., p. 5.
47 Ibid., p. 8.
48 Narrator: Madhu (journalist), Peechamkod.
49 K. Panur, *Keralathile Africa*, Kottayam: Sahitya Pravarthaka Sahakarana Sangam, 1963, pp. 20, 21.
50 E.A. Karunakaran, *Pazhassiyude Priya Bhoomi*, Kottayam: Current Books, 2000.
51 O.K. Johnny, *Wayanad Rekhakal*, Calicut: Olive Publications, 2001, p. 102.
52 Narrator: K.K. Annan (former MLA), of the Kurichya community.
53 Narrator: K.K. Annan.
54 Narrator: Kelupittan, Thalappuzha.
55 O.K. Johnny, *Wayanad Rekhakal*, Calicut: Olive Publications, 2001, p. 102.
56 *Thirunelly Mahatmyam*, Thirunelly Devaswom, p. 8.
57 *Thirunelly Mahatmyam*, Thirunelly Devaswom, pp. 7, 8.
58 O.K. Johnny, *Wayanad Rekhakal*, Calicut: Olive Publications, 2001, p. 102.
59 Narrator: Chandrasekharan, Vasdevan (Trikkaipatta).
60 James George Frazer, *The Golden Bough* (abridged ed.), London: Macmillan, 1983, p. 52.
61 Narrator: E.T. Raju, Sulthan Bathery.
62 Narrator: Kariyan, Trissileri.
63 Ramesan K., 'Adiyanmar' story from Alavu song, in *Jeevithavum Samaravum*, Vol. 1.
64 Narrator: P.K. Kalan, Trissileri.

65 Quoted in D. Chacko Kannatumodi, *Kurichyarude Lokam*, Thiruvanathapuram: Kerala Bhasha Institute, 1994.
66 Kumaaran Vayaleri, *Kurichyarude Jeevithavum Samskaravum*, Kottayam: Current Books, 1996, p. 16.
67 K. Panur, *Malakal, Thazhvarakal, Manushyar*, Kottayam: National Book Stall, 1971, p. 61.
68 Narrator: Ampupittan, Sulthan Bathery.
69 M.R. Pankajakshan, *Wayanattile Adivasikalude Pattukal*, Thrissur: Kerala Sahitya Akademi, 1989, p. 407.
70 Narrator: Mathai, Trissileri; in K. Panur, *Keralathile Africa*, pp. 23, 24.
71 Narrator: Narayanan, Temple Priest, Iruppu temple, Kodagu district.
72 Narrator: Raman Chetti, Pulpally.
73 Narrator: K.K. Annan, Kammana.
74 Narrator: P.K. Kariyan, Trissileri.
75 Narrator: P.K. Kariyan, Trissileri.
76 Narrator: K.K. Annan, Kammana.
77 *Thirunelly Mahatmyam*, Thirunelly Devaswom, p. 5.
78 *Thirunelly Mahatmyam*, Thirunelly Devaswom, p. 6.
79 K.C. Radhakrishnan in *Mathrubhoomi Weekly Supplement*, 23 July 2006.
80 *Thirunelly Mahatmyam*, Thirunelly Devaswom, p. 6.
81 *Thirunelly Mahatmyam*, Thirunelly Devaswom, p. 7.
82 Narrator: Lakshmikutty Teacher, Kalindi Anganwadi.
83 Mundakayam Gopi and K. C. Radhakrishnan, 'Thirunelly Pazhama', *Mathrubhoomi Weekly Supplement*, 23 July 2006, p. 32.
84 Narrator: Kappukunnu Chami.
85 Narrator: Madakundu Surendran.
86 Narrator: Theyyamkuni Chakkan.
87 Narrator: Padacheni Chanthu.
88 M.R. Pankajakshan, *Wayanattile Adivasikalude Pattukal*, Thrissur: Kerala Sahitya Akademi, 1989, pp. 19–38
89 Ibid., pp. 62–63.
90 O.K. Johnny, *Wayanad Rekhakal*, Calicut: Olive Publications, 2001, p. 17

91 Raghavan Payyanad, *Folklore*, Thiruvananthapuram: State Institute of Languages, 1986, p.123.
92 M.P. Veerendrakumar, 'Thalarunna Thazhavarakalum Valarunna Nadikalum', *Mathrubhoomi Weekly*, 2-18 June 2005.
93 Nellikkal Muraleedharan, *Viswasahitya Darsanangal*, Kottayam: DC Books, 1997, p. 252.
94 E.D. Hirsch, Jr, 'Three Dimensions of Hermaneutics', *New Literary History*, Vol. 3, No. 2, 1972, pp. 245-261
95 Ibid.
96 K.R. Raman Namboothiri, *Vedahrithayathiloode*, Calicut: Poorna Publications, 2006, p. 101.
97 Ibid.
98 P. Rajendran, *Journal of Kerala Studies*, Vol. 4, December 1977.
99 Christoph von Furer-Haimendorf, *Tribes of India: The Struggle for Survival*, Berkeley: University of California Press, 1982.
100 Sadhu Krishnanda, *Thirunelly Puranam*, Thirunelly: Njanamargam Books, 2006, p. 14.
101 James George Frazer, *The Golden Bough* (abridged ed.), London: Macmillan, 1983, p. 52.
102 Kaarle Krohn and Julius Krohn, *Folklore Methodology*, Austin: University of Texas Press, 1971, p. 160.
103 M.V. Vishnu Namboothiri, *Folklore Chinthakal*, Calicut: Poorna Publications, 2005, p. 98.
104 P.G. Padmini, *Kattu Jeevithathinte Spanthana Thalangal*, Thalassery: Akam Samithi, 2001, p. 76.
105 M.R. Pankajakshan, *Wayanatile Adivasikalude Pattukal*, Thrissur: Kerala Sahitya Akademi, 1989, pp. 13, 14.
106 Manu Jose, *Mullakurumarude Kalipattukal*, Cuddalore: Adivasi Munneta Sangam, 2001, p. 11.
107 Rao Bahadur C. Gopalan Nair, *Wayanad: Janangalum Parambaryavum*, Madras: Higginbotham & Co., 1911, pp. 47, 50, 54.
108 C. Unnikrishnan, 'Eviduthe Kattinu eradikalude impam', in *Indian Labour Rashtriya Vartha Masika, Punaprathishta*

Mahotsava Supplement by the Ponkuzhy Sri Rama Kshektra Samuchayam, 2004.

109 C. Hwaykas, *The Old Javanese Ramayana*, 1958.
110 Camille Bulcke, *Ramakatha Uthbavavum Valarchayum*, Thrissur: Kerala Sahitya Akademi, 1999, p. 263.
111 Himamsubhooshana Sarkar, *Indian Influence on the Literature of Java and Bali*, Calcutta: Greater India Society, 1934.
112 Book on the Birth Centenary of Royal Bathevian Society, Bethevia, 1929, p. 423.
113 F.W. Thomas, 'A Ramayana Story in Tibetan, Indian Studies', M. Lalu, *Journal Asiatic*, 1936, p. 560.
114 Camille Bulcke, *Ramakatha Uthbavavum Valarchayum*, Thrissur: Kerala Sahitya Akademi, 1999, p. 273.
115 M.P. Veerendrakumar, *Ramante Dukhom*, 1993, pp. 85, 86.
116 Camille Bulcke, *Ramakatha Uthbavavum Valarchayum*, Thrissur: Kerala Sahitya Akademi, 1999, p. 273.
117 Ibid.
118 'The Rama Jathaka', *Journal Siam Society*, Vol. 36, p. 1.
119 Camille Bulcke, *Ramakatha Uthbavavum Valarchayum*, Thrissur: Kerala Sahitya Akademi, 1999, p. 275.
120 *Bulletin Ecole Francaise Extreme Orient*, Vol. 17, p. 101.
121 G.P. Kanor, 'The Ramayana in Burma', *Journal Burma Research Society*, Vol. XV, p. 80; K.B. Iyyer, Yamapve Triveni, Vol. XIV, p. 239.
122 Lalan Prasad Vyas (ed.), *The Ramayana Global View*, quoted in R. Prasannan, *Bhashaposhini*, September 1995, p. 10.
123 Fernau Hall, 'Gagaku and Bugaku', Delhi: Sangeet Natak Akademi, 1971.
124 *Journal of Oriental Research*, Vol. 6, pp. 117–148.
125 C.K. Moosath, *Ramakatha—Malayalathil*, Kerala Sahitya Akademi, 1989, p. 8.
126 English translation of the Chinese Ramayana, Saraswathivihar Granthamala-8, 1938.
127 Dineṣa-Chandra Sena, *The Bengali Ramayanas*, p. 7.
128 Monier Williams, *Indian Wisdom*, p. 316.
129 J.T. Wheeler, *The History of India* (Part 2), p. 74.
130 Dineṣa-Chandra Sena, *The Bengali Ramayanas*, p. 7.

131 A. Weber, *On the Ramayana*, p. 11.
132 Ibid.
133 A.B. Keith, *Sanskrit Literature*, p. 43.
134 M. Winternitz, *History of Indian Literature*, Part 1, p. 497.
135 Paumacharitham, Bhaganagaram Version of H. Jacobi, 1914.
136 Sisir Kumar Das, *A History of Indian Literature, 500-1399: From the Courtly to the Popular*, Delhi: Sahitya Akademi, 2005, p. 122.
137 B. Surenda Rao, 'Pala Ramayanangal', *Bashaposhini*, No. 5, October 2003.
138 H. Jacobi, Encyclopedia of Religion and Ethics, Part 7.
139 Paumacharitham (canto 15–18), quoted in Camille Bulcke, *Ramakatha Uthbavavum Valarchayum*, 1971.
140 Camille Bulcke, *Ramakatha Uthbavavum Valarchayum*, 1971, p. 87.
141 Ibid., pp. 92, 93
142 Nathuran Premi, *Jaina Sahitya Aur Ithihas*, p. 183.
143 Quran, 10:47.
144 Quran, 35:7.
145 Quran, 35:24.
146 Quran, 4:164.
147 Sri Sri Ravishankar, *Hinduism, Islam: The Common Thread*, Vyakti Vikas Kendra - India publication division, 2002, pp. 5, 6, 7.
148 Ibid., p. 12.
149 Khuda Baksh, *Hinduism During the Mughal India of the 17th century*, Patna: Oriental Library, p. 185; Cited in Anand, 'Vettakkaranum Virunnukaaranum', p. 30.
150 Prof. Balarama Panicker, Thoolika Chalanangal (Part 2), p. 39.
151 M. Venkata Ratnam, *Rama, The Greatest Pharaoh of Egypt*, p. 73.
152 Kavitha Balakrishnan, Ramayanavum Kalacharithravum, *Navamalayali*, 4 September 2019.
153 Camille Bulcke, *Ramakatha Uthbavavum Valarchayum*, p. 285.
154 Ibid., p. 267.

155 Ibid., p. 267.
156 Anwar Ibrahim/A. Rasheedudhin, Interview, *Madhyamam Daily*, 11 April 2005 (Malayalam).
157 N.V. Krishna Warrier, Kumkumum Varika, 17 October 1982.
158 Juan R. Francisco, 'Maharadia Lawana', *Asian Studies*, Vol. 3, No. 2, pp. 186–249.
159 *Kambaramayanam palakandam, Arruppatalam, Sri Kambaramayanam palakandam*, ed. Vai. Mu. Kopalakirusnamacaryar Kampeni, Chennai, 1964. [Vasudha Narayanan, 'The Ramayana and its Muslim Interpreters', in *Questioning Ramayanas: A South Asian Tradition*, Paula Richman (ed.), p. 269.]
160 *Cirappuranam, villattattu kantam, Nattu patalam*, 12 [Vasudha Narayanan, 'The Ramayana and its Muslim Interpreters', in *Questioning Ramayanas: A South Asian Tradition*, Paula Richman (ed.), p. 270.]
161 John Richardson Freeman, 'Marriage Offers: Mappila Ramayana of Hassankutty ("The Mad")', in *Ramayana Stories in Modern South India: An Anthology*, Paula Richman (ed.), Bloomington: Indiana University Press, 2008.
162 The marriage contract in Islamism.
163 C.N. Ahmed Maulavi and K.K. Mohammed Adbul Karim, *Mahathaya Mappila Sahityaparamparyam*, Azad Bookstall, 1978, p. 193.
164 Ouli: Arabic for saint.
165 /r/→/l/ substitution (Rhotacism); Ramayana becomes Lamayana, Ravana becomes Lamana, Rama becomes Lama.
166 Last month in the Malayalam Calendar. (July–August). The Ramayana is recited in households during this time.
167 Refers to the Azaan, where the muezzin plugs his ears with his fingers during his call to prayer.
168 Nikah: marriage contract.
169 Due to his three wives being barren, Dasaratha offers a special yajna for having sons (Putrakameshti), after which the wives who drank the payasam would bear children.
170 One of the wives drank the payasam twice, and bore two sons.
171 Refers to Shiva.

172 Refers to Sita; the old practice of child marriage is being alluded to.
173 Parashurama, who was a devotee of Shiva, confronted Rama after the Sita swayamvar, for breaking the bow of Shiva.
174 Manthara, the hump-backed maid of Kaikeyi. She convinced Kaikeyi to persuade King Dasharatha to crown her son Bharatha as king instead of Rama.
175 /b/→/v/ substitution (Rhotacism); Baratha becomes Varatha
176 Derived from Bibi (Arabic), respectful title for a woman; lady.
177 Umma: term used for Amma (mother) by Muslims in Kerala (there's an /a/→/u/ umlaut here).
178 Probably because Shurpanakha is depicted as a demoness or she-devil.
179 *Neolamarckia cadamba*. Radha and Krishna are supposed to have conducted their love-play in the hospitable and sweet-scented shade of the kadamba tree.
180 *Magnolia champaca*.
181 Referring affectionately to Sita.
182 Hanuman.
183 Acharya Narendra Bhushan, *Ayodhyayile Sreeraman*, Rainbow Book Publications, 2004, p. 109.
184 O.M. Karuvarakundu/Azeez Tharuvana, Interview, *Pacchakuthira Masika*, September 2018.
185 Kamel Ibnu Ibrahim Kilani was born to a well-known engineer in Cairo in 1897. He memorised the Quran at a young age, and after obtaining his BA, showed his talent in English, Arabic and French. Kilani, who was an alumni of the Al Azhar University, excelled in Arabic syntax (nahw), morphology (sarf) and logic (mantiq). He was an official in the Ministry of Awqaf from 1922 to 1954, and at the same time was the editor of *El-Ragaa* newspaper. He also was the chairman of Modern Actors' Club and secretary of the Arabic Liteature Society.
186 M.N. Karaserry, 'Arabiyile Ramayanam', *Mathrubhumi*, 03 October 2010.
187 *Journal of the Bihar and Orissa Research Society*, Vol. 11, pp. 41–53.

188 Edward Tuite Dalton, *Descriptive Ethnology of Bengal*, Calcutta: Office Of The Superintendent Of Government Printing, 1872, p. 140.
189 S.C. Roy, *The Oraons of Chota Nagpur*, Ranchi: Crown Publications, 1925.
190 Walter G. Griffiths, *The Kol Tribe of Central India*, Calcutta: Royal Asiatic Society of Bengal, 1946.
191 Camille Bulcke, *Ramakatha Uthbavavum Valarchayum*, Thrissur: Kerala Sahitya Akademi, 1999, p. 496.
192 Gopal Lal Varma, *Santhali Nadodippattukalil Sreeraman*, Delhi, 1960, pp. 43–45.
193 Verrier Elwin, *Myths of Middle India*, London: Oxford University Press, 1949, p. 129.
194 Saratchandra Mitra, 'On the Karuna Dharma Festival of North Bihar and its Munda Analogues', *Journal of the Department of Letters*, Vol. 4, p. 303.
195 Sarat Chandra Roy, *The Birhors: A little-known Jungle Tribe of Chota Nagpur*, Ranchi: Man in India Office, 1925.
196 Shamrao Hivale, *The Pardhans of the Upper Narbada Valley*, London: Oxford University Press, 1946.
197 Stephen Fuchs, *The Gond and Bhumia of Eastern Mandla*, Asia Publishing House, 1960, pp. 421–422.
198 'Among the Primitive Tribes', *Bulletin of the Tribal Research Institute*, Chhindwara, Vol. 1, No. 2.
199 *Bharathiya Sahityam*, Vol. 3, p. 94, cited in Camille Bulcke, *Ramakatha Uthbavavum Valarchayum*, p. 591.
200 Verrier Elwin, *Myths of the North-East Frontier of India*, 1958, pp. 131–132.
201 C.P. Rajan (Attapady), 'Sreerama Kushalava Natakam', *Gothrasmriti Smaranika*, Kerala Saksharatha Samithi, pp. 237–328.
202 B. Surenda Rao, 'Pala Ramayanangal', *Bashaposhini*, No. 5, October 2003.
203 Velcheru Narayana Rao, 'A Ramayana of Their Own: Women's Oral Tradition in Telugu', *Many Ramayanas: The Diversity of a Narrative Tradition in South Asia*, Paula Richman (ed.), Berkeley: University of California Press, 1991.

204 B. Surenda Rao, 'Pala Ramayanangal', *Bashaposhini*, No. 5, October 2003.
205 Velcheru Narayana Rao, 'A Ramayana of Their Own: Women's Oral Tradition in Telugu', *Many Ramayanas: The Diversity of a Narrative Tradition in South Asia*, Paula Richman (ed.), Berkeley: University of California Press, 1991.
206 Nabaneeta Dev Sen, 'A Women's Retelling of the Rama-Tale', *Narrative: A Seminar*, Amiyadev (ed.), Delhi: Sahitya Akademi, 1994.
207 Bala Kanda, cantos 1–4.
208 Cantos 16 and 47.
209 In another part of the *Dakshinatya Ramayana* (Uttara Kanda-111,11), it is mentioned that Valmiki is the son of Prachethas (Gujarathi Printing Press, Mumbai, Southern Impression).
210 *Dakshinatya Ramayana*, 'Uttarakanda', canto 96, verse 20.
211 Camille Bulcke, *Ramakatha Uthbavavum Valarchayum*.
212 *Oriya Mahabharatha*, 'Sabha Parvam', Cuttack: Radharaamana Book Stall, 1954, p. 250.
213 *Tribes and Castes*, Part—I, pp. 262–263
214 B. Surenda Rao, 'Pala Ramayanangal', *Bashaposhini*, No. 5, October 2003.
215 William Crooke, *Tribes and Castes of the North Western India*, Vol. 1, 1896, pp. 263, 268.
216 Vettam Mani, *Puranik Encylopedia*, Kottayam: Current Books, 1993, p. 1037.
217 'Das Ramayana', cited in Camille Bulcke, *Ramakatha Uthbavavum Valarchayum*, Thrissur: Kerala Sahitya Akademi, 1999, p. 101.
218 Vettam Mani, *Laghu Purana Nikhandu*, Kottayam: National Book Stall, 1999, p. 520.
219 Ibid., p. 14.
220 Ibid., p. 33.
221 M.P. Veerendra Kumar, 'Puranakathakalude Niravil: Hanuman Ghatti', *Mathrubhoomi Weekly*, January 2006, 1–7.
222 A.V. Schlegel, 'Date of the Ramayana', *German Oriental Journal*, Vol. 3, p. 379.

223 G. Gorresio, 'Part 10, Introduction', in *Rāmāyaṇa, poema indiano di Valmici*, Paris: Stamperia Reale, 1843–1870.
224 C.V. Vaidya, *The Riddle of the Ramayana*, Asiatic Society, 1955.
225 A.B. Keith, 'The Date of the Ramayana', *Journal of Royal Asiatic Society*, 1915
226 Camille Bulcke, *Ramakatha Uthbavavum Valarchayum*, p 53, Kerala Sahitya Akademi, 1999.
227 Hermann Jacobi, *Das Ramayana*, 1893
228 A.V. Schlegel, *Valmiki Ramayana*, Bonn, 1829
229 G. Gorresio, *Rāmāyaṇa, poema indiano di Valmici*. Paris: Stamperia Reale. 1843–1870.
230 *Kamba Ramayana*, trans. Padma Sundaram, Delhi: Penguin, 2002.
231 Romila Thapar, 'The Ramayana Syndrome', Seminar 353, January 1989; *The Past As Present: Forging Contemporary Identities Through History*, Delhi: Aleph Book Company, 2014.
232 Acharya Narendra Bhooshan, *Sri Rama of Ayodhya*, p. 102.
233 Mikhail Bakhtin, *Problems of Dostoevsky's Poetics*, University of Minnesota Press, 1984.

GLOSSARY

Adivasi: (Literally, 'original dweller') This is a collective term for the indigenous tribes of India. Adivasis are considered to be the original inhabitants of the Indian subcontinent, who sought refuge in the hills and forests during various invasions. Often alienated from the mainstream society and denied education, they live as hunters and foragers in the forests. After 1950, they are referred to as Scheduled Tribes (see also, *Scheduled Tribes*).

***Adivasi deities* (Kerala)**: The deities worshipped by the Adivasis are different from Hindu deities. The Adivasis engage in animism and worship their forefathers, forest fairies and so on. Each tribe and community has different deities. Recently, there have been attempts to link the Adivasi deities to the Hindu deities, based on certain similarities in their descriptions or legends.

Deities of the Adiyas: Sidhappa, Nanchappa, Mathappadeivam, Malakkari, Mallappan, Pookkari, Magatheyyam, Tirunelli Jogiyachan, Karichathan, Chikkamma, Valuramma.

Deities of the Kurichyas: Malakkari, Bhagavathy (Pothi), Muthachi (Pegithi) and Muthappan.

Deities of the Wayanad Chettis: Athirukalan, Arupuli, Kandanpuli, Bammadan, Kaikolan, Thampiratti.

Adiyas: (singular Adiyan. Literally, 'slave') A prominent tribal sect in Wayanad. Until 1977 when it was banned by law, the landlords in Wayanad used to sell and buy the Adiyas as slaves during the annual festival at Valliyoorkavu. The tribe speaks a dialect which is a mixture of Kannada and Malayalam. It has no alphabet. The Adiyas have a rich lore of folk songs, which are sung as ritual and as entertainment. These songs contain allusions to a glorious past and their degradation after becoming slaves. The songs have references to a past without any racial, religious or ethnic exploitation.

Ashram: A hermitage or monastery in the forest inhabited by ascetics for meditation.

Asura: In Indian mythology, a class of divine or semi-divine beings, demigods or super-humans with good or bad qualities. They are often described in opposition to the devas or Suras (see also, *Deva* and *Rakshasa*).

Bhadrakali: A Hindu Goddess worshipped especially in Kerala. Bhadrakali is the benevolent form of Mahakali (Goddess of destruction), who protects the good. Bhadrakali's slaying of the demon Darika to liberate the universe from evil is believed to have taken place in Madayi, Kannur district, Kerala. Bhadrakali is worshipped as the daughter of Lord Shiva, from whose third eye she sprung to defeat the demon. (Note the similarity with Malakkari.) She is considered as the protector of women.

Bhagavathy (Also Bhagwati): Honorific title for female deities in Kerala. Male deities are referred to as Bhagavan/Bhagwan (see also, *Deva*).

Brahmins: One of the four social classes (Varnas) in Hinduism, based on occupation. The highest in the hierarchy of classes, the Brahmins were Vedic scholars, priests, teachers and Ayurvedic physicians (see also, *Nambuthiri, Varnas*).

Caste System (Jathi): Division of specific communities based on occupation. Endogamy (marrying within the same group), hereditary occupation, specific traditions and rituals, social hierarchy and social inclusion (or exclusion) are the major features of castes. Castes were also classified as 'upper'/'higher' and 'lower' castes based on hierarchy. The Brahmins and the Kshatriyas were at the top, and castes that performed hard labour were at the bottom of the rung. The lower castes were forbidden to interact with the upper castes, an offence which could result in death (see also, *Purity and Pollution*).

Dalit: (Literally, 'broken') The unofficial term for communities outside the traditional Hindu caste hierarchy. The term was popularised by Dr B.R. Ambedkar, social reformer and architect of the Constitution of India (and a Dalit as well), who included all subjugated people irrespective of their caste into the definition (see also, *Harijan* and *Scheduled Castes*).

Dasaratha: (Literally, 'ten chariots') In Ramayana, the king of Kosala and the father of Rama. His kingdom's capital was known as Ayodhya. He had three wives: Kausalya, Kaikeyi and Sumitra. He acquired the name Dasaratha as his chariot could move in all ten directions.

Deva: (Literally, 'divine') In Hinduism, male deities are called devas, and female deities are called devis. In Indian mythology, benevolent supernatural beings are called devas or suras. They represent the forces of nature, specialised knowledge, creative energy, magical powers or moral values. Some examples are: Brahma (creator), Vishnu (preserver), Shiva (destroyer), Varuna (rain), Agni (fire), Yama (death), Indra (thunder), Surya (sun), Chandra (moon). They are often described in opposition to the asuras; the devas represent the good, and the asuras the bad (see also, *Asuras* and *Rakshasas*).

Devaswom: (Literally, 'belonging to God') Socio-religious trusts in Kerala that oversee Hindu temples and their assets, and ensure their smooth operation in accordance with traditional rituals and customs. The properties of each temple are deemed to be the personal property of the presiding deity of the temple, and are managed through a body of trustees that comprise members nominated by both the government and the Hindu community.

Edanadan and Mandadan Chettis: A sub-group of the Wayanadan Chettis. The Chetti community has around eighteen and a half sub-groups. The Edanadan and Mandadan Chettis, numbering lesser than 1,000, make up only a tiny fraction of the Chetti population. (The other 'half sub-group' are the Wayanadan Chettis.) The Edanadan and Mandadan Chettis are also heavily backward in terms of education and economic status. Their belief systems are the same as the Wayanadan Chettis (see also, *Wayanadan Chettis*).

Ghaddika: The practice of sorcery and the dance of the Adiyas. This is performed in order to ward off diseases, death and danger. As the Adiyas believe that these misfortunes happen due to the scourge of the evil goddesses, the Ghaddika is a form of offering or worship to get rid of these afflictions. There are three kinds of Ghaddika—Cheriya (Small) Ghaddika, Pooja Ghaddika and Naattu (Village) Ghaddika. Cheriya Ghaddika is performed in household settings, with only the family members participating. Pooja Ghaddika is in a larger setting, with relatives participating, and Naattu Ghaddika is where the whole village takes part in the ceremony to ward off evil.

Harijan: (Literally, 'children of God') A term popularised by Mahatma Gandhi to refer to Dalits. However, many Dalits, including Dr B.R. Ambedkar, found the term patronising and even derogatory, as it tended to view them inside the framework of Hinduism, rather than as an independent community. This term is used usually by members of the upper castes to refer to the Dalits (see also, *Dalit* and *Schedule Caste*s).

Indrajith: The eldest son of Ravana, also called Meghanada. He was named Meghanada (lord of the skies) after his birth, because his birth cry sounded like thunder. During the battle between the devas and Ravana, Indra (God of thunder, and king of the heavens) accompanied by all other devas captured Ravana. To rescue his father, Meghanada attacked Indra and his elephant Airavata, and defeated all the devas, including Indra. Thus he was named Indrajith (conqueror of Indra). Meghanada is considered the fiercest warrior in Ravana's army after Ravana himself.

Irulas: (Literally, 'dark') An Adivasi tribe in the Palakkad district of Kerala. The Irulas are the second largest Adivasi tribe in Kerala, and are found mostly in the Attapadi region. The name likely refers to their dark skin. The language they speak is also called Irula. Their chiefs are called Oorumooppan, Vandari, Kuruthala and Mannookkaran. They worship the tiger as their God. There are tribes very similar to the Irulas living in the Nilgiri hills and in the regions of Coimbatore. The Irulas are expert catchers of snakes and rodents, and also honey-gatherers.

Janaka: In Ramayana, king of Videha and the foster father of Sita. King Janaka was intensely spiritual and was detached from the material world. His adopted daughter Sita is also called Janaki mata.

Jatayu: In Ramayana, the younger son of Aruṇa and Shyeni, the brother of Sampati and a friend of Dasaratha, Rama's father. He is in the form of a vulture. Jatayu tried to rescue Sita while she was being carried off to Lanka by Ravana. However, as he was very old, he could not withstand Ravana, who clipped his wings. Jayatu fell onto the rocks in Chadayamangalam. Rama and Lakshmana, while on the search for Sita, came across the dying Jatayu, who informed them of Sita's whereabouts. Rama performed his funeral rites.

Kolkali: Also called Kambadikali, this is a folk art of the Malabar region of Kerala. Kolkali is performed by the Mandadan Chetti, Wayanad Chetti, Kurumas and the Kurichyas as entertainment. The dance is performed under the guidance of a 'guru'. It begins only after an offering or tribute (gurudakshina) is given to the guru. The dancers move in a circle around a lamp, striking small sticks and keeping rhythm with special steps. The circle expands and contracts as the dance progresses. The accompanying music gradually rises in pitch and the dance reaches its climax. The songs narrate episodes from the Puranas. Kolkali has its origins in Kalarippayattu, a martial art form of Kerala.

Kurichyas: A tribe in the Wayanad and Kannur districts of Kerala. They are also called the Malai (Hill) Brahmins. They are expert archers, and when a man dies, an arrow is buried with the body. The Kurichyas are heirs to a valiant tradition of waging sustained wars alongside Pazhassi Raja against the domination of the British. They speak a singsong type of Malayalam. They maintain untouchability with the other communities except the Brahmins. Food cooked by others is prohibited to them. Their main livelihoods are farming and hunting. There is a mooppan (elder) called 'Pittan' in each Kurichya settlement. The Kurichya colonies are known as mittam. The Kurichyas worship gods such as Malakkari, Bhagavathy (Pothi), Muthachi (Pegithi) and Muthappan. Bow and arrows are the weapons of the God Malakkari. Recently, the Kurichyas have started worshipping the Hindu gods.

Kurumas (Mullukurumas and Uralikurumas): This is the oldest tribal sect in Wayanad. There are two sects of the Kurumas—the Mullukurumas and the Vettakurumas (Uralikurumas). Until

2002, these were considered a single tribe. They are found mostly in the regions of Bathery, Meenangadi, Poothadi, Mullan Kolli, Pulpally and Noolpuzha. Amongst the Adivasi tribes of Wayanad, the Kurumas are equivalent in almost all respects, including education, economic and social status, with the Kurichyas. Like the Kurichyas, they are expert archers. They speak a dialect that is a mixture of Kannada and ancient Malayalam. They live in groups, and their main occupation is farming. Many of them have their own land. Their settlements are generally very close to their farms. They practice untouchability with the other communities. Along with the Kurichyas, the Kurumas were also actively involved in the war of Pazhassi Raja against the British. They believe that they are the descendants of the Kuruma dynasty that once ruled Wayanad. Though they have their own gods, they go to Hindu temples. They have recently taken to the practice of worshipping Hindu gods.

Lakshmana Rekha: In Ramayana, a magical perimeter line drawn by Lakshmana to protect Sita, while he went searching for Rama. Rama had gone in chase of a golden deer (which was actually the rakshasa Maricha in disguise), and had not returned for a long time. Sita ordered Lakshmana to leave in search of his brother. He did so on the condition that Sita would not cross the protective line he drew. Anybody other than Rama, Sita and himself attempting to cross the line would be burnt by flames erupting from the line. Once Lakshmana left in search of Rama, Ravana came in the form of a mendicant and asked Sita for alms. Not expecting a trick, she unsuspectingly crossed the Lakshmana rekha to give alms and Ravana kidnapped her.

Lakshmana: In Ramayana, the younger brother of Rama, and the son of Dasaratha with Sumitra. He is also the husband of Urmila, Sita's sister. Lakshmana joined Rama and Sita in their exile for fourteen years.

Mahabali (also Maveli/Mavothi): An Asura king and the grandson of Prahlada. In Kerala, Mahabali is considered to be the noblest and most prosperous ruler, who transformed his kingdom into a heaven-like place. His legend is a major part of the annual Onam festival in the state of Kerala. In the days of his rule, all people lived as one. There was no cheating or deceit. Everyone lived contented lives. The gods, who were envious of the prosperous rule of Mahabali, sought the help of Vishnu. While Mahabali was performing the Viswajith yajna, to gain the power to go to heaven and enjoy the pleasures there, Vishnu took on the form of Vamana, a dwarf Brahmin boy. He asked for three paces of land. As soon as Mahabali agreed, Vamana began to grow to immense proportions. With his first footstep, he covered the heavens. With his second footstep, he covered the earth. Vamana then asked Mahabali where his third footstep should be placed, and Mahabali lowered his head and offered it. When Vamana placed his final footstep onto Mahabali's head, he pushed Mahabali into the netherworld. Mahabali's final request that he be allowed to visit his subjects once a year was granted by Vishnu. Therefore, it is believed that on the Thriruvonam day during the festival of Onam, Mahabali visits his subjects.

Malabar Migrations: Refers to the large-scale migration of Syrian Christians from southern Kerala to Malabar in the nineteenth and twentieth centuries. When the Christians of central Travancore, who lived on agriculture, felt the scarcity of land for farming, they first migrated to places in the north-eastern hilly regions, like Arakkulam, Moolamattam, Velliamattam, Udambannoor, Peerumedu, Mundakkayam, Kattappana and Kumali. During the Second World War, food scarcity intensified in Kerala. The first batch of migrants to Malabar went in search of land for paddy cultivation. They took land on lease and alongside rice they cultivated tapioca, pepper, cocoanut and areca nut. Migration to Malabar began in the early 1900s. The pace of migration slowed down in the 1930s due to death and disease. It picked up momentum in the mid-1940s, and by the 1960s, around five lakh people had migrated to Malabar from the southern regions of Kerala. This resulted in a major change in the demography of Malabar. The Christian population, which had been mostly insignificant, grew to a substantial number.

Mali: A fierce female deity with blood dripping from her tongue. Mali appears as the agent of the gods who divided the men into castes. The castes got their names according their reactions to the fierce

Mali. She appears again as the agent of Pakkathappan, to imprison the first parents of the Adiyas and keep them as Pakkathappan's slaves. Once, Melorachan and Keeyorithi, the first parents of the Adiyas, were running far away into the unknown. When they reached the place called Undayangadi near Mananthavady, they decided to take rest. At this moment, Mali came there with her bloody tongue out and her dark eyes bulging. She came in anger, her dark tresses hanging loose. The sudden apparition shocked the duo. They cried aloud and tried to run away. They tried to hide among the trees, stones and bushes. Wherever they went, Mali followed them and drove them out. And she drove them to Pakkathappan's castle. Pakkathappan was pleased with Mali. He told her, 'Follow the Adiyas everywhere and I will give you nine garlands. I will give you tender coconuts to drink. I will give you hens to be killed and eaten. You should go wherever they go and move wherever they move. In the river and in the lakes, into the whirlpool you should follow them. Follow them even amidst the screw pine bushes. Like the little mouse which says "chi, chi", you should frighten them.' Thus saying, Pakkathappan again put Melorachan in charge of the cattle and Keeyorithi in charge of the kitchen.

Manram: A clan of Adiya families linked by blood kinship. The Adiyas of Wayanad are known by their clans. They live as separate manrams. The following are the main clans: Thurunelli Manram, Vadakku Manram, Katchala Manram, Puthur Manram, Kalikku Manram, Kalakkod Manram, Veleppu Manram, Chaintha Manram, Nalappa Manram, Putharu Manram, Ulankudi Manram, Muthukutti Manram and Momatta Manram. It is believed that among these, Thirunelly Manram, Vadakku Manram and Pootharu Manram are of higher status. The tribal elders (mooppans) belong to these manrams. The members of the Nalappa and Kamamatta Manrams are believed to be of lower status. These people do the work of burying the dead, and are known as Kanaladikal. In addition to the mooppans, there are several chemmams, who reside over the rituals connected to birth, marriage and death. The chemmams also function as priests, magicians and singers. The mooppan has the ultimate authority.

Those who disregard the views and disobey the decisions of the mooppan are ostracised. The Adiya community is hierarchically structured as the mooppan, chemmakaran, kanaladi, family and individual. Each clan of the Adiyas has its own God.

Mappilapattu (also Mappila songs): A Muslim folk-song genre sung by the Mappila Muslims of the Malabar region in Kerala. The lyrics are set to a melodic framework called an ishal. The language of these songs is Arabi Malayalam with words from Persian, Hindustani and Tamil also used. Mappilapattus are sung during marriages, birth and death. There are different types of Mappilapattu songs based on themes such as love, faith, satire and heroic acts. The Malappattu are songs in praise of pious personalities, Urudi are songs narrating the events of battles and Khessukal are romantic ballads. The earliest recorded text of a Mappilapattu is the *Muhyidheen Mala*, written in 1607 by Khasi Muhammed of Kozhikode about the Sufi saint Muhyidheen Abdul Khader Gilani.

Maramayappattu: Song sung by the Kurichyas about the Malakkari deity. The song is about how Malakkari took on the role of the saviour of the tribe. This is a derivation of the Mahabali story (see also, *Mahabali*).

Munootans: A community that performs the ritual dance form of Thira. They have an extensive repertoire of songs. There are a lot of sorcerers/magicians (shamans) in this community. They perform the Thira dance, dressing up as the deities Uchita, Karuval, Vasoori, Nagakaali, Thalachil, Kariyathan, Elavalli, Karivalli, Malakkari, Marppulian, Veerabhadra, Poothadi and so on.

Nambuthiris (also Nambudiri, Namboodiri, Nampoothiri): Brahmins of Kerala. They owned significant areas of land in the region of Malabar. The custom of primogeniture, where only the eldest son could marry a Nambuthiri woman and inherit the family assets, was followed very strictly. The other sons had a kind of concubinal relationship (sambandam) with women of other castes, especially the Nairs.

Pakkatheyyam/Pakkathappan: Pakkam is a place near Pulpally in Wayanad. The Adiyas believe that Pakkathappan lived here. (Pakkathappan means the Lord of Pakkam.) Currently, there is a temple in the custody of the Nair community. Pakkam Daivam is a God in the Vaishnava tradition. The members of the Kalanadi sect even today have a ritual dance in which the form of Pakkam is presented. The songs of the Adiyas mention that their God was born in the Chenthamarappalkadal, the ocean of lotus milk. Pakkatheyyam/Pakkthappan occupies a prominent place in the beliefs and songs of the Adiyas. He is mentioned in the stories relating to the slavery of the Adiyas. Melorachan and Keeyorithi, the first parents of the Adiyas, started their journey from the Karippoorru Kotta (castle) in the Moodal country. They were not travelling in search of fruits or game but running away in search of freedom. And they reached a place called Pakkam in Wayanad. At Pakkam lived the Pakkathappan. This Lord caught hold of them using Mali and made them his slaves. Melorachan was assigned the cattle and Keeyorithi the kitchen (see also, *Mali*).

Paniyas: The largest tribal sect in Kerala. According to the 1991 census, their number is 67,948. Most of them live in Wayanad. They are also found in the districts of Kozhikode, Kannur and Malappuram. Among the tribals of Kerala, the Paniyas are the poorest, most illiterate and most backward. Their dialect is a mixture of Tamil and Tulu. The physical features of Paniyas resemble those of black Africans. Until quite recently, the landlords had the right to buy, sell and mortgage the Paniyas. Until the close of 1970, the landlords enjoyed the right of engaging them in work for one year by giving them a slave allowance called Nippupanam. The records of Thukkidi Munsif show that Subharaya Pattar mortgaged a Paniyan by the name of Kaippadan for eight annas (fifty paise). This community, which has all along been denied all human rights and brutally oppressed, is today a victim of the policies of globalisation.

Pelappatu: A ritual song of the Adiyas. This song is about the origins of the Adiyas, and how they became slaves. It contains the story of Melorachan and Keeyorithi (the first parents of the Adiyas), how Mahabali (the ruler of the Adiyas) was tricked and killed, and how the Adiyas were enslaved with the help of the fierce Goddess Mali (see also, *Mahabali, Mali, Pakkatheyyam*).

Pooja (Puja): Worship; acts of devotion with fruit, flame and water offered to the deity.

Purity and Pollution: The 'upper' castes maintained a strict distance from other castes. Touching or even coming within a certain distance of the 'lower' castes was considered as polluting. In some cases, even the sight of a lower-caste person was considered polluting. Lower-caste people were to use separate paths and their houses were in places where they could not be seen. If a lower-caste person saw an approaching Brahmin or higher caste, they had to make a loud howling sound to warn them from getting near until they went away or climbed up a tree. In Kerala, the Pulayas were considered as the lowest caste, and even members of the other lower castes did not interact with them. The higher castes could kill a Pulaya if they came across them on the paths, even by accident. Robin Jeffrey, in *The Decline of Nayar Dominance: Society and Politics in Travancore 1847–1908,* quotes, '. . . a Nair can approach but not touch a Namboodiri Brahmin: a Ezhava must remain thirty-six paces off, and a Pulayan slave ninety-six steps distant.'

Putrakameshthi yajna: A sacrifice in order to beget sons. Payasam (a sweet dish) is prepared during this yajna, and given to the wife to eat. King Dasaratha held such a yagna. When the payasam was passed around, Kausalya ate half, Sumitra ate a quarter, and Kaikeyi ate some and passed the pot back to Sumitra, who consumed the kheer for a second time. Kausalya gave birth to Rama. Kaikeyi gave birth to Bharata. Sumitra, who had consumed the kheer twice, gave birth to Lakshmana and Shatrughna.

Rakshasa: (Literally, 'demon') In Hinduism, a malignant supernatural being, often considered a 'man-eater'. They are very often depicted as fierce, enormous, monstrous, with insatiable desires. In the Ramayana, Ravana, Shurpanakha and Tadaka are described as rakshasas (see also, *Deva* and *Asura*).

Rama: In Ramayana, son of Dasaratha with Kausalya; husband of Sita. He is the seventh avatar of Vishnu. Rama had three brothers: Lakshmana, Bharatha and Shatrughna. Kaikeyi, the mother of Bharatha, was the powerful warrior who had saved the life of King Dasaratha during a war. In return, she was granted two boons by him. After Rama was chosen to be crowned as king, Kaikeyi's mind was poisoned by Manthara, her maid. As one of her boons, Kaikeyi demanded that Bharatha be crowned king and Rama be sent to the forest for fourteen years. Rama went to the forest with his wife, Sita, and his brother Lakshmana. There, Sita was abducted by Ravana. Rama, with the help of Sugriva and Hanuman and their monkey army, freed Sita and slew Ravana. After fourteen years, Rama returned to Ayodhya and was crowned king.

Ravana: In Ramayana, king of Lanka, husband of Mandodari, and the father of Indrajith. Ravana is depicted and described as having ten heads. He was one of the most ardent devotees of Shiva, in addition to being a learned scholar of astrology and Siddha medicine, ruler and a maestro of the veena (a stringed instrument). Ravana was the eldest son of Sage Vishrava and the rakshasi Kaikeshi. He abducted Rama's wife, Sita, and carried her away to his kingdom of Lanka, where he held her as a prisoner in Ashoka Vatika, until Rama, with the help of the vanara (monkey) King Sugriva and his army of vanars, including Hanuman, attacked Ravana and slew him.

Rishi: In Hinduism, great sages who composed Vedic hymns and texts. They were also involved in intense meditation and had great magical powers (see also, *Saptarishis*).

Sampathi: In Ramayana, elder brother of Jatayu and the son of Aruṇa and Shyeni. He had the form of a vulture. Sampathi and Jatayu used to compete as to who could fly higher. Once, Jatayu flew so high that he was about to be burnt by the sun. Sampathi saved his brother by spreading his own wings and shielding Jatayu. Sampathi lost his wings in this incident. Later on, when Hanuman and his party, searching for Sita reached the end of the land, exhausted, with only the sea before them, Sampathi rejoiced at the sight of so much easy prey. At that time, one of Hanuman's party, Jambavan, lamented that the vulture Sampathi who was about to feed on them, was of the same kind as vulture Jatayu, who had defended Sita. On hearing Jatayu's name, Sampathi froze and revealed that he is Jatayu's brother, and also revealed to Hanuman's search party that Sita had been taken across the ocean to Lanka.

Saptamathas: (Literally, 'seven mothers') In Hinduism, a group of seven mother goddesses who are always depicted together. They are associated with the major gods as their energies (shaktis). Thus, Brahmani emerged from Brahma, Vaishnavi from Vishnu, Maheshvari from Shiva, Indrani from Indra, Kaumari from Skanda, Varahi from Varaha and Chamunda from Devi. They are described as the assistants of the Shakta Devi (Goddess) in her fight with demons. They are also called goddesses of the battlefield. They are depicted as being frightening and ferocious, as well as beautiful. They are described as living in trees, crossroads, caves and funeral grounds.

Saptarishis: (Literally, 'seven sages') In Hinduism, a list of seven primary sages who are mentioned in the Vedic texts. They are the sages Atri, Bharadvaja, Gautama, Jamadagni, Kashyapa, Vasistha and Vishwamitra.

Savarnas: The communities and castes included in the first three classes (varnas). They include the Brahmins, the Kshatriyas and the Vaishyas.

Scheduled Castes: Communities within the framework of the Hindu caste system who have historically faced deprivation, oppression and extreme social isolation in India on account of their perceived 'low status'. They were considered outside the Savarna system, and hence were forced into hard labour, such as disposal of animal carcasses, cleaning of excreta and other tasks deemed as 'unclean'. These communities were 'untouchables'. They were prohibited from living in areas frequented by the 'higher' castes, had to move away to a specific distance when a member of a higher caste came across their way, and were prohibited from taking water from water sources such as wells or ponds that were used by the other castes. The offenders were beaten, and often times, killed. They were frequently exploited and abused, forced to live as slaves and agricultural labourers with little to no wages, and the women were frequently subjected to sexual abuse, though they were 'untouchables'. They are also called Dalits and Harijans (see entries above).

Scheduled Tribes: In the Constitution of India, many Adivasi communities are listed as Scheduled Tribes, based on factors such as primitive traits, geographical isolation, distinct culture, shyness of contact with others communities and economic backwardness, as targets for social and economic development. Since the framing of the Constitution, the Adivasis of India have been known officially as Scheduled Tribes.

Shurpanakha: In Ramayana, sister of Ravana. The name literally means 'with fingernails like winnowing fans'. Valmiki describes her as ugly, old and pot-bellied. However, Kampar describes her as being attractive. Shurpanakha secretly married Vidyutjihva, the prince of the Kalkeya Danava clan, who were the enemies of Ravana. Later, in a fight, Ravana killed Vidyutjihva. Seeing his sister's grief, Ravana asked her to search for another husband, and that he would agree to her match. On coming across Rama in the forests, she was enamoured of him. But he rejected her. She tried her luck with Lakshmana, but he too refused her. Frustrated, she tried to attack Sita, but Lakshmana cut off her nose and breasts. Shurpanakha complained to her brother Khara, who tried to attack Rama with his army but was killed. She then went to Ravana to complain and also told him that Sita is beautiful. In retaliation for Shurpanakha's disgrace and humiliation, Ravana abducted Sita.

Sita: In Ramayana, wife of Rama. Sita was the daughter of Goddess Bhumi (Earth), and was brought up by King Janaka. King Janaka proclaimed that Sita would be wed to the man who could lift and string he Shiva's bow (Shiva Dhanush, a very heavy bow gifted by Shiva), in what was called the Sita swayamvara (a practice where the girl chose her groom from a list of suitors after a test). Sita married Rama, the only one who not only lifted and strung the bow, but also broke it. During Rama's exile, Sita accompanied him and his younger brother Lakshmana to the Dandaka forest. There, she was abducted by Ravana, the king of Lanka. She was held hostage in Ashoka Vatika in Lanka until she was rescued by Rama, who slew Ravana. After the war, Rama made Sita undergo an agni pariksha (a test by fire), to prove her purity. Unsure of her purity, Rama exiled a pregnant Sita to the forest again, where she gave birth to Lava and Kusha in the ashram of Valmiki. After her sons were united with Rama, Sita pleaded that her humiliation might end and south refuge in the arms of her mother, Bhumi (earth). The earth opened up, and Sita disappeared within.

Slavery of the Tribals: Tribal groups like the Adiyas and Paniyas were treated as slaves by the landlords. In the beginning, this was perennial slavery, which meant that one slave had to be with one landlord for life. Later, the Valliyoorkavu system began be followed, where the term of one slave's life under a master was from one festival to the next festival at Valliyoorkavu. The festival lasted for fourteen days. During that period, the Paniyas and Adiyas of Wayanad visited the temple. Each landlord selected a group of Paniyas and Adiyas, much like selecting cattle, on the condition that they do slave work under him for one year, starting with that year's festival and ending with the next year's. The contract was signed in front of the Goddess Vallooramma. A certain amount was given as slave allowance. Vallooramma (Goddess of Valliyoor) was much feared by the tribals. They believed that the Goddess causes as well as removes illnesses. Hence, they believed that it was their sacred duty to honour the contract made in the presence of the Goddess. A slave would be allowed to put up his hut near the field of the landlord. In 1977, the government of Kerala abolished this through legislation.

Tharavadu: Malayalam word for ancestral home, usually used as the common house for the joint family system practised by Nairs, Ambalavasis, Syrian Christians and Namboothris of Kerala.

Theyyam: (Literally, 'God') A ritual dance form of worship, prevalent in the north Malabar region of Kerala. Each deity is worshipped in a different manner. The Malakkari Theyyam is performed in worship of Malakkari by the Kurichyas and the Adiyas. The Kurichyas wear an elaborate costume, whereas the Adiyas wear a much simpler costume. The image of the deity is drawn on the body using rice flour, and a white headdress is worn. Silk is worn on the forehead, and anklets on the legs. Since each clan has a different deity, there are around 400 different types of Theyyam. The Theyyam of the Kurichyas is performed by the dancers of other communities. The Anjootan Theyyam is performed in the worship of Kannavath Moothappan. Two of the important Theyyams that are relevant to this current study are the Manavalan and Manavatti Theyyams. Manavalan (meaning bridegroom) Theyyam and Manavatti (meaning bride) Theyyams are performed at the Sree Madiyan

Koolom temple near Kanhangad in the Kasaragod district of Kerala and at Srirama Vilyakazhakam. The deities worshipped in this Theyyam are modelled on the characters of Rama and Sita. These Theyyams are staged by people of the Vannan (washermen) caste. Parts of the Ramayana are sung during the ritual dances.

Thira: A ritual folk-dance form of northern Kerala, where the dancers dress up as goddesses. The word 'Thira' means vision of God. Dr Hermann Gundert defined it as an 'offering'. Thus, it can be considered as an offering to God in the form of a dance.

Thiyyas: A Hindu community in north Malabar. The Thiyyas are a forward caste, and placed next to Nairs in the hierarchy. They were also permitted to carry weapons. They take pride in their casteist superiority and the glory of their ancestral families. The Chekavars of Malabar also belong to this community. They are also firm devotees of the ritual dance-worship form of Theyyam. They are also known as Mannanars, Emprans, Gurukkals, Panikkars and Karanavars.

Vadakkan Pattu (also Vadakkan Pattukal/ Ballads of North Malabar / Songs of the North): A collection of Malayalam ballads of medieval origin. The songs present the exploits of heroes and heroines such as Aromal Chekavar, Thacholi Othenan and Unniyarcha who belong to two families: the Puthooram family and the Thacholi manikkoth family, whose members are warriors and martial artists. They are in the form of folk songs, and were spread by the Panans, a nomadic singing community. They existed in oral form for centuries and were handed down through generations. The texts of these songs can be traced back to the sixteenth century.

Vaishnava Tradition: A major Hindu denomination, which considers Vishnu as the Supreme Being. The Vaishnavite tradition is known for the loving devotion of an avatar of Vishnu. Rama is an avatar of Vishnu, and is taken as the model of the 'ideal king', based on the principles of dharma, morality and ethics. The Mahabharata and the Ramayana showcase the Vaishnava philosophy and culture through legends and dialogues.

Varnas: (Literally, 'classes' or 'colours') Social classes in India categorised into occupations, based on Hindu texts (especially the *Manusmriti*). There are four classes in the Varna system:

1. Brahmins (temple priests, scholars of scripture, teachers, physicians), 2. Kshatriyas (rulers, warriors), 3. Vaishyas (agriculturalists [landlords, not labourers], traders, merchants), 4. Shudras (artisans, peasants). Communities belonging to the first three of these four varnas are called Savarna. Communities outside these four varnas are called Avarna. Each class is further subdivided into castes based on specific occupation and region (see also, *Savarna, Avarna, Caste System*).

Vattakali: A dance form performed by the Kurumas, Wayanad Chettis and the Mandadan Chettis for entertainment. Vattakali is usually performed on festival days. There are different dances for men and women. Women perform this dance only in a household environment. This starts off as a slow dance, with the performers in a circle, and with gentle movements. The whirling movements become faster as the dancing reaches a climax. Vattakali is done exclusively by men in public, who step in a circle around a sacred lamp, first slowly, and then gradually increasing speed until unable to hold together the circle. While the dance is going on, the Theyyam of the Kurumas also joins the dancers. The Vattakali is usually performed at the Karingali Kavu temple near the Karnataka border. The Vattakali is also performed by the Urali Kurumas, and is closely linked to their lifestyle. The songs are usually about the different foods.

Wayanadan Chettis: A Dalit group found in the regions of Wayanad. The *Wayanadan Chetti*s are a distinct community found exclusively in the district of Wayanad and in the adjacent areas in the Nilgiri district of Tamil Nadu. Historical records and studies suggest that these are people who migrated into Wayanad from Dharapuram in Coimbatore district in Tamil Nadu. The Wayanadan Chettis have no relation to the Chettis in other parts of Kerala. Traditionally, they engage in agriculture and trading. They speak the Chetti language, which is based on Malayalam, but has a distinct alphabet and a literature of its own. The cultural world of the Wayanadan Chettis is built around spiritual links and rituals connected to several places related to epic stories and legends populated by Rama, Sita, Lava and Kusa. They believe in an ancestry embracing Chedattilamma (Sita) and Munikumar

(Lava and Kusa). Wayanadan Chettis traditionally had no statues or gods in the Hindu pantheon nor did they have temples. Their practice was to clean the surroundings of a tree or a stone, put a lamp there, and perform worship. They did not depend on other communities for performing religious rituals; they did it themselves. The abode of the gods was called matam or kavu. The practice of worshipping Hindu gods has been initiated recently.

Yagna: (Literally, 'sacrifice') In Hinduism, a ritual done in front of a sacred fire, often with mantras. Here, Agni (God of fire), acts as a medium between man and the gods. Yagna is usually performed to invoke the gods for obtaining blessings and favours from them.

Yuga: In Hinduism, epochs. There are four yugas, each yuga's length decreasing by a quarter (25 per cent), in the ratio of 4:3:2:1. The first is Satya/Krita Yuga (1,728,000 years), the age of truth, when humanity is governed by gods, and every manifestation or work is close to the purest ideal and humanity will allow intrinsic goodness to rule supreme. The second is Thretha Yuga (1,296,000 years); the third is Dvapara Yuga (864,000 years), characterised by compassion and truthfulness; and the fourth Kali Yuga (432,000 years), the present age, characterised by conflict and sin.

SELECTED BIBLIOGRAPHY

Bulcke, Camille, *Ramakatha Uthbavavum Valarchayum*, trans. Abayadev, Thrissur: Kerala Sahitya Akademi, 1999.
Crooke, William, *Tribes and Castes of the North Western India*, Vol. I, 1896.
Dalton, Edward Tuite, *Descriptive Ethnology of Bengal*, Calcutta: Office Of The Superintendent Of Government Printing, 1872.
Das, Sisir Kumar, *A History of Indian Literature, 500-1399: From the Courtly to the Popular*, Delhi: Sahitya Akademi, 2005.
Elwin, Verrier, *Myths of the North-East Frontier of India*, Shillong: North-East Frontier Agency, 1958.
Elwin, Verrier, *Myths of Middle India*, London: Oxford University Press, 1949.
Francisco, Juan R., 'Maharadia Lawana', *Asian Studies* Vol. 3, No. 2, 1969, pp. 186–249.
Frazer, James George, *The Golden Bough* (abridged ed.), London: Macmillan, 1983.
Fuchs, Stephen, *The Gond and Bhumia of Eastern Mandla*, Asia Publishing House, 1960.
Furer-Haimendorf, Christoph von, *Tribes of India: The Struggle for Survival*, Berkeley: University of California Press, 1982.
Gorresio, G., 'Part 10, Introduction' in *Rāmāyaṇa, poema indiano di Valmici*, Paris: Stamperia Reale, 1843–1870.
Griffiths, Walter G., *The Kol Tribe of Central India*, Calcutta: Royal Asiatic Society of Bengal, 1946.
Hivale, Shamrao, *The Pardhans of the Upper Narbada Valley*, London: Oxford University Press, 1946.
Hwaykas, C., *The Old Javanese Ramayana*, 1958.

Jacobi, Hermann, *Das Ramayana*, Bonn: Verlag Von Friedrich Cohen, 1893.

Johnny, O.K., *Wayanadan Rekhakal*, Calicut: Olive Publications, 2001.

Jose, Manu, *Mullakurumarude Kalipattukal*, Cuddalore: Adivasi Munneta Sangam, 2001.

Kannatumodi, D. Chacko, *Kurichyarude Lokam*, Thiruvanathapuram: Kerala Bhasha Institute, 1994.

Kanor, G.P., 'The Ramayana in Burma', *Journal of Burma Research Society*, Vol. XV, p. 80.

Karunakaran, E.A., *Pazhassiyude Priya Bhoomi*, Kottayam: Current Books, 2000.

Keith, A.B., *A History of Sanskrit Literature*, London: Oxford University Press, 1920.

Keith, A.B., 'The Date of the Ramayana', *Journal of Royal Asiatic Society*, 1915.

Krohn, Kaarle and Julius Krohn, *Folklore Methodology*, Austin: University of Texas Press, 1971.

Lallan Prasad Vyas (ed.), *The Ramayana: Global View*, South Asia Books, 1996.

Mitra, M.C., 'The Munda Legend about Sita and Sitali', *Journal of Department of Letters*, Vol. 4, pp. 303–304.

Moosath, C.K., *Ramakatha – Malayalathil*, Thrissur: Kerala Sahitya Akademi, 1989, p. 8.

Muraleedharan, Nellikkal, *Viswasahitya Darsanangal*, Kottayam: DC Books, 1997.

Nabaneeta Dev Sen, 'A Women's Retelling of the Rama-Tale', *Narrative: A Seminar*, Amiyadev (ed.), Delhi: Sahitya Akademi, 1994.

Nair, Rao Bahadur C. Gopalan, *Wayanad: Janangalum Parambaryavum (Wayand: Its Peoples and Traditions)*, Madras: Higginbotham & Co., 1911.

Namboothiri, K.R. Raman, *Vedahrithayathiloode*, Calicut: Poorna Publications, 2006.

Namboothiri, M.V. Vishnu, *Folklore Chinthakal*, Calicut: Poorna Publications, 2005.

Nivat, Dhani and H.H. Prince, 'The Rama Jathaka a Lao version', *Journal of the Siam Society*, Vol. 36, p. 1.

Padmini, P.G., *Kattu Jeevithathinte Spanthana Thalangal*, Thalassery: Akam Samithi.
Pankajakshan, M.R., *Wayanattile Adivasikalude Pattukal*, Thrissur: Kerala Sahitya Akademi, 1989.
Panur, K., *Keralathile Africa*, Kottayam: Sahitya Pravarthaka Sahakarana Sangam, 1963.
Panur, K., *Malakal,Thazhvarakal, Manushyar*, Kottayam: National Book Stall, 1971.
Payyanad, Raghavan, *Folklore*, Thiruvananthapuram: State Institute of Languages, 1986.
Rao, Velcheru Narayana, 'A Ramayana of Their Own: Women's Oral Tradition in Telugu', *Many Ramayanas: The Diversity of a Narrative Tradition in South Asia*, Paula Richman (ed.), Berkeley: University of California Press, 1991.
Ratnam, M. Venkata, *Rama, The Greatest Pharaoh of Egypt*, 1934.
Richman, Paula (ed.), *Questioning Ramayanas: A South Asian Tradition*, Berkeley: University of California Press, 2001.
Richman, Paula (ed.), *Ramayana Stories in Modern South India: An Anthology*, Bloomington: Indiana University Press, 2008.
Roy, Sarat Chandra, *The Birhors: A little-known Jungle Tribe of Chota Nagpur*, Ranchi: Man in India Office, 1925.
Roy, Sarat Chandra, *The Oraons of Chota Nagpur*, Ranchi: Crown Publications, 1925.
Sarkar, Himamsubhooshana, *Indian Influence on the Literature of Java and Bali*, Calcutta: Greater India Society, 1934.
Schlegel, A.V., 'Date of the Ramayana', *German Oriental Journal*, Vol. III, p. 379.
Schlegel, A.V., *Valmiki Ramayana*, Bonn, 1829
Sena, Dineṣa-Chandra, *The Bengali Ramayanas*, University of Calcutta, 1920.
Thapar, Romila, 'The Ramayana Syndrome', Seminar 353, January 1989
Thapar, Romila, *The Past As Present: Forging Contemporary Identities Through History*, Delhi: Aleph Book Company, 2014.
Thomas, F.W., 'A Rāmāyaṇa Story in Tibetan from Chinese Turkestan' in *Indian Studies in Honor of Charles Rockwell Lanman*, Cambridge, Mass: Harvard University Press, 1929, pp. 193–212.

Vaidya, C.V., *The Riddle of the Ramayana*, Bombay: Asiatic Society, 1955.
Varma, Gopal Lal, *Santhali Nadodippattukalil Sreeraman*, Delhi, 1960.
Vayaleri, Kumaaran, *Kurichyarude Jeevithavum Samskaravum*, Kottayam : Current Books, 1996.
Veerendrakumar, M.P., *Ramante Dukhom*, 1993.
Weber, A., *On the Ramayana*, Bombay: Thacker, Vining, 1873.
Wheeler, J.T., *History of India From the Earliest Ages*, London: Trübner & Co., 1874.
Williams, Monier, *Indian Wisdom: Examples of the Religious, Philosophical, and Ethical Doctrines of the Hindus*, Cambridge University Press, 1875.
Winternitz, M., *History of Indian Literature*, Part 1, University of Calcutta, 1927.

www.ingramcontent.com/pod-product-compliance
Lightning Source LLC
LaVergne TN
LVHW010312070526
838199LV00065B/5536